PLYMOUTH ARGYLE

101 Golden Greats

Plymouth Argyle: 101 Golden Greats	1-874287-47-3
Stoke City: 101 Golden Greats	1-874287-46-5
Stoke City: The Modern Era – A Complete Record	1-874287-39-2
Ipswich Town: The Modern Era – A Complete Record	1-874287-43-0
Bristol City: The Modern Era – A Complete Record	1-874287-28-7
Colchester Utd: Graham to Whitton – A Complete Record	1-874287-27-9
Halifax Town: From Ball to Lillis – A Complete Record	1-874287-26-0
Portsmouth: From Tindall to Ball – A Complete Record	1-874287-25-2
Portsmouth: Champions of England – 1948-49 & 1949-50	1-874287-38-4
Coventry City: The Elite Era – A Complete Record	1-874287-51-1
Coventry City: An Illustrated History	1-874287-36-8
Luton Town: The Modern Era – A Complete Record	1-874287-05-8
Luton Town: An Illustrated History	1-874287-37-6
Hereford United: The League Era – A Complete Record	1-874287-18-X
Cambridge United: The League Era – A Complete Record	1-874287-32-5
Peterborough United: The Modern Era – A Complete Record	1-874287-33-3
Peterborough United: A Who's Who	1-874287-48-1
West Ham: From Greenwood to Redknapp	1-874287-19-8
West Ham: The Elite Era – A Complete Record	1-874287-31-7
Wimbledon: From Southern League to Premiership	1-874287-09-0
Wimbledon: From Wembley to Selhurst	1-874287-20-1
Wimbledon: The Premiership Years	1-874287-40-6
Aberdeen: The European Era – A Complete Record	1-874287-11-2
The Story of the Rangers 1873-1923	1-874287-16-3
The Story of the Celtic 1888-1938	1-874287-15-5
History of the Everton Football Club 1878-1928	1-874287-14-7
The Romance of the Wednesday 1867-1926	1-874287-17-1
Red Dragons in Europe – A Complete Record	1-874287-01-5
The Book of Football: A History to 1905-06	1-874287-13-9
England: The Quest for the World Cup – A Complete Record	1-897850-40-9
Scotland: The Quest for the World Cup – A Complete Record	1-897850-50-6
Ireland: The Quest for the World Cup – A Complete Record	1-897850-80-8

PLYMOUTH ARGYLE
101 GOLDEN GREATS

Series Editor: Clive Leatherdale

Andy Riddle

Desert Island Books

First Published in 2001

DESERT ISLAND BOOKS LIMITED
89 Park Street, Westcliff-on-Sea, Essex SS0 7PD
United Kingdom
www.desertislandbooks.com

© 2001 Andy Riddle

The right of Andy Riddle to be identified as author of this work has been asserted
under The Copyright Designs and Patents Act 1988

British Library Cataloguing-in-Publication Data
A catalogue record for this book is available from the British Library

ISBN 1-874287-47-3

Printed in Great Britain
by
Bookcraft, Midsomer Norton

Photographs in this book are reproduced by kind permission of:
Dave Rowntree, Don Smith, Paul Curtis and Paul Hobbs

~ Contents ~

~ *Preface* ~

Andy Riddle is a bit of an unsung hero when it comes to Plymouth Argyle. He works diligently for the club every other Saturday afternoon – a true dyed in the wool 'Green' for many a season. So, when he asked me to write something of a note for his book, I had no hesitation. Anybody writing about Argyle in any shape or form deserves the freedom of the City! And to write about the best 101 players . . . wow . . . that is some task. Many players down the years have graced Argyle with pride! What a task Andy has given himself. So well done you!

Having spent only four years at Home Park, my players of distinction are well known. Who will ever forget TT . . . yes, Tommy Tynan. But then there is Kevin Hodges, Geoff Crudgington, and so many more.

How do you pick the best? Forwards score goals and win games and probably remain immortal, but defenders graft away for 90 minutes every game and get all the blame for losing matches. How unfair football is sometimes.

And what about Gordon Nisbet, that shrewd player on and off the park? Who could forget him standing on his toes in the dressing room trying hard to guess the size of the crowd through the little window. And would you believe it, he would be right; right up to the nearest hundred. Nissie had the knack of assessing a situation. Don't forget the players had a crowd bonus in those days. Well done, PC Nisbet.

Andy, I think you have done a wonderful job with this book, but there are so many players who have tried very hard over the years to help Argyle achieve its potential. I have a strong sense of this 'potential' inside me again, and I firmly believe that Paul Sturock will realise it.

DAVE SMITH

~ *Author's Note* ~

Players. They are what football revolves around. Spectators pay to watch them, journalists scribble about them, and managers live and die by them.

Since 1966 I have been hooked on Plymouth Argyle. I can vaguely recall my first game at Home Park, a midweek fixture against Coventry. The floodlit arena, the clatter of supporters' 'rattles', but mostly the roar of the crowd every time Argyle scored. In fact, I heard that roar on four occasions that evening, two of them sparked by goals from my new hero, Mike Bickle. The next day in the park, I was Bickle, outclassing my schoolmates – Greaves, Charlton and Best.

Since then, I have had other heroes, all of them Pilgrims, and I am delighted to be asked to pay my tribute to them. Sadly, Argyle did not get into the habit of scoring four goals every time I saw them, and when discussing this project with friends I received the tart reply: 'Are there 101 great Argyle players?' In fact my short-list contained about 200 names. To prune them to the requisite figure has, I admit, caused heartache and soul-searching. I have suffered numerous guilt trips as I crossed off names which many other supporters would surely have left in.

I do not pretend that my 101 is definitive. Many players achieved stardom after they left Argyle. David Jack and Tony Book spring to mind. Others were great players before joining Argyle, such as Peter Shilton and Bruce Grobbelaar. Apart from the occasional indulgence – when finding room for a personal favourite – I trust that my final selection will not be judged too perverse.

While I hope to stimulate argument about the good sense or absurdity of my selection, I say this to all Pilgrims, past and present. If you have ever worn the green of Argyle, be it once or 500 times, you are a hero of mine. But this book also reflects how life and soccer have changed over the decades. My overriding wish was to be transported back in time, to revisit some of the characters who have served the club over the years.

I would like to thank my publisher, Clive Leatherdale, for proposing this book to me and for his guidance and support; Leigh Edwards for his statistical input; Dave Rowntree, Don Smith, Paul Curtis and Paul Hobbs for their photographic contributions; Dave Smith for his preface; and finally my wife, Joy-Anne, who has endured countless evenings of keyboard-tapping and willingly sacrificed family outings.

ANDY RIDDLE

Chapter One

~ *The Team that Jack built* ~

No 1. **ROBERT JACK**
Debut: v Northampton, 5 September 1903
Farewell: v Brentford, 28 April 1906

It is debatable whether 'Bob' Jack merits inclusion in a survey of 'great' players of Plymouth Argyle. There are probably others who have greater claims, yet it seems remiss not to include him in any work related to Argyle, given his overall contribution to the club.

Born at Alloa, Scotland, on 4 April 1876, Jack had been groomed for a career in law but, displaying a talent for soccer from an early age, the opportunity to pursue a career in the game proved irresistible, and aged fifteen he began playing for his local side, Alloa Athletic. He was transferred two years later to Bolton Wanderers, where he spent six seasons, and also had spells at Preston North End and Burslem Port Vale prior to signing for the Pilgrims in 1903.

The Argyle manager at that time was an Irishman, Frank Brettell, an experienced administrator who was given the task of building a professional club fit to join the Southern League – a task he had achieved at Tottenham and Portsmouth. Election to the Southern League was attained and Jack ensured a permanent place in Argyle history as the first player to sign professional terms with the club.

Playing at outside-left, he appeared in Argyle's first game as a professional club, a Western League fixture at West Ham on 1 September 1903 which resulted in a single goal victory.

As a winger, speed was his main gift. The Argyle handbook of 1904-05 describes him as a 'flier'. His pace caused many a defender problems and he played in all but two of the 57 Southern League, Western League and FA Cup-ties of 1903-04. He scored four goals, including two in a 5-3 victory at Southampton, who went on to lift the championship.

That first season in the Southern League saw the side finish ninth, which drew praise from all quarters. The 1904-05 handbook includes a tribute in the form of a poem by Albert Webb. Each player's contribution is highlighted, with one line reading 'For many clubs in by-gone days beneath Jack's genius fell'.

The following season began with Jack at outside-left, although he lost his place to Hodgkinson. The directors had other plans for Jack and it was to him that they turned when Brettell left in 1905, having accomplished his objectives. Jack was appointed the club's first player-manager.

He picked himself for the first game of 1905-06 and scored in a 2-0 win over Norwich, but in the main preferred to administer tactics and encouragement from the sidelines, limiting himself to only nine appearances. A poor run in mid-season, when Argyle earned only two points from six games, pegged them back to fifth, but there was an air of optimism for the following season.

To the dismay of supporters, Jack then fell out with the board and became the first player-manager-secretary of Southend United, a newly formed semi-professional club who had secured a place in the Southern League Division Two. Like Argyle three years earlier, Southend were prepared to dig deep to achieve their dreams, and Jack led the Essex club to two Southern League Division Two titles.

Argyle did not replace Jack, the team being selected by committee instead. To the modern mind this seems unthinkable, but Argyle immediately finished runners up. Two mediocre seasons followed, however, and in 1910 the club persuaded Jack to return to fulfil the joint roles of manager and secretary, his playing days now behind him. Thus began an association which spanned a further 28 years, a record unlikely ever to be surpassed, given the modern day *penchant* for hiring and firing managers on a chairman's whim.

Under Jack's leadership, Argyle lifted the Southern League title in 1912-13. In 1920, with the Football League's decision to expand with a Third Division, split into North and South, Jack became the Pilgrims' first Football League manager.

A canny Scot, Jack had the ability to 'wheel and deal' on transfers, which in the long term put the club on a firm financial footing. As an example of this, his eldest son, David, who played for Argyle between 1919 and 1921, was sold to Bolton Wanderers for the princely sum of £3,000. David touched the heights with Bolton and Arsenal, becoming the first player to score in a Wembley Cup final and earning nine England caps.

Jack's two other sons, Rollo and Donald, were also on Argyle's books, Rollo playing seventeen games between 1922 and 1924, although Donald never made the first team.

In the mid-1920s, Jack's Argyle sides created a heartbreaking record of finishing runners-up in Division Three (South) for six successive seasons. Only the champions were promoted in those days, although Jack eventually led Argyle to the title in 1929-30. The club consolidated in Division Two until Jack's retirement from the game in 1938.

He spent his final years back in Southend, where he was tempted out of his slippers by son David, then Southend manager. Jack Snr became scout and 'outside representative'.

Jack was good at bowls, winning the Essex singles title. Despite being a Scot, he represented the English Bowlers against Scotland in 1922. He passed away on 6 May 1943 in Southend, but his long association with Argyle was commemorated by the scattering of his ashes over a Home Park pitch which was, by then, devastated by German bombs.

Magic Moment: *Jack finally secured the Division Three (South) title in 1929-30 in style. Argyle scored 98 goals in 42 matches.*

Worst Nightmare: *During the sequence of second places, Argyle fans accused Jack's sides of lacking ambition to progress into a higher division, an accusation that has also been levelled at the club recently.*

ARGYLE RECORD	Appearances	Goals
Southern League	60	7
FA Cup	11	—

No 2. **JOHN SUTCLIFFE**
Debut: v West Ham, 18 March 1905
Farewell: v Brentford, 8 April 1912

John William Sutcliffe, or 'JW' as he was known, cemented his name in sporting history as the last player to win international caps for England at both soccer and Rugby Union.

Born in Shibden near Halifax on 14 April 1868, Sutcliffe excelled at all sports. He was a talented cricketer and excellent athlete but it was rugby that he took seriously, in 1886 joining Bradford, where he became a regular in the first fifteen, usually at full-back or a three-quarter. Two years later he joined Heckmondwike and showed sufficient prowess to be selected for Yorkshire, the North of England, and ultimately, the full England side, for whom he played his only rugby international against New Zealand in 1889.

With rugby an amateur game, Sutcliffe's career was halted when Heckmondwike were accused of professionalism and found themselves suspended. As one of the club's stars, Sutcliffe was linked with the allegations but these were never substantiated.

Unable to further his rugby career, Sutcliffe was confident that he could switch from the oval to the round ball. So it proved, and in

September 1889 he signed for Bolton Wanderers, initially as a centre-forward. His robust style, however, upset officials and opponents alike, and in order to preserve Sutcliffe's career and the club's reputation, he was persuaded to try his hand in goal.

It proved to be an inspired decision. His grounding in rugby had blessed him with agility and excellent ball-handling skills. At 6ft in height and a muscular 12st 10lbs, his powerful frame was a help in an age when goalkeepers were afforded minimal protection by referees from onrushing opponents.

He soon established himself in Bolton's first team and won the first of five international caps in 1893 against Wales at Stoke. He had little to do: England won 6-0. Indeed, he was never on a losing England side. He also played for Bolton in the 1894 FA Cup final.

By 1898 it was said that his wage was a respectable £5 a week. It was a dispute over wages that provoked his departure from Burnden Park in April 1902. Relegated Bolton anticipated lower gates and refused to meet his wage demands and his request for a benefit game. In total he had played 332 League games for one of the country's top clubs. He joined Manchester United, via Southern League Millwall Athletic, but lost his place to the promising Harry Moger.

In January 1905 Sutcliffe was signed by Argyle manager, Frank Brettell, who wanted him as cover for first-choice keeper 'Tich' Horne. Now 37, it was logical to think that Sutcliffe's playing career was winding down and the fact that he did not actually visit Plymouth until three months after signing seemed to substantiate this. He kept a clean sheet in a 2-0 debut win over West Ham in the Southern League, and retained his place for the remaining nine games of that season.

Sutcliffe kept up his fitness and agility, which prolonged his career. Horne, his goalkeeping rival, was also highly rated and, as the club did not wish to lose him, Horne was occasionally given a run in the first team. JW continued playing for Argyle until 1912, when at the age of 44 he finally called time on his playing career, having made 170 Southern League and FA Cup appearances for the club. Horne's patience was rewarded when he became first choice for the next three and a half years.

That summer, the still ambitious Southend United appointed Sutcliffe as coach, a position he held until World War I brought soccer to a halt at the end of the 1914-15 season. It was around this time that John's brother, Charles, 22 years his junior, made his League debut, also as a goalkeeper, for Rotherham County.

JW became one of the first Englishmen to move into Continental soccer when he was appointed coach of Dutch side Arnhem. Once hostilities ceased and the English leagues resumed in 1919, he returned to his native Yorkshire, becoming trainer at Bradford City before finally retiring. He continued to indulge his sporting skills in such diverse activities as billiards and ice-skating. He died in Bradford on 7 July 1947, aged 79.

Magic Moment: *Early in his career, playing at centre-forward for Bolton reserves, Sutcliffe was challenged hard by the goalie. He picked up his assailant and threw him across the goalmouth.*

Worst Nightmare: *JW had four goals put past him in the 1894 FA Cup final by rank outsiders Notts County, who thereby created one of the earliest 'giant killing' acts in Cup history.*

ARGYLE RECORD	Appearances	Goals
Southern League	166	–
FA Cup	4	–

No 3. **SEPTIMUS ATTERBURY**
Debut: v Northampton, 2 September 1907
Farewell: v Portsmouth, 13 April 1921

In 1907-08 Sutcliffe was joined by two full-backs, Jack Butler and the Dickensian sounding Septimus Atterbury. The trio formed the basis of an Argyle defence reputed to be one of the meanest in the Southern League.

Atterbury was born at Allestree near Derby on 18 October 1880 and started his soccer career with Loughborough, before moving to Kettering and subsequently Leicester Fosse. Aged 25 he joined Argyle's Southern League rivals, Swindon. Playing at left-back, his reputation was enhanced during 1906-07 when Swindon conceded only eight home goals and kept a clean sheet against Argyle.

Atterbury was persuaded to join Argyle by the management committee and so began an association with the club that was to endure for 30 years. His debut came in the opening match of 1907-08, and a 1-0 win was a sign of things to come. Only two goals were conceded in the first eight games and Argyle let in just 31 in 38 games throughout the season.

Atterbury rarely neglected his defensive duties, so it was a surprise when, in his second season, he scored in the 1-1 home draw with Reading. To general astonishment he notched five goals in 1909-10, including successive strikes against Brighton and Brentford. Usual order was subsequently restored, however, and he never scored again in first-team football. Though an elegant player, he had a ruthless streak and was sent off at Luton in 1921 for a robust shoulder charge on winger Higginbotham. Atterbury was pelted by the crowd as he trudged off.

Injury aside, Atterbury and Butler were automatic full-backs up to the Great War. Top League clubs were rumoured to covet both players, and the fact that Robert Jack, with his eye for selling if the price was right, resisted such temptation shows how highly they were thought of.

Atterbury remained at the club and when Argyle were elected to Division Three (South) in 1920, he wore No 3 for the historic opening fixture against Norwich. He captained the side for much of that season. But the four-year interruption had deprived Atterbury of his best years and he was now offered the position of assistant trainer at the club, having made 343 appearances. In November 1921 he was granted a benefit and was permitted to retain the proceeds of a reserve-team fixture against his former club, Swindon. Although only classed as a second-team match, a crowd of 7,000 ensured a fair reward.

With the expansion of the Football League, the Southern League was reformed to accommodate the reserve sides of the respective clubs. As well as trainer, Atterbury continued to play in the second team, where his experience guided younger players. Such was the quality of his performances for the reserves that, despite his years, he was selected for a Southern League representative side.

During his time as a trainer, Atterbury worked with some of the most gifted players ever to have worn the green of Argyle. Much of this can be credited to the vision of Robert Jack in assembling such a side, but the success and style of play of those teams in the 1920s and 30s was also down to their fitness. Atterbury and the club's other trainer, Tommy Haynes, employed methods which were effective if unconventional, concentrating on stamina-building.

Financially, League football was taking its toll on Argyle. Wages were higher and distances travelled greater, yet attendances were static. With the country suffering low wages and high unemployment, a hike in admission charges was not prudent. The long-serving board resigned *en bloc* and a new board was appointed on the pledge of injecting funds. Inevitably, this meant changes to both the playing and backroom staff, and in 1937, after seeing the departure of various players with whom he had worked closely, Atterbury retired. He passed away in 1964.

Magic Moment: *Atterbury outplayed legendary Manchester United forward Billy Meredith in an FA Cup-tie at Home Park in 1913. Despite Atterbury's efforts, Argyle were defeated 0-2.*

Worst Nightmare: *Atterbury was blamed for the goal Argyle conceded on their Football League debut. Reports said he was slow to react to a cross and Norwich's Whitham sneaked ahead of him to score.*

ARGYLE RECORD	Appearances	Goals
Southern League	294	6
Football League	30	–
FA Cup	19	–

No 4. **FRED CRAIG**
Debut: v Crystal Palace, 9 November 1912
Farewell: v Luton, 15 March 1930

Fred Craig was a colleague of Septimus Atterbury in the Argyle defence either side of World War I. A study of Craig's record, which shows him scoring five goals in 467 League and Cup games, belies one fact – Craig was a goalkeeper.

All five came from the penalty spot, but the notion of keepers striding up to the other end was at that time alien to the game. Craig was not always successful with his kicks, and one can imagine the panic that ensued on those occasions as he quickly backtracked.

Born in Larkhall in Scotland, he began his career with Larkhill Thistle, Scotland's oldest amateur club, where he caught the eye of Robert Jack on one of his scouting trips north of the border. Jack beat off interest from Partick Thistle to sign Craig in 1912.

For his first two seasons at Home Park, Craig was second choice to 'Tich' Horne and most of his appearances were for the reserves in the Plymouth and District League. It was not until part way through 1914-15 that he established himself in the first team.

With war intervening, Craig played for Motherwell and Hamilton Academicals, and was selected for an Anglo Scots side versus the Home Scots in 1917. Fortunately for Argyle, Craig was persuaded to return to the West Country for the 1919-20 season.

He was ever present in Argyle's first season in League football, and over the next decade it was rare to see Argyle take the field without the tall Craig between the posts.

Over the years, his penalty-taking prowess has overshadowed the qualities that made him an outstanding goalkeeper. At 6ft tall, he was a confident catcher of crosses, but he also had great agility. He was so assured of his place in the first team that he was known to slip away during the half-time team talk for a cigarette.

His ability to make match-winning saves was typified in an FA Cup-tie at Swansea in January 1921. With Argyle 2-1 ahead, a late penalty was awarded against Greens' defender Jimmy Logan. Before a hushed crowd of 22,000, Craig dived full length to his right and diverted the ball for a corner. Even the partisan Welsh crowd applauded him from the field at the end.

Another of Craig's outstanding features was his nose, which provided much scope for local cartoonists. One depicted Craig with the caption 'No one "*nose*" more about goalkeeping'.

Craig also played in each of Argyle's nine matches during their pioneering summer tour of the Argentine and Uruguay in 1924. The club had been invited to teach the South Americans the basics of the game. Such a trip at that time was almost unheard of. Some considered it foolhardy – a journey into the unknown. In the 1920s even European soccer was a distant dream, but the tour was a success both in terms of results and building team-spirit. Among the three wins, three draws and three defeats was a 4-0 victory over the Uruguayan national side that six years later would win the World Cup! The tour lasted five weeks. On his return, Jack expressed surprise at the high standard of South American soccer, declaring it the equivalent of the English Third Division.

The first of Craig's five successful penalties came at Newport on 15 January 1927. The Welsh club were vying with Argyle for the Division Three (South) title, but the Pilgrims had scored two early goals before inside-forward Freddie Forbes was fouled and a spot-kick awarded. Craig trotted up to strike the ball past the Newport keeper and give Argyle an unassailable lead. They won 4-1.

Craig was now entrusted with penalties in crunch situations. Later that season he scored in successive home games against Brentford and Charlton, the former proving to be the match-winner in a 2-1 win.

Honours finally came Craig's way when he won a Third Division (South) champions medal in 1929-30. He also had the honour of captaining Argyle for much of that season. He departed that summer and moved north to join Barrow.

Magic Moment: *Not content with scoring his first penalty, Craig hit it with such force that the ball flew through the net and into the crowd. This was even more remarkable considering the sodden pitch and heavy old-style leather ball.*

Worst Nightmare: *In a game at Luton, Craig sustained a cut head after being hit by a stone thrown by a Luton fan. The intended victim had been his team-mate, Moses Russell.*

ARGYLE RECORD	Appearances	Goals
Southern League	78	–
Football League	361	5
FA Cup	28	–

No 5. **MOSES RUSSELL**
Debut: v Brighton, 2 September 1914
Farewell: v Gillingham, 8 February 1930

The intended victim of the 'Luton missile' that struck Craig was Moses Russell. It was not the first time that he had angered opposing supporters or players. This was partly due to his muscular style, and partly to his shiny cranium, which made him the subject of derision at away grounds. Nevertheless, Russell was an effective defender. He won 23 Welsh caps, twenty of them as an Argyle player, which still remains a club record.

But for some astute detective work by Robert Jack, Russell may have slipped the net. He had been playing for Southern League Merthyr and had already won three Welsh caps. Several clubs had shown an interest, which cooled in the belief that the pipe-smoking baldie was too old. Jack travelled to Russell's birthplace, Tredegar, to obtain a copy of his birth certificate. Proving that appearances can be deceptive, it revealed that the Welshman had been born on 20 May 1888 and was therefore just 26. In 1914, a fee of £400 brought Russell to Argyle. Russell later divulged that his baldness had been caused by rheumatic fever in his youth.

During 1914-15 Russell played 27 Southern League and FA Cup-ties, appearing in both full-back positions, at centre-half, and also at left-half, the position in which he played in his first international for Wales.

Following the War he played at right-back, partnering Septimus Atterbury. When Atterbury retired in 1921, Russell switched to left full-back and it was as No 3 that he played most of his remaining matches for Argyle and Wales.

Russell only stood 5ft 8in, but he was an excellent header of the ball. On many occasions his distinctive head would rise above taller opponents to clear. It was, however, his tenacious tackling and uncompromising approach that made him the player he was, and which saw him involved in various 'incidents'.

The stone-throwing at Luton was a consequence of Russell's tactics. Argyle were protecting a slim lead but had been reduced to ten men through injury. Russell's answer was to belt the ball as far into touch as possible at every opportunity. On another occasion in another game, he was assaulted by a spectator as he left the pitch at the end.

His forays into other countries provoked a similar reaction. Whilst playing for Wales during their 1929 international tour of Canada, a spectator, enraged by Russell's tackling, drew a gun before being overpowered by police.

Russell almost provoked a diplomatic incident during Argyle's 1924 South American tour. During a 'friendly' against Boca Juniors in Buenos Aires, supporters invaded the pitch when their favourites scored and carried all eleven shoulder high around the stadium, forcing the disbelieving Argyle players to retreat to the dressing rooms. After a half-hour delay the match resumed, but a further invasion was sparked when referee Fred Reeve – a Plymothian who had travelled with the Greens' party – awarded a penalty against the home side. Once again the Argyle players had to seek sanctuary. From the safety of the dressing room it was decided, in the interests of all concerned, that Pilgrims winger Patsy Corcoran would take the spot-kick and miss. On the resumption he placed the ball, but before Corcoran could kick it the ultra competitive Russell shoved him aside and blasted it into the net. Unsurprisingly, the Boca fans invaded the pitch yet again, and this time the match was abandoned.

Russell's Argyle and international career continued to blossom and in his later years he became club captain. All his official caps were awarded against the other Home Countries, the last of which was aged 40, against England in 1929. By then, wear and tear had taken their toll and Russell lost his place in the Argyle first team, ironically during the season when they finally won the Division Three (South) title.

In 1930, Russell joined the Thames Association side that had just been elected to Division Three (South). He spent two seasons with the London club, but by now his defensive qualities had deserted him. During his second year, the club conceded 109 goals in 42 games, which saw them drop out of the Football League. After retiring from the playing side, Russell returned to his beloved Plymouth and became a publican in the Union Street district. He passed away in 1946 at the relatively early age of 58.

Magic Moment: *Russell clinched Wales' first Home International Championship in 1924, scoring the only goal (a penalty) in a 1-0 win in Belfast, thus completing a 'clean sweep' of three victories.*

Worst Nightmare: *After signing for Plymouth, Russell was due to move into a house in the city. His friend and future Argyle player, Jack Fowler, offered to help redecorate it, but after some hours, paint-brushes in hand, they realised they were in the wrong house.*

ARGYLE RECORD	Appearances	Goals
Southern League	61	–
Football League	314	5
FA Cup	25	1

No 6. **JACK HILL**

Debut: v Crystal Palace, 8 September 1920
Farewell: v Newport County, 28 April 1923

Joining Moses Russell in the Argyle defence for that historic first season of League football was 'Jack' Hill. Despite spending only three seasons at Home Park, he is regarded as one of the outstanding players in Greens' history.

John Hill, to give him his correct Christian name, was born at Hatton-le-Hole in the North East on 2 March 1897. He left school for the mines and played amateur soccer for Durham City. His early life contributed to his physical development, and by the time he signed as a professional with Argyle he was a powerfully built, 6ft 3in centre-half.

Once again it was Robert Jack, scouring the country, who spotted Hill's potential. Jack offered him £5 a week. Hill held out for £6. Jack suggested spinning a coin to resolve the deadlock. Hill lost, but in reality the choice between the mines and football cannot have been difficult.

Hill was not selected for Argyle's baptismal League game and had to wait until the fourth match of 1920-21 to make his debut in a 0-1 home defeat by Crystal Palace. He was then dropped, but was recalled a month later to score the only goal at Gillingham. Finding the transition to League football relatively easy, he quickly made the No 5 shirt his own. He scored twice more that season, and with the Pilgrims finding goals hard to come by, only two players finished the season with a higher tally.

With a shock of red hair, Hill was, predictably, nicknamed 'Ginger'. His hair, added to his height, made him an imposing figure on the pitch. His height was an advantage in both defence and attack, where he induced panic at corners and free-kicks, but for such a large man he was also extremely skilful. He liked to dribble out of defence before delivering a pinpoint pass to either wing or surging forward to test the opposing goalkeeper with a long-range shot.

His strength was an asset, not only in dealing with opposing forwards, but also at times off the pitch, as one local boxer could testify when coming off second best in a public house brawl.

During his time at Home Park, Hill was selected for a South against North trial match, which suggested that some form of international honour was not far away. Whilst the Argyle faithful were resigned to losing him, it was still a huge disappointment when in 1923 a fee of £5,450 took him to Burnley, giants of the game, who three years earlier had won the First Division championship.

The higher standard in which he now found himself made no difference to Hill. He quickly became the kingpin of the Clarets' defence and it came as little surprise when he was selected for his England debut in 1925 against a Welsh side that contained his former Argyle team-mate Moses Russell. A further ten England caps came his way, as well as the England captaincy.

In 1928 Hill returned to the North East to sign for Newcastle, with whom he made his final three England appearances. Without him, Burnley were promptly relegated. In 1931, aged 34, he joined Hull City, where his experience helped them claim the Third Division (North) title. In 1934 he was appointed Hull's manager, but when relegation followed he switched to scouting. Later he was in charge of the pools system at Scarborough before retiring in 1963. He died in 1972, aged 75.

Magic Moment: *Against mighty Chelsea in a home FA Cup-tie in 1921, Hill faced Jack Cock, an England forward and future Pilgrim. The even-tempered Cock became so frustrated at his failure to outplay Hill that he was cautioned for 'questionable play'.*

Worst Nightmare: *After uprooting himself from his family in Durham to move to Plymouth, Hill doubted the wisdom of his decision when he initially found himself in the reserves.*

ARGYLE RECORD	Appearances	Goals
Football League	102	10
FA Cup	10	—

No 7. **PATSY CORCORAN**

Debut: v Brighton, 6 November 1920
Farewell: v Exeter, 26 December 1925

A beneficiary of Hill's long passes out of defence was winger Patsy Corcoran. Despite his Irish-sounding name, he was yet another of the many Scots who donned the green of Argyle in those early years.

A Glaswegian, Corcoran was born on 10 June 1893. He first signed for Glasgow Celtic, who offloaded him to Bathgate, at that time members of the Scottish League. He joined Argyle just prior to the club's entry into Division Three (South) and soon displaced fellow Scot, Jimmy Kirkpatrick, on the right wing, scoring on his debut.

At 5ft 10in and 11st 7lbs, Corcoran was not the ideal build for a winger, and he was not particularly quick either. He did, however, possess excellent ball control. He was not afraid to try his luck from all angles, as his 27 goals, a fair return for a winger, testifies.

For six seasons, Corcoran missed few matches. He was even invited to take part in a Scottish international trial. After losing his place in 1925-26, he moved to Torquay, then a non-league club, before being transferred to Luton. Strangely, he never made the Hatters' first team, as a result of which Corcoran quit football and returned to Scotland.

Magic Moment: *First Division Everton paid Corcoran the compliment of travelling to Devon for his benefit game in 1926.*

Worst Nightmare: *Corcoran was dropped after playing in the first twenty games of 1925-26, of which Argyle only lost two.*

ARGYLE RECORD	Appearances	Goals
Football League	188	27
FA Cup	10	—

No 8. **JACK LESLIE**
Debut: v Merthyr Tydfil, 19 November 1921
Farewell: v Fulham, 29 December 1934

One of Patsy Corcoran's early wing partners was Jack Leslie, who became one of the outstanding figures in Argyle's history. The story might have been different, however, if Leslie had remained as a winger.

Born of a Jamaican father in Canning Town, London, on 17 August 1901, Leslie was during his time at Argyle the only black player in England. He had begun with east London side Barking, a top non-league outfit, playing with team-mates Frank Richardson and Alf Rowe. Argyle offered contracts to all three. Just twenty, Leslie was in two minds about whether to uproot, but after being shown photos of Plymouth and the surrounding area he was persuaded to sign.

Richardson made an immediate impact, scoring 31 goals in his first season in League football, though both Leslie and Rowe had to wait for their first-team opportunities. Following a goalless home draw with Merthyr, Leslie enjoyed a run of nine games before being dropped in favour of the man he had replaced, Billy Baker. The consensus amongst

Argyle fans and, it seems, manager Robert Jack, was that Leslie would not make the grade.

Leslie languished in the reserves until January 1923 before he returned for just one game. But late that season Jack picked Leslie again, this time at inside-left. Three goals in the final five games suggested that perhaps he was more suited to an inside role.

The 1923-24 season saw Leslie make seventeen appearances, scoring five goals, but it was the following year that he began to make his mark, coinciding with the arrival of diminutive winger Sammy Black. With Leslie at inside-left and Black outside him, the duo formed an immediate understanding. Their first game together saw Argyle crush Brentford 7-1 with Leslie scoring twice. Later that season he scored a hat-trick in another 7-1 victory, this time over Bristol City.

In tandem with Black, Leslie was unrecognisable from the raw winger he had once been. He was as much a maker of chances as a taker, his clever passing and interplay with Black creating many opportunities for his fellow forwards. The scoring exploits of colleagues such as Jack Cock and Ray Bowden owed much to Leslie's creativity.

He could also be relied upon to score his share, regularly reaching double figures and twice notching 21. His fourteen goals in 1924-25 made him the club's top scorer that season. He scored three hat-tricks for Argyle and went one better against Nottingham Forest in October 1931, scoring four of Argyle's five against a single reply from Forest.

When injuries forced a reshuffle, Leslie was employed as an emergency centre-half. Jack considered switching him to defence permanently, but his contribution to the front line was irreplaceable.

Although playing in Division Three, Leslie and Black were often described as one of the finest match-winning combinations in League football. Leslie was touted as a possible England cap. Jack once told the local press that it had been whispered to him that Leslie was in line for the full England side. Confirmation, however, was never received. Cynics suggested that the selectors had shied away from choosing a black player to represent England.

Rumours abounded that top clubs were keen on Leslie. Fortunately for the Argyle faithful, if not for the club's bank balance, a move never transpired and Argyle would remain Leslie's only club.

His 1933-34 season was ended prematurely by a serious eye injury and by the time he was ready to return the following year age was beginning to tell. He played just once in 1934-35 when, fittingly, both he and Black scored in a 3-1 home win over Fulham. Leslie retired from soccer and moved to Cornwall to become a publican, before eventually returning to

East London as a boilermaker. He continued working into his 70s. In his later years he worked in the boot room at West Ham, where he cared for the boots of great England internationals such as Bobby Moore and Geoff Hurst. He died in London in 1988.

Magic Moment: *With the Argyle goalkeeper injured and the side down to ten men, Leslie gave a commanding performance in defence to ensure a shock 2-0 victory over Tottenham in 1930.*

Worst Nightmare: *Leslie was part of the Argyle side that suffered a club record 1-9 defeat at Everton only a few weeks later.*

ARGYLE RECORD	Appearances	Goals
Football League	383	131
FA Cup	17	3

No 9. **FRANK SLOAN**
Debut: v Charlton, 18 April 1924
Farewell: v Hull, 8 February 1936

Whilst it would be foolish to compare Frank Sloan to his fellow inside-forward, Jack Leslie, Sloan's contribution to Argyle's attractive football played during the 1920s and 30s should not be overlooked.

Yet another Scot brought in by Robert Jack, Sloan was born on Boxing Day 1904 at Chapelhall near Airdrie. Prior to joining Argyle in 1923 he had turned out for Shieldmuir Celtic, where one of his team-mates was Jimmy Healy, later to join him at Home Park.

After debuting on Good Friday 1924 against Charlton, Sloan played in the final six games of that season. He netted four goals, including a hat-trick in the final game against Southend, the Pilgrims winning 7-1.

During the following season he made the inside-right position his own and scored eight goals in 31 appearances. Only 5ft 7in and spindly legged, Sloan was nevertheless blessed with good balance and excellent ball control. When the ball was at his feet, he was capable of the unexpected. Against Tottenham in 1933 he scored one of the greatest goals ever seen at Home Park. Receiving the ball from the kick-off, he dribbled past several bewildered defenders before finding the net. He then promptly retrieved the ball and dribbled it back to the centre spot.

Sloan's failing was his work-rate. Whilst his skill with the ball was undoubted, his commitment to the cause was questionable. He loved the ball at his feet and, at times, he would hold play up or lose possession.

This would frustrate Jack to the extent that Sloan failed to establish a place for any length of time. In thirteen years at the club his appearance record should have been much higher.

The arrival in 1935 of another inside-forward, Jackie Smith, suggested that Sloan's days at Home Park were numbered. He left the club in 1936 to join Luton. After his playing days, he returned to Argyle as a member of the groundstaff. He also trained Argyle's third team, which competed in the South Western and subsequently Western Leagues.

The Sloan connection with Argyle continued for several years when his son, Francis, reported on matches under the *nom de plume* 'Spectator' for the local *Independent* newspaper.

Frank Sloan passed away in April 1976.

Magic Moment: *Sloan scored at home against Watford as Argyle won the 1929-30 Division Three (North) championship shield.*

Worst Nightmare: *Former Argyle star Alex Govan recalls the team coach returning from a match. A player asked the result of the University Boat Race. 'Oxford' came the reply. 'Who did you back, Frank?' asked someone. 'Cambridge' retorted Sloan, in his thick Scottish accent, 'but I'm nae bothered, I had them each way!'*

ARGYLE RECORD	Appearances	Goals
Football League	208	49
FA Cup	6	1

No 10. **SAMMY BLACK**
Debut: v Brentford, 6 September 1924
Farewell: v Swansea Town, 29 January 1938

'The greatest winger I've ever seen.' That is how Sammy Black is described by Wilf Hoskin, a lifelong Argyle supporter, who watched his first game at Home Park in 1921 and is able to fondly recollect many of the early Argyle heroes. To the modern fan it may seem an over-statement, but had Sammy been given the opportunity to play at a higher level he may well now be a household name to rank alongside Finney and Matthews. It was Argyle's good fortune that such a move never materialised and Black goes down in history as possibly the greatest player ever to don the green shirt of the Pilgrims.

Born on 18 November 1905, Black was yet another addition to the Scottish contingent at Home Park, having been born in Motherwell and been discovered by Jack playing for Glasgow-based Kirkintilloch Rob Roy. He arrived at Argyle in 1924 and scored on his debut, a 7-1 thrashing of Brentford.

Black never looked back. Just 5ft 6in and sporting size four boots, he epitomised the tanner-ball winger of the day, small, fast, tricky, and with dazzling skills. He rarely tracked back and his heading ability was non-existent. It was not uncommon for him to shirk an aerial challenge but, unlike today, wingers were not expected to do anything other than torment opposing full-backs. Black did that on a regular basis but there was more to his game than fancy footwork. It was his eye for goal that made him stand out from other wingers. In only three of fourteen seasons at Home Park did he fail to reach double figures, and he was the club's top scorer on five occasions. He could shoot with either foot and many of his goals came from unlikely angles. He placed shots just inside the post and it was said that he always aimed for the stanchion. Another of Black's idiosyncrasies was to play with a cigarette stub tucked behind his ear.

In his first season, he scored thirteen goals, including a hat-trick in a 5-0 home defeat of Norwich. Three other hat-tricks followed during his Argyle career, including a memorable trio against Blackpool in an FA Cup-tie in 1929, watched by a crowd of 30,000. In 1935 he went one better by scoring all four Pilgrims' goals in a 4-1 defeat of Port Vale.

Black became the darling of the Argyle crowd and his partnership with inside-left Jack Leslie became legendary. Their clever exchanges would leave defenders chasing shadows. Leslie would play the ball inside the full-back for Black to run onto or alternatively pass it to his feet to allow Black to attack the defender or cut inside to shoot. When transfer rumours reached fever pitch, a 'Sammy Must Not Go' campaign sparked demonstrations and public meetings. Overwhelmed by this public outcry, Jack and the directors resisted all offers and Black remained an Argyle asset.

Equally remarkable was the fact that Black was never capped, Scottish selectors presumably reasoning that the gulf between Third Division soccer and the full Scottish side was unbridgeable.

Black's final career statistics pay homage to his contribution to the Argyle cause. His 491 games remained an Argyle record until the 1990s, and his 185 goals for the club remains unbeaten to this day. The fact that he played so many games is testimony to both his fitness and ability as, on many an occasion, opposing defenders resorted to roughhouse tactics in an attempt to subdue Black or put him out of the game. The sight of the diminutive Black skipping past a burly defender endeared him to the Argyle fans even more. It was only during his last two seasons that injury restricted his appearances. It is also, perhaps, more than coincidence that Black was less effective when not partnered by Jack Leslie. Indeed, after Leslie had retired, Black was for a time employed at inside-forward.

Black moved to Queens Park Rangers in 1938 but made only a handful of appearances for the London club before War terminated both League football and Black's career.

During hostilities Black returned to Plymouth to work in the Royal Naval Armament Depot as a storehouse assistant. There he showed the same loyalty as he did to the city's football club and continued to work for the establishment for many years. In 1966 he was awarded the Imperial Service Medal for his contribution to the depot. He passed away in 1977 at the age of 72.

Magic Moment: *During a Cup-tie against mighty Huddersfield in January 1934, Black's dazzling wing play saw his opposing full-back, England international Roy Goodall, endure a torrid time.*

Worst Nightmare: *In another FA Cup-tie, in January 1932, Black missed a completely open goal against Manchester United. His blushes were saved however, as the Greens stormed to a 4-1 victory.*

ARGYLE RECORD	Appearances	Goals
Football League	470	176
FA Cup	21	9

No 11. **JACK COCK**
Debut: v Watford, 14 March 1925
Farewell: v Torquay, 5 November 1927

One of the main beneficiaries of Sammy Black's classic wing play was John 'Jack' Gilbert Cock. Unlike many of Robert Jack's early signings, Cock was already an established player, having played top-flight football for some years and even represented his country. It was somewhat of a surprise that such a big name could be attracted to Home Park, but Cock was a Cornishman by birth and no doubt reasoned that a return to the South West would afford him hero status.

Cock was born at Hayle on 14 November 1893. The first records of his soccer career show him playing as an amateur for West Kensington United, Forest Gate, Old Kingstonians and Brentford before signing professional terms with Huddersfield prior to World War I. During the conflict he saw action in the front line and was wounded. His bravery saw him awarded the Military Medal and at one time he was mistakenly reported as being killed in action.

In 1917 he was posted as a sergeant-major with the Army gymnastics staff based at Aldershot. This allowed him to resume his soccer career with Brentford, for whom he guested in friendly matches.

When League football resumed, Cock joined Huddersfield Town. He represented the Football League against the Scottish League, and won his first full England cap, and scored a goal, in a Victory international against Wales.

Chelsea then paid £2,500, a huge sum, for the centre-forward. During his time at Stamford Bridge he won two further caps and netted in a 5-4 win over Scotland at Hillsborough in April 1920. After three years with Chelsea he moved to Everton, scoring 31 goals in 72 games. Cock, along with team-mate Fred Forbes, joined Argyle in a double signing in March 1925, and both debuted together.

Cock's seven goals in the final ten games of that season was a sign of things to come. In the opening game of 1925-26 he bagged a hat-trick in a 6-2 thrashing of Southend. Two goals followed four days later as Argyle defeated Crystal Palace by the same score. Assisted by the talents of arguably Argyle's greatest ever forward line – Corcoran, Forbes, Leslie and Black – Cock scored goals for fun. He scored four in one match against Norwich and finished that campaign with 32 goals from only 36 games.

Whilst Cock was fortunate to be at Argyle with other great players, he was master of his own destiny. He was a fitness fanatic. Once the stamina-building training sessions were finished, Cock volunteered for more. This additional work paid off. He was a strong leader of the line who adopted a direct style of play. His stamina allowed to him to pressure defenders for 90 minutes, often forcing errors in dangerous areas of the pitch.

Cock's scoring form continued into 1926-27. He registered two further hat-tricks in a total of 33 goals from 40 games, setting an Argyle scoring record for a single season which still stands today.

He started 1927-28 on the injured list. After playing six games and scoring two goals, Cock, to the dismay of Argyle fans, returned to the capital to join another Third Division (South) side, Millwall. His departure ended a short but extraordinary spell with Argyle. His tally of 74 goals from 92 starts remains the best goals per game ratio in the Pilgrims' history.

Cock was no less prolific at Millwall, for whom his 77 career goals was not bettered until the 1970s. After enduring three runners-up places at

Home Park, Cock finally won a Third Division championship medal with Millwall, his final League club. After leaving the professional game he played for non-league Folkestone. On retirement from football he edited a publication 'Copes Chat', tipping the outcome of matches for Football Pools punters.

After World War II, Cock chose to return to Millwall as manager, but the Lions were shortly relegated and he was dismissed. His elegant appearance, combined with his fine tenor voice, saw him briefly embark on a stage career, as well as gain a small part in a film, 'The Great Game'. Cock remained in London until his death in Kensington on 19 April 1966.

Magic Moment: *Cock scored for Argyle against one of his former clubs, Chelsea, in a 1926 FA Cup-tie. But the Pilgrims lost 1-2.*

Worst Nightmare: *During his managerial spell at Millwall, Cock oversaw a club record 1-9 defeat by Aston Villa.*

ARGYLE RECORD	Appearances	Goals
Football League	90	72
FA Cup	2	2

No 12. **FREDDIE TITMUSS**
Debut: v Brighton, 13 February 1926
Farewell: v Chesterfield, 7 May 1932

As with Jack Cock, Freddie Titmuss was an experienced pro and former international when he joined Argyle. Born at Pirton in Hertfordshire on 15 February 1898, Titmuss had played as an inside-forward for Pirton United, Luton Alliance and Hitchin Town when, aged eighteen, he was drafted into the Great War. A posting to France with the King's Liverpool Regiment gave rise to a set of circumstances that were to shape his later life.

Titmuss was asked to play full-back for a scratch side against the first choice Battalion XI. His performance earned selection for various Army representative sides, where his fellow full-back partner was Southampton's trainer, Bert Lee. After the war, Lee invited Titmuss for a trial with Southampton – then Southern League rivals of Argyle – and he signed for them in May 1919.

Titmuss quickly made his mark and was twice chosen for a South of England XI to face the full England side. He won two full England caps

– against Wales in 1922 and 1923 – whilst a Southampton player. He also won a Third Division (South) championship medal in 1922, ever present, as the Saints pipped Argyle to the title on goal-average.

In February 1926, Jack paid £1,750 to secure Titmuss's services, a then record transfer fee for Argyle. He was one of a number of signings made around that time in an attempt to secure the championship. Although the title (and promotion) eluded Argyle for a further four years, Titmuss was a fixture in the No 3 shirt. A gentleman both on and off the field, he was not the fastest of defenders but was a superb tackler. He often appeared to be beaten by his winger, only to execute his specialist sliding tackle to clear the ball or regain possession. He also preferred creative passes to team-mates rather than resort to long speculative clearances. The fact that he failed to score during his Argyle career also shows that he rarely ventured upfield.

Titmuss was captain when the club finally won the Third Division (South) title. That side was built around a solid defence which conceded only 38 goals in 42 games, with Titmuss and his full-back partner, Harry Bland, forming a resolute combination.

It was unfortunate that promotion had been achieved so late in Titmuss's career. At 32, his best years were behind him and during his final two seasons he was no longer assured of a regular place. His last game brought a 4-0 win over Chesterfield that saw Argyle clinch its highest ever finish of fourth in Division Two. Earlier that season, Titmuss played at Arsenal in an FA Cup-tie in front of a 65,000 crowd. Argyle gave the Gunners a few scares before losing 2-4.

Titmuss remained in the West Country, playing for Cornish side St Austell. He continued to live in Plymouth and subsequently became a publican at The Cherry Tree, close to Home Park, and later The Laira Hotel. Away from football, he excelled at golf, tennis and cricket. Titmuss died in October 1966.

Magic Moment: *Titmuss took over in goal from the injured Harry Cann against Tottenham in December 1930. Several fine saves, plus a little luck, saw him keep a clean sheet. Argyle won 2-0.*

Worst Nightmare: *Whilst Titmuss was with Southampton, the Saints reached the semi-finals of the FA Cup. But flu meant Titmuss missed the game.*

ARGYLE RECORD	Appearances	Goals
Football League	166	–
FA Cup	11	–

No 13. **FRED McKENZIE**
Debut: v Reading, 27 February 1926
Farewell: v Bradford City, 14 April 1934

Fred McKenzie joined Argyle around the same time as Freddie Titmuss. Born at Lochee, near Dundee on 13 November 1903, McKenzie was yet another lured from Scottish junior football to Home Park. Unlike most other Scots who joined Argyle, however, McKenzie had previous experience in English League soccer.

He had started with local junior side Lochee United, but in 1924 moved south to join one of Argyle's Division Three rivals, Newport. He played 66 times over two seasons for County, scoring once, but with the local economy in decline and attendances falling, Newport had to sell in order to survive.

Robert Jack was intent on strengthening a porous defence that threatened to spoil Argyle's promotion challenge. Scoring goals was no problem, as the League tally of 107 in 1925-26 confirms, but three games in which thirteen goals were conceded, six of them at Aberdare Athletic, convinced Jack that new blood was needed. By mid-March the signings of Titmuss, McKenzie, and another experienced half-back, Alec Hardie, had been completed. McKenzie's fee, £1,500, was at that time a record for Newport.

A strong, physical player, equally comfortable at half-back or centre-half, McKenzie was seen as the ideal type to shore up Argyle's leaky defence. The timing of McKenzie's signature was fortunate, as it was followed by Welsh international centre-half John Pullen suffering a long-term injury.

McKenzie played at right-half on his debut, at home to Reading, the Pilgrims losing 1-3. He reverted to centre-half for the rest of that season, scoring his first goal in a 3-1 home win over Bristol Rovers.

The following season saw McKenzie establish himself at No 5, playing 31 games and missing others through injury. He scored five goals during that campaign. His muscular frame proved useful at corners and free-kicks and, whilst speed was not his main asset, he always looked to initiate attacks by playing accurate passes to team-mates rather than hit long, hopeful balls.

The 1927-28 season was probably McKenzie's best for Argyle in terms of personal performances. He played in all 43 League and Cup games, although the team's run of six runners-up places came to an end. This time Argyle finished third. Honours finally came his way when Argyle won the Third Division (South) title in 1930.

Although McKenzie played the majority of his games at centre-half, whenever Pullen was fit he was preferred in the No 5 shirt and McKenzie would switch to left or right-half. During the side's first season in Division Two, McKenzie found it increasingly difficult to break into the first team. Pullen stayed clear of injury, Hardie had established himself at left-half, and another of Jack's signings, Norman Mackay, had successfully switched from inside-forward to right-half. McKenzie was used mainly as cover for the next four years. In 1934 he was released and, ironically, rejoined Newport County, notching up a further 22 appearances for the Welsh side.

After retirement from soccer McKenzie returned to live and work in Plymouth. He became a publican and continued to follow Argyle's fortunes. The family's sporting prowess was continued by one of McKenzie's sons who, while at school in Devonport, was selected for the England Schools rugby side. Fred McKenzie passed away on 22 November 1979 at the age of 76.

Magic Moment: *McKenzie established himself as Argyle's penalty king, missing only once from twelve spot-kicks.*

Worst Nightmare: *After a bout of blood poisoning, McKenzie had a toe surgically removed, although this clearly did not impeded his ability.*

ARGYLE RECORD	Appearances	Goals
Football League	203	13
FA Cup	11	–

No 1. Robert Jack, with white hat and cigarette, greets new signing David Hill at Plymouth North Road railway station

No 3. Long-serving Septimus Atterbury

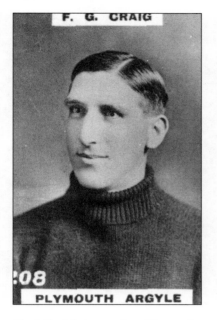

No 4. Fred Craig, penalty-takling goalie   No 5. Moses Russell, Argyle international

No 6. Jack Hill, future England captain   No 8. Jack Leslie, England's only black player

No 9. Frank Sloan, one of Argyle's many Scottish signings

No 11. Sammy Black, Argyle's all-time record goalscorer

POPULAR FOOTBALLERS
N° 11

S. BLACK
(Plymouth Argyle)

Forward, with plenty of speed, Sammy Black turned out for the Argyle in 34 league matches last season (1934-35). Native of Motherwell, first played for Kirkintilloch Rob Roy, a Scottish junior club, in 1925. Joined Argyle in following season. Described as one of the best left wingers in English football. An attractive personality in the game to-day.

A SERIES OF 48

ISSUED BY
CARRERAS LIMITED
ARCADIA WORKS, LONDON, ENGLAND.

KEEP THIS SERIES OF 48 PICTURE CARDS IN THE CARRERAS "SLIP-IN" ALBUM OBTAINABLE FROM ALL TOBACCONISTS (PRICE ONE PENNY)

Chapter Two

~ *League Pioneers* ~

No 14. **ALF MATTHEWS**
Debut: v Bristol Rovers, 13 March 1926
Farewell: v Notts Co, 25 March 1933

Right-winger Alf Matthews joined Argyle around the same time as Fred McKenzie. A Bristolian by birth, Alfred William Matthews was born on 28 April 1901. A promising schoolboy player, captaining his school side, Parson Street School, he signed as an amateur with Bristol City, helping their reserves win the Southern League title in 1921-22. As a professional he played one League game before moving to Exeter City, for whom he made 153 appearances, scoring seventeen goals (nine of them penalties). He also played in a Grecians' club record 117 consecutive games.

When Robert Jack signed Matthews in March 1926 for £750, he saw him as a foil to left-winger Sammy Black. Matthews was as quick, if not quicker, and had already proved he could score goals. Outside-right had been a problem to Jack. The remainder of the front line picked itself, but Patsy Corcoran and Jimmy Healy had tried on the No 7 shirt without success. Matthews scored five times in the final twelve games, although just one point from the final two games saw Argyle pipped for promotion.

The following season Matthews was ever present, scoring eight goals. He also featured in the first sixteen matches of 1927-28, before injury terminated a sequence of 71 consecutive games.

Although Matthews continued to score vital goals, his main asset was creating chances with accurate and dangerous crosses. Jack Cock's prolific goal tally was in no small way thanks to the number of incisive passes played into the opposition penalty area by Matthews.

In the third game of 1929-30, at home to Brentford, Matthews took a knock on the knee. His replacement, Tommy Grozier, seized his chance, scoring four times in one match against Crystal Palace, and with the team hitting peak form – losing only four times to clinch the Division Three (South) title – Matthews was out on a limb. In his last four years at Home Park he made only sporadic appearances, leaving the club in 1933. Fittingly, his contribution to Argyle was rewarded with a benefit match against his former club, Exeter City.

He played eight games for Doncaster Rovers, scoring once, before joining Crystal Palace. He failed to make the first team and retired. He returned to live and work in Plymouth, playing bowls and a round of golf or two at Yelverton Golf Club. Up until his death in Plymouth in February 1985, Matthews retained his affection for Argyle and was a keen follower of the club's fortunes.

Magic Moment: *In his fifth game, Matthews scored against his first club, Bristol City. Argyle won 3-1 before a crowd of 27,000.*

Worst Nightmare: *During his time at Exeter, a fire destroyed the grandstand and everyone's kit. For the next game Matthews had to 'break in' new boots and use a local pub for changing facilities.*

Argyle record	Appearances	Goals
Football League	142	30
FA Cup	5	2

No 15. **RAY BOWDEN**
Debut: v Merthyr Tydfil, 12 March 1927
Farewell: v Stoke, 25 February 1933

Another player to benefit from Alf Matthews' wizardry was Raymond Bowden. Argyle already boasted several capped players but hitherto these had been established internationals. Bowden became the first player to come through the ranks at Argyle and go on to full international honours.

Born at Looe in Cornwall on 13 September 1909, Bowden shone even as a schoolboy. He compensated for his short stature by a determination to succeed. It is said that he each day he hopped to school on one leg and home on the other in order to improve his balance. By fifteen he was a prolific scorer for Looe in Cornish senior soccer, once scoring more than 100 goals in one season. Argyle swooped after Bowden scored ten in Looe's 11-0 crushing of Tavistock in a Plymouth & District League match in October 1925. Robert Jack signed him on amateur terms and rather boastfully claimed that he had 'discovered' Bowden.

At that time, Bowden had been articled to an auctioneer but was persuaded to sacrifice that potential career. As well as training with Argyle he was employed by the club in the secretary's office, commuting from home on his motorcycle.

He first played for Argyle reserves in September 1926, and scored in a 3-2 victory over Exeter reserves. One local scribe was not impressed, claiming that 'Bowden's physique is not quite robust enough for the class of football to which he has been promoted'.

In December he played for the first team in a friendly against Queens Park Rangers, scoring four goals in a 6-1 win, and shortly afterwards signed professional terms.

His League debut came some weeks later, in a 1-1 home draw with Merthyr. It was his only outing that season. He had to wait over a year for another chance, scoring both Argyle goals in a 2-2 draw at Bournemouth. Two weeks later, in the final game of the season, he scored two more in a 4-0 win over Luton.

Not surprisingly, the No 9 shirt was his for the kick-off of the 1928-29 campaign. Bowden responded by scoring 23 goals in 32 League and Cup matches to finish as the club's top scorer. Bowden was not just an out and out goalscorer. He was a graceful player with supreme ball control, and was equally at home at centre- or inside-forward. Indeed, it was in the latter position that he made his greatest impact.

Word soon spread of Bowden's ability and the big clubs soon sent spies. In 1931, whilst still an Argyle player, he toured Canada with an FA select side. For the first game, Bowden was called up at the last minute and scored five goals.

He stayed with Argyle until March 1933, when he signed for all-powerful Arsenal under legendary manager Herbert Chapman. The Gunners had won the League title in 1931, but Chapman was looking for fresh faces to brighten an ageing side, a decision, no doubt, made easier by a shock FA Cup defeat by lowly Walsall.

Chapman had made three trips to Devon to watch Bowden, and three times invited him to sign. Twice Bowden refused. Arsenal could only offer the same maximum wage, £8, that he was earning at Plymouth. On the third occasion he accepted Arsenal's offer and a fee of £4,500 secured the transfer.

Herbert Chapman died in 1934, Bowden being his last major signing. Chapman's successor, George Allison, used Bowden at inside-right in a legendary Arsenal forward line that included such names as Cliff Bastin, Ted Drake and Alex James. Ironically, the man Bowden replaced at No 8 was former Argyle star, David Jack.

Bowden won major honours during his time at Highbury. Arsenal clinched the First Division championship shortly after he joined them, although he played too few games to be awarded a medal. He did, however, score on his debut, against Wolves. He played a major part in the next two championship-winning seasons. In the first of these he finished joint top scorer with Bastin, with thirteen goals from 32 games, and the following season scored fourteen times in 24 starts, including a hat-trick in a 8-1 demolition of Liverpool. He played in Arsenal's Charity Shield-winning side of 1934, as well as earning an FA Cup winners medal in 1935, as the London side defeated Sheffield United by a single goal. It was thanks to Bowden that Arsenal reached the final, as he had scored the semi-final winner against Grimsby Town.

International honours followed. He made his England debut in 1935 against Wales at Highbury. International appearances boosted his weekly wage by £6 per game. Later that year the same venue saw Bowden become one of a record seven Arsenal players to represent England. The opponents were the World Cup holders, Italy, in a game dubbed 'the Battle of Highbury'. England won 3-2 but at the cost of a broken nose, a suspected broken arm, a gashed leg and a damaged hand. Bowden remained relatively unscathed by 'keeping out of the way'.

He earned six full England caps in all, a modest total for such a talented player whose play impressed almost all who saw him. His tireless running and intelligent passing earned him the nickname of 'Football's Professor'.

Bowden played a total of 123 League games for Arsenal, scoring 42 goals, before he was transferred to Newcastle in November 1937 for £5,000. He was appointed captain, but World War II curtailed his career. In what proved to be his last game, he scored a hat-trick against Swansea.

He subsequently returned to live in Plymouth and for many years, along with his brother, ran a sports shop in the city. After his wife's death he spent his last years in a residential home in Plymouth. Although he never returned to Highbury, Arsenal kept in contact. Among his treasured possessions was a letter from Arsène Wenger, saying how proud the French manager was to serve a club that had been graced by the likes of Bowden.

Bowden was a true gentleman, both on and off the field. In later life, he harked back to an early game when, as a teenager, he was selected for the Argyle first team. As he recalled: 'I looked across at the player whose place I was taking and thought how unkind it was. I didn't like putting a married man out of a job and I'll never forget the look on his face as he watched me lace up my boots.'

Up to his death on 23 September 1998, at the age of 89, Bowden continued to receive letters from fans, young and old who were enthralled to read of his exploits.

Magic Moment: *The manner of Bowden's signing for Argyle was 'Boy's Own' stuff. The day after scoring ten goals for Looe, he was kicking a ball with friends after attending church when he was told to return home. Argyle boss Robert Jack wished to speak to him.*

Worst Nightmare: *An inauspicious League debut for Argyle sowed doubts in Bowden about his physique. He feared that, perhaps, he was too small for the rigours of Third Division football.*

ARGYLE RECORD	Appearances	Goals
Football League	145	83
FA Cup	8	4

No 16. **NORMAN MACKAY**
Debut: v Coventry, 28 January 1928
Farewell: v Swansea Town, 5 May 1934

Compared to Ray Bowden's modest debut for Argyle, Norman Mackay's career at Home Park could not have begun more spectacularly. Born on 26 May 1902 in Edinburgh, Mackay's first club was Edinburgh Royal. He made his way via Scottish non-league Broxburn, Hibernian, and Aston Villa (for whom he made two first-team appearances) to join Welsh non-leaguers Lovells Athletic. The club was based around a toffee producing firm and Mackay combined his part-time football career with selling Lovell's products.

Robert Jack gave Mackay the opportunity to resurrect his League career, Lovells receiving the sum of £200. He was selected at inside-right for his debut and scored a hat-trick in Argyle's 4-0 win over Coventry. This feat is all the more remarkable, given that he scored only another eleven goals in 240 more games for the club. Indeed, he failed to find the net in his last four seasons, which comprised 157 games. In mitigation, most of his appearances were at half-back, although he was on occasions employed in the forward line to deputise for absent colleagues.

A small, stocky player with a receding hairline, Mackay was living proof that appearances can be deceptive. He was a 'terrier like' player who never stopped running and was renowned for his tackling. This made him a great favourite with both the crowd and with Robert Jack. So much so that he became an integral part of Jack's teams over the following six years, when only the occasional injury prevented him from lining up in the first team. His energy and zest for tackling made him an obvious half-back, and once he had wrested the No 4 shirt from fellow Scot Jimmy Logan early in 1928-29 it was his for keeps.

A Division Three (South) championship medal in 1930 was fitting reward for Mackay, and over the next two seasons he missed only one game. He gave one of his finest performances in January 1932 when Argyle demolished Millwall 8-1, which still stands as the club's record win. Although he did not claim a goal, Mackay's powerful presence in the half-back line created chances for the Argyle forwards. To even things up, Mackay also had the 'distinction' of playing in Argyle's record defeat, a 1-9 hammering at Everton in December 1930.

Mackay served the club admirably until the end of 1933-34, when he moved to Southend United. He played only 34 games for the Essex side before joining the Clydebank club that was a forerunner to the Scottish League side of today that bears the same name.

Magic Moment: *Mackay was popular with team-mates off the pitch too. Like ex-Argyle player Jack Cock, he had a fine singing voice and would entertain them on long trips to and from away matches.*

Worst Nightmare: *After his stunning performance in the 8-1 win over Millwall, Mackay missed the next match through injury.*

ARGYLE RECORD	Appearances	Goals
Football League:	227	14
FA Cup	14	–

No 17. **HARRY CANN**
Debut: v Bournemouth, 21 May 1928
Farewell: v Southampton, 6 May 1939

Argyle have over the years been blessed with some outstanding goal-keepers, and Harry Cann, a team-mate of Norman Mackay, can certainly be considered in that category.

A Cornishman, Cann was born in Tintagel on 31 March 1905. In his early days he played for the local village side and was selected for the Cornwall county team. His reputation as the best keeper in Cornwall brought him to Argyle's attention and he signed for the club in 1927.

With Fred Craig the established first choice, Cann had to be patient. During his first two years at the club he made only three League appearances. But when Craig departed towards the end of 1929-30, Cann seized his opportunity. Apart from a spell when Bill Harper was preferred, he remained the Pilgrims' custodian until World War II.

With the Pilgrims again chasing the title in 1929-30, it came as a shock to Argyle fans when Craig departed. Cann, however, filled the void. He played in the final twelve games, with Argyle winning eleven and con-ceding just ten goals. It was a run that belatedly secured the Third Division (South) title and established Cann as a crowd favourite.

Cann's main assets were his bravery and agility. At 5ft 11in, he was not particularly tall for a goalkeeper, but, at a time when the game was much more physical, Cann's courage was undeniable. Many a time the crowd would wince as Cann plunged headlong at an onrushing forward's feet to smother the ball. Inevitably, he took his share of knocks, and on more than one occasion Cann was forced to go off for treatment. With substitutes a distant thought, this led to temporary disarray, as Argyle were forced to reshuffle to cover their goalkeeper's absence.

Cann was ever present during Argyle's inaugural season in Division Two, during which he featured in that notorious 1-9 defeat at Everton. There were mitigating circumstances. The previous day, Argyle had beaten Cardiff 5-1 before undertaking a ten-hour overnight train journey to Liverpool. They arrived at 6am and, after a short rest, travelled to the ground in torrential rain. The pitch was so waterlogged that the referee had the two captains toss the coin on the touchline! Everton, with the legendary Dixie Dean in their line up, had not been in action the previous day, and with a gale-force wind at their backs were two goals up within five minutes. Dean went on to score four, and the scoreline remains Argyle's record defeat.

The following season, Cann missed a number of games through injury. His immediate replacement was reserve George Stanbury, but the opportunity to sign former Scottish international keeper Bill Harper was too good to miss, and when Harper arrived in December 1931 he was immediately given the No 1 jersey. Cann was thus dismissed to the reserves and had to content himself with only the odd first-team game until midway through 1933-34, when he was restored on merit. That summer it appeared at one stage that Cann would leave, and only after protracted negotiations did he agree to sign a new contract.

Cann remained at Argyle until the end of the 1938-39 season. By that time Robert Jack had finally departed the scene and a new manager, Jack Tresarden, had been appointed. Tresarden considered that Cann, now 34, was dispensable and granted him a free transfer. He joined Fulham, only for the onset of World War II to put paid to League football. Cann was restricted to playing in wartime matches only. He was called up to join the Army but remained based in London. He also guested for West Ham in a number of wartime friendlies.

Come peacetime, Cann returned to his birthplace, Tintagel, where he owned a sports shop. He worked for the National Trust and became a qualified FA coach, spending much of his time until his retirement coaching in Cornish schools. He coached Cornish Senior League side Wadebridge before returning to coach Tintagel and play for the side until the age of 50. Cann was a keen badminton player and a four-handicap golfer. He remained in north Cornwall until his death on 9 May 1980.

Magic Moment: *Despite conceding nine goals at Everton, Cann was applauded by home fans at half- and full-time. It was reportedly 'the greatest ovation ever given to a goalkeeper at Goodison'.*

Worst Nightmare: *In a vital match against Spurs in December 1930, Cann dived at a forward's feet and emerged bloodied from a head wound that forced him off the pitch. The ten men then scored twice to win the game. Cann only returned for the last five minutes.*

ARGYLE RECORD	Appearances	Goals
Football League	225	–
FA Cup	7	–

No 18. **JACK VIDLER**
Debut: v Southend, 2 March 1929
Farewell: v Sheffield United, 4 February 1939

Whilst Harry Cann was stopping goals, one of those scoring them was Jack Vidler. Born in Portsmouth on 13 June 1906, Vidler had served in the Army, but Robert Jack negotiated his release and Argyle paid the required fee in order to obtain his signature on a professional contract.

At first Vidler was second fiddle to a forward line that contained Bowden, Leslie and Black, but his ability to play at inside-forward, centre-forward or on the left wing ensured that he was called upon if any of the aforementioned trio were absent.

Vidler certainly never let the side down and in his first full season scored nineteen goals in 31 League and Cup appearances, including a hat-trick against Watford in the FA Cup, and all four Argyle goals against Norwich. It was a comfort to the manager that he had such an able deputy for any of his forwards.

Vidler missed four months of the following season through injury, but announced his return with a hat-trick against West Brom. Once Ray Bowden was switched to inside-right, Vidler seized the opportunity to make the No 9 shirt his own. He scored nineteen goals in 1931-32, including another hat-trick in Argyle's record 8-1 rout of Millwall, although the following two seasons saw a slump in his form which suggested that perhaps his best days were behind him. The 1934-35 season saw him gain a second lease of life and, despite playing for much of the time at outside-left, he easily finished as the club's top scorer with 21 goals to his name.

Predominantly left-footed, Vidler was a distinctive figure on the pitch. At 5ft 9in, he was a not a big man but he sported a hairstyle that was 'short back and sides' in the truest sense. He invariably played with sleeves rolled up around his elbows. He would hustle and bustle, rather than exhibit any real skill on the ball. His style of play was effective though, as many defenders would testify.

Vidler continued to give excellent service until the end of 1938-39, when he was released. He played three games for Bristol City before war intervened, but he continued to play for City in regional league matches and twice returned to Home Park for games against Argyle. Neither proved to be a happy experience for him, with the Pilgrims following up a 6-0 victory in the first encounter with a 10-3 win later in the season.

Vidler died in 1953 at the early age of 47.

Magic Moment: *In an FA Cup-tie at Highbury in January 1932 before a crowd of 65,000, Vidler gave Argyle a fifth-minute lead. A Jack Leslie shot struck the bar and Vidler netted the rebound.*

Worst Nightmare: *In the same match, Vidler had a great chance to make it 2-0 when, from only five yards out, he trod on the ball and the chance was lost. Argyle went on to lose the game 2-4.*

ARGYLE RECORD	Appearances	Goals
Football League	243	95
FA Cup	13	8

No 19. **BILL HARPER**
Debut: v Bury, 26 December 1931
Farewell: v Blackburn, 22 April 1939

Argyle's goalkeeper in that famous cup-tie with Arsenal in 1932 was Bill Harper, a former 'Gunner', making a nostalgic return to Highbury.

At his peak, Bill Harper was a formidable keeper and whilst it is fair to say that he was past his best by the time he joined the Pilgrims, no publication on Argyle could ignore his overall contribution to the club in many capacities.

Born on 19 January 1897 at Winchburg, West Lothian in Scotland, Harper's early career with Edinburgh Emmett and Winchburg Violet spanned World War I. He trained as a blacksmith and during the conflict proudly served in the Scots Guards. It was there that he displayed his all-round sporting prowess, becoming the Guards heavyweight boxing champion and captaining their rugby side to the Brigade championship.

After the war, he reverted to soccer and first came to prominence with Hibernian, whom he joined in 1920. While with Hibs he established himself as Scotland's first-choice goalkeeper. His international record was impressive and he was fortunate to play during one of the most successful spells in Scotland's soccer history. His first cap came in March 1923 as Scotland won 1-0 in Belfast, and he played in eleven of twelve internationals played by Scotland up to April 1926. He featured in a losing Scotland side just once and made his farewell appearance for his country at Old Trafford in a 1-0 Scottish win over England.

The last two of these international appearances were made with Arsenal, who had signed him in November 1925 for a fee of £4,500, then a record for a goalkeeper. The Gunners reached the 1927 FA Cup final, against Cardiff, but Harper was injured and missed out. Ironically, his replacement, Dan Lewis, made the crucial mistake which led to the only goal and took the famous trophy out of England for the only time.

After a brief spell in the United States with Fall River, Harper returned to Highbury and won a League championship medal in 1930-31. Losing his first-team spot to Frank Moss, in December 1931 he was persuaded to move to Plymouth. Then aged 34, he was expected by most critics to be employed as a back-up only. Indeed, Harper initially played for the reserves, but upon saving two penalties in a Christmas Day fixture he was upgraded for his full Argyle debut the following day. Argyle triumphed 5-1 and Harper retained his place for the remainder of the season, keeping out fit-again regular keeper Harry Cann.

Harper missed only five games the following season, and while he had lost some of his agility, his renowned handling and courage had not been diminished by age. He was also as strong as an ox, due to his early background, and could leather the ball to yonder parts. He had also gained over the years a reputation for impeccable behaviour on the pitch, a reflection not only of his demeanour away from football, but also his love for the standards and values of the game.

He held his first-team place until halfway through 1932-33, but, with Cann fully fit, the club turned to Harper to take over as trainer from the recently retired Tommy Haynes. Harper retained his registration and made the occasional first-team appearance when the need arose. Towards the end of 1938-39, aged 41, he played his final three League games, although in 1940 he turned out in the wartime South West Regional League when raising eleven players was, at times, difficult. During hostilities, Harper returned to Scotland and to his original trade, serving as a blacksmith in Rosyth Dockyard.

After the War, Harper continued to serve the club, firstly as a groundsman and later as a laundryman, as well as carrying out various other sundry duties around Home Park. Fittingly, in 1972 Argyle awarded him a testimonial against his former club, Arsenal, who were, again, at that time dominating the English game, having completed the 'double' the previous year.

Long afterwards Harper remained a familiar figure around Home Park. He was always willing to talk about the game and would vividly recall matches and players from bygone years. His death in April 1989 at the age of 92 saw the passing of one of the most popular figures ever to serve Argyle. But Bill Harper's name will remain part of the club for many years to come. One of his Scotland caps is to this day displayed at the club, and the training pitch adjacent to Home Park is aptly named 'Harper's Park'.

Magic Moment: *Some 40 years after first gracing Home Park, Harper received a marvellous reception from the crowd – many of whom had never seen him play – at his testimonial against Arsenal.*

Worst Nightmare: *In February 1924, during his only losing appearance for Scotland, Harper inexplicably dropped the ball, allowing Wales to score their second goal to clinch a shock 2-0 win.*

ARGYLE RECORD	Appearances	Goals
Football League	78	–
FA Cup	4	–

No 20. **ARCHIE GORMAN**
Debut: v Bristol City, 16 September 1932
Farewell: v Sheffield Wednesday, 2 September 1939

Another of Argyle's Scots was MacDonald Archibald Gorman, who was to assist Bill Harper on and off the pitch during his time at Home Park. Born in Lochore, Gorman had been playing for Edinburgh City when he was brought to the West Country by Robert Jack in 1931.

Initially, Gorman had to be content with the reserves, making just one first-team appearance in his first season. He gradually established a regular place, and was equally assured at right- or left-half. At only 5ft 7in and weighing a mere 10½st, he was the smallest player on the Argyle staff but this did not deter him. Tenacious in the tackle, he would be described in the modern game as a 'terrier-like' player, always running and harrying. As can be noted from his record, goalscoring was not his *forte* but his ability to win the ball and deliver it to a team-mate set up countless chances for Argyle forwards over the years.

It is perhaps easy to overlook Gorman's playing contribution. From 1933 until World War II he was almost an automatic choice and it must be remembered that he played all his football in the Second Division against some powerful teams. The 1934-35 season was arguably Gorman's best for the club. He missed only one game during the season and even scored a rare goal, against Bradford.

The War effectively ended Gorman's League career. Argyle took their place in a newly formed South West Regional League, Gorman playing in all but one of 28 matches, but with the city a prime target for enemy bombs, the club were forced to withdraw from this competition after only one season.

Upon Hitler's defeat, Argyle entered an interim Football League South for the 1945-46 season as a precursor to the resumption of a full league programme the following year. Guest players were permitted and the club used new fewer than 61 players during that campaign. With new faces appearing in every game, the club won only three matches to finish bottom, although relegation was not a concern. Gorman came out of retirement in the second half of that season, when finding eleven available players was often a problem. He made sixteen appearances, the majority of them at centre-half.

When Argyle resumed their place in Division Two for the 1946-47 season, Gorman was appointed assistant trainer to Bill Harper, a position he continued to hold until the early 1950s. He later became a publican, running the Blue Monkey pub in Plymouth and later the George Hotel at Buckfastleigh. Gorman passed away at Tavistock on 18 September 1992.

Magic Moment: *Gorman scored the first of his rare goals for the club in October 1933 in a 3-3 draw with Bury.*

Worst nightmare: *Despite playing on the winning side in his debut, Gorman was immediately dropped and had to wait another fifteen months before making his next appearance.*

ARGYLE RECORD	Appearances	Goals
Football League	240	2
FA Cup	10	–

No 21. **JIMMY RAE**

Debut: v Oldham, 27 August 1932
Farewell: v Sheffield Wednesday, 2 September 1939

Completing an all-Scottish left side for Argyle for much of the 1930s –
alongside Archie Gorman and Sammy Black – was Jimmy Rae, who was
to give great service to Argyle both as a player and manager. Born in
Blackmill, Argyllshire, Rae was an outstanding player as a youngster. He
captained the Scottish schoolboys team and at the age of seventeen
signed as a part-time professional with Scottish side King's Park, which
also allowed him to complete his apprenticeship as an electrician.

In 1927 he moved to Partick, where he played more than 100 League
matches, not to mention the 1929-30 Scottish Cup final at Hampden Park
– Partick losing to Rangers 1-2 in a replay after a scoreless first game.

Clearly an outstanding prospect, Rae drew admiring glances from a
number of clubs. In a time when full-backs were, at best, expected to win
the ball at all costs and despatch it quickly upfield, Rae would attempt to
extricate himself from defensive situations by employing superior skill.
He was confident enough in his own ability to calmly retain possession in
his own penalty area, for which he drew plenty of flak.

Rae came to the attention of Argyle manager Robert Jack when
Partick played at Home Park in a benefit match for Alec Hardie in 1932.
At the time, it appeared that Rae would be heading for Glasgow Rangers,
but whilst the Scottish giants dithered, Jack invited Rae back to Plymouth
for talks. The astute Jack employed a trick which he had successfully
employed previously when luring Jack Leslie away from London, by
showing Rae photographs of Devon and Cornwall beauty-spots. This
was not the only thing that persuaded Rae to move south. He was
impressed by Jack the person and later described him as 'one of the greatest managers in the game'.

Rae returned to Glasgow without having signed on the dotted line and
Rangers came in with a last-minute bid. But Rae remained good to his
word and, confirming his admiration for Jack, later revealed that 'I had
given my word and would not break it to a man so obviously sincere and
honest'.

Incidentally, another Partick player to turn out in Hardie's benefit
match was John Simpson, who joined Argyle at the same time as Rae.
Simpson was not one of Jack's better signings and played only five games
for the club before retiring.

Having moved to Plymouth in the summer of 1932, Rae went straight
into the side for the new season. He stayed there with few absences for

seven years, never varying from the left-back position. Many considered him unfortunate not to win a full Scottish cap. On three occasions he was put on 'standby' but the magic call never came.

On paper, Rae's playing record for Argyle seems unremarkable. He never scored and did not win any honours, but he was the sort of player any manager likes to have – always reliable and one less position to worry about when team selection is made. He might have gone on for ever, but for the War, in which he was restricted to twenty games in the South West Regional League.

Afterwards, Rae was appointed Argyle's assistant manager to Jack Tresarden. When Tresarden left the club early in 1947-48, the Argyle directors turned to Rae, whose time in charge at Home Park attracts contrasting views. His term of office spanned eight years, which saw relegation from Division Two in 1949-50. Several other seasons were also spent in the wrong half of the table, yet, interspersed with this, was one of the most successful spells in the club's history. Rae masterminded the winning of the Third Division (South) title in 1951-52 and the rise to the heady heights of fourth place in Division Two the following season.

Undoubtedly, Rae's main legacy was the number of outstanding players – such as Neil Dougall and Jack Chisholm – that he brought to Home Park. His shrewd buys were reminiscent of those of Robert Jack, whom he so admired. Rae was criticised, however, for allowing players to leave at a time when the team needed strengthening to build on its success.

After two seasons of struggle in Division Two, Rae resigned part way through 1954-55 at a time when discord in the boardroom was beginning to intensify. To replace him, the directors opted for a star name, Jack Rowley, the Manchester United and England forward. Ironically, Rowley's record was no better than Rae's over a period of five seasons.

After leaving Argyle, Rae moved to the Midlands to manage a pub in Solihull but kept an eye on the fortunes of the club he served for over twenty years. He died on 4 July 1958, only four years after leaving Home Park.

Magic Moment: *In May 1954, Rae led an Argyle tour to play a series of games in the USA. The tour was a great success and included a 16-2 trouncing of Colorado 'All Stars'.*

Worst Nightmare: *At Aston Villa in February 1937, with only three minutes remaining, Rae hesitated when attempting to tackle the Villa winger. The subsequent cross saw the home side score the winner in a 5-4 victory, Argyle having led 3-0 after half an hour.*

ARGYLE RECORD	Appearances	Goals
Football League	249	–
FA Cup	10	–

No 22. **GEORGE SILK**
Debut: v Coventry, 18 December 1937
Farewell: v Watford, 10 January 1951

George Silk has a unique connection with Jimmy Rae, being the only Argyle player to take the field alongside Rae the player and under Rae as manager. In fact, Silk was one of the few players to turn out for Argyle both before and after World War II.

The connection does not end there, as Silk's Argyle debut was made at left-back, replacing the injured Rae. Where it is hard to find any connection is in their styles of play. Whereas Rae loved to play the ball out of defence, Silk's policy was to win the ball, no questions asked, and clear upfield without fuss. Whilst this was not to the football purists' liking, the Argyle fans loved it. Silk possessed the qualities needed to effect his style. His philosophy on opposing wingers was that they were an inconvenience, and his tackling could be described as tough, not to say reckless. Had Silk been a player in the modern game, he would certainly have seen his share of yellow and red cards, but in his day physical contact was part and parcel of soccer.

Silk's approach was exemplified in October 1949 against Preston, who had the famous Tom Finney on the right wing and another England international, Bobby Langton, on the left. Whilst Silk's full-back partner, Pat Jones, used more conventional methods to nullify the threat of Finney, Silk's early challenge on Langton left the winger so badly shaken that he posed no threat thereafter.

The other vital quality to Silk's game was his powerful kick. During his schoolboy days he was a centre-forward, the position in which he played for Liverpool Schools. His fierce shot was a useful weapon, and he once wore No 9 for Argyle, in a defeat at Swansea in April 1939. This owed more to desperation on the part of manager Jack Tresarden than a shrewd tactical ploy, given that Argyle had scored only one goal in their last seven games.

Born in Bootle on 18 October 1916, Silk played for Bootle Miranda before joining Southport in September 1935. He remained there for two years, playing fourteen League games, before joining Argyle in August 1937. Silk took time to establish himself in the Argyle side and during his first two seasons at Home Park played only ten games.

He remained in Plymouth during the War and was the club's only ever present during its one season in the South West Regional League. During the succeeding war years, he played occasionally for Millwall as a 'guest'.

After a five-year break, Argyle resumed competitive football in the Football League South. Silk was one of the few players young enough, and still available, to continue his career. He missed only one match in 1945-46, but when the League proper was revived for the following season, Silk had to wait until after Christmas for a run in the side. 1947-48 was a personal disappointment for Silk as he made only three first-team appearances, by which time Jimmy Rae had succeeded Tresarden as manager. In 1948-49, Rae stuck by Silk as first-choice right-back in preference to Paddy Ratcliffe, a Tresarden signing from Wolves. Silk played in all but the final five matches that season. With the irrepressible Pat Jones, Silk formed one of the fiercest full-back partnerships in the lower divisions.

The 1949-50 season saw Argyle struggle to stay in Division Two. Having won only four games up to Christmas, a reshuffle saw Ratcliffe replace Silk at right-back. It was the beginning of the end of Silk's Argyle and professional career. He played only twice in the 1950-51 before retiring from full-time football.

He subsequently moved to Cornwall where he worked at the Blue Star garage in Newquay, before becoming landlord of The Farmers Arms public house at St Columb Minor. He stayed in the game as player-manager of a Newquay side that dominated Cornish soccer at the time. After running the Cross Mount guest-house in Newquay, he returned to Plymouth to become steward of the Stuart Social Club in Pennycomequick before his premature death in 1969 at the age of 53.

Magic Moment: *Silk's only goal for Argyle was a legacy of his powerful kick. Against West Ham in February 1949, Silk belted the ball from just over the halfway line. Opposing keeper Ernie Gregory misjudged the flight and the ball sailed over him into the net.*

Worst Nightmare: *A Cup-tie in January 1949 against Notts Co – who included the famous Tommy Lawton – was in extra-time when County gained a corner. Silk on the near post and goalkeeper Bill Shortt left the ball for each other, leaving Jackie Sewell an easy header.*

ARGYLE RECORD	Appearances	Goals
Football League	86	1
FA Cup	4	–

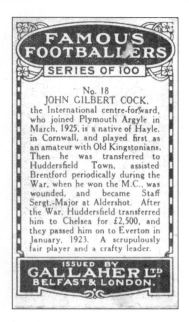

No 11. Jack Cock, England international forward

No 12. Full-back Fred Titmuss, Argyle's record signing in 1926

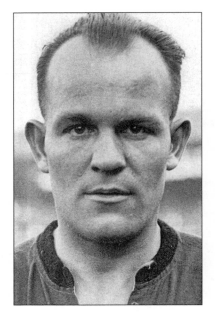

No 16. Norman Mackay had a fine voice   No 17. Harry Cann, Cornwall's finest keeper

No 18. Jack Vidler was a prolific scorer   No 19. Bill Harper, Scottish international goalie

~ *The Glory Years* ~

No 23. **BILL SHORTT**
Debut: v West Ham, 31 August 1946
Farewell: v Bristol Rovers, 2 April 1956

The goalkeeper involved in the mix-up with George Silk which led to that Notts County winner was Bill Shortt. It is perhaps a harsh introduction to someone who became one of the great keepers in Argyle history.

William Warren Shortt was born in Wrexham on 13 October 1920. He spent his early years with Hoole Alexandra before joining Chester in May 1939. War arrived before he had played a game. Army service brought him to Plymouth, for whom he 'guested' on a number of occasions, as Argyle's regular keeper, Matt Middleton, had to travel from his Derbyshire home.

When Shortt was released from the Army, Chester sold him to the Pilgrims for a fee of £1,000. He played eighteen times in 1945-46. With Argyle's ever changing defence conceding 120 goals, Shortt was not 'short' of practice.

Fortunes improved little the following season in Division Two, with the club shipping 96 goals. But for Shortt, it would have been worse. He made 38 appearances that season and for the next nine years made the Argyle No 1 jersey his own. Looking back, he was the archetypal goalkeeper of the time. Not particularly tall, he could best be described as well built. His photographs display him as a jovial character, invariably wearing a thick roll-neck jersey, usually in the red of Wales. His physique certainly helped protect him from battering-ram forwards. His Argyle team-mate, Alex Govan, who played both with and against top-class keepers in Europe, rates 'Shortty' as the best he has seen. Govan recalls that it was rare to see Shortt dive to stop a shot, as his positioning was so good.

Shortt was renowned for plucking crosses out of the air. Time and again, attacks were foiled by Shortt leaping above taller forwards and safely gathering the ball. He could also kick a dead ball vast distances.

Whilst his ability made him a crowd favourite, he exhibited an element of showmanship that enhanced his popularity. It was not unknown for him, for example, to chat with the crowd behind his goal when the ball was in distant parts.

It was early in Shortt's Argyle career that he caught the eye of the Welsh selectors, and he made his full international debut in a Victory international against Northern Ireland in 1946. He went on to win twelve caps, but played understudy for much of that time to Wolves and Liverpool custodian Cyril Sidlow. His best international season was 1951-52, when as the regular keeper he helped Wales tie with England as co-winners of the Home International Championships. He also played against the 'Rest of the UK' in a match won by Wales.

Back at Home Park, manager Jimmy Rae, having endured relegation in 1949-50, was assembling a strong side. The defence and half-backs were virtually unchanged for two seasons, a factor which helped Argyle storm to the Division Three (South) title in 1951-52. Shortt was the backbone of a side that used only seventeen players all season. Twelve months later the Greens finished in their highest ever position of fourth in Division Two. Shortt missed only four games, but with the club on the verge of breaking into the big time, that winning side was disintegrating.

In 1953-54, the patient reserve keeper Les Major was given his opportunity and, although Shortt was soon recalled, Major later regained his place. Although Shortt was now in his mid-30s, he was not finished yet. He participated in Argyle's tour of North America in May 1954 and played 34 times during the following season as the club narrowly avoided relegation.

1955-56 marked the end of the road for both Argyle and Bill Shortt. The Greens went down and Shortt retired. He was in goal for the 0-6 drubbing at Bristol City in December, a result all the more remarkable considering that Argyle had thrashed the Robins 5-0 at home the day before. Shortt's retirement was ironic only because Les Major, now the preferred No 1, also had to quit, in his case through injury.

Shortt had a spell with Tavistock and, like many other ex-players of the time, he went into the publican trade. He ran the Duke of York public house in Tavistock before taking over as licensee of the Golden Hind Hotel. Now in his 80s, he still lives in Plymouth.

Magic Moment: *At home to Everton in November 1952, Argyle conceded a penalty, but Shortt saved from Irish international Tom Clinton, pushing the ball on to a post, grabbing the rebound, and getting a kick in the ribs in the ensuing melee.*

Worst Nightmare: *After a 1-2 home defeat by Leeds in November 1949, Shortt was the innocent victim of crowd trouble. The referee required a police escort because of his controversial decisions. Missiles were thrown, one of which hit Shortt on the head and drew blood.*

ARGYLE RECORD	Appearances	Goals
Football League	342	–
FA Cup	14	–

No 24. **BILL STRAUSS**

Debut: v West Ham, 31 August 1946
Farewell: v Leeds, 16 September 1953

Alongside Bill Shortt in Argyle's first post-War League side was a South African, Bill Strauss – a surname that was a headline writer's dream.

Born in the Transvaal on 6 January 1916, Strauss had represented South Africa at soccer and had impressed ex-Aberdeen player Eddie Swan, who recommended Strauss to his former club. He arrived in Britain in December 1935 on board the *SS Arundel Castle*, and scored six times in his first two games for the Dons, despite playing on the left wing instead of his preferred centre-forward role. Strauss's 25 goals in 1936-37 helped Aberdeen to second place behind Rangers and their first Scottish Cup final, where they lost to Celtic in front of a record Hampden Park attendance of over 144,000.

World War II saw Strauss serve in the Royal Signals and then the Commandos. He then returned to Pittodrie, and totalled in his Aberdeen career 53 goals from 94 League and Cup appearances. Argyle boss Jack Tresarden travelled to see Aberdeen in a Scottish League Cup semi-final. It was not his intended target who caught his eye, but Strauss, who at the age of 30 was brought to Plymouth in time for the commencement of the 1946-47 campaign.

A 25,000 home crowd witnessed his debut, and Strauss became an instant hit, scoring twice in a 3-1 victory over West Ham. Seven goals in his first ten games showed that he had lost none of the goalscoring prowess he had displayed at Aberdeen, but injury curtailed his season.

In the days when wingers seemed glued to the touchline, Strauss was unorthodox in roaming elsewhere, thereby confusing the opposition, who were unsure how to respond. Combined with his venomous shooting, these tactics go some way to explaining Strauss's impressive scoring feats.

The following season saw Strauss miss just one game, although his scoring touch had deserted him somewhat. Nevertheless, his five goals made him second top scorer. Jimmy Rae had replaced Tresarden in the hot seat, but kept faith with evergreen Strauss. Towards the end of 1948-49 he played a few games on the opposite flank and the following season wore the No 7 shirt on a regular basis.

Relegation meant changes were inevitable, and the emergence of two young wingers, Gordon Astall and Alex Govan, saw Strauss gradually fade from the scene. Despite their rivalry for the wing positions, Strauss was always willing to advise and help the two youngsters.

After being granted a testimonial against his former club, Aberdeen, in May 1951, Strauss played nine times during the Division Three (South) title-winning season, scoring once, but had to be content with reserve team football for the whole of the next season. Aged 37, he made two appearances early in 1953-54 before quitting the game.

Strauss's sporting prowess was not confined to the soccer pitch. He was good at badminton and a fine cricketer, playing for Plymouth Cricket Club and for Devon Minor Counties. The highlight of his cricket career was scoring a century for Devon against the Surrey Second XI at the Oval.

He remained a well-known figure around the city For a time he worked on the administrative side at Home Park, before working for the local Gas Board and taking over as the landlord of The Tandem Inn public house in the Octagon, Union Street. Bill Strauss passed away in 1987.

Magic Moment: *Strauss scored against Crewe in an FA Cup-tie in December 1950. His half-volley from wide on the right was so fierce that some of the Crewe players joined in the applause.*

Worst Nightmare: *A young Alex Govan, who eventually took over from Strauss on the Argyle left wing, once revealed to Strauss that he skipped school on one occasion to watch him play for Aberdeen.*

ARGYLE RECORD	Appearances	Goals
Football League	158	40
FA Cup	8	2

No 25. **ALEX GOVAN**
Debut: v Coventry, 5 October 1946
Final Farewell: v Stoke, 27 February 1960

The story of Alex Govan, the man who eventually succeeded Bill Strauss in the Argyle No 11 shirt, reads like a 'Boy's Own' serial, recounting as it does his early days, kicking a ball around the back streets of Glasgow, to playing in a Wembley FA Cup final.

Govan was born in Glasgow on 16 June 1929 and starred for the Bridgeton Boys Club team. Dundee United, Motherwell and Queens Park all invited him for a trial, and Celtic and Rangers were also said to be interested.

Govan had been picked for a Scotland Youth versus Wales fixture at Swansea with a morning kick-off. A non-playing reserve for Scotland that day, incidentally, was another future Argyle star, Jimmy Gauld. Argyle were playing at Swansea that afternoon and manager Jack Tresarden took in the youth international. After the game he pressed Govan to come for a trial.

Govan had no idea where Plymouth was, but he was eventually persuaded, and was one of four Scottish youngsters who made the long train journey to Plymouth. After the trial, the four were called in turn to learn their fate. Tresarden told the first three that their services would not be required, so Govan, last to go in, feared the worst. He was wrong. Tresarden wanted him to sign, but Govan said 'no', on the basis that Plymouth was too far from home.

Former Argyle player Alec Hardie, then the club's Scottish scout, arranged for Govan to play higher-grade football with Kilsyth Rangers. The step up made no difference to Govan and Hardie reported this back to Home Park. A second trial at Plymouth was agreed, this time with Govan's father coming along. Father and son were treated royally and were accommodated in the Grand Hotel, then owned by Argyle director Bob Heath.

Govan remained unconvinced and returned to Scotland yet again. Finally, Argyle made him an offer he could not refuse, £6 a week, with an extra £1 for first-team appearances, a handsome wage in those days for an untried youngster. As a bonus, Govan registered as an apprentice joiner with the building contractor, Dudley Coles, another Argyle director. This exempted Govan from National Service on the basis that he was providing valuable skills to a city that was rebuilding after the wartime devastation.

Govan began his Argyle career in the reserves, scoring twice on his debut. Each day he would make a token gesture to his other 'job' as an apprentice joiner by turning up for work for an hour before leaving to attend training.

By October, he confronted Tresarden to demand why he was languishing in the reserves. To his credit, Tresarden responded by giving the lad his first-team debut. Govan gave a good account of himself, playing at inside-left, but was immediately dropped again. The manager explained that he wanted to nurture Govan's rare talent.

It was much the same the following season. Then, to the surprise of Govan, he was summoned for National Service. The club investigated and discovered that as part of his apprenticeship Govan should have been registered for, and attended, night school. As this had not happened, his call up was enforced and he joined the RAF.

Govan was finally sent to an RAF station at Gloucester, purely on the basis of his football ability. This was the base for the RAF soccer team and he found himself billeted with other professional players. Provided his displays on the pitch were up to scratch, he was told he could remain there for the duration of his service. Govan played for the full RAF side against top class opposition, including an England Select XI.

An unexpected bonus came along when Govan was released from the RAF after completing only nineteen months of his two-year stint. As the soccer season had finished, he served no real other purpose to the Air Force.

By this time, he had converted from inside-forward to outside-left, and, on his return to Home Park, found himself a regular spot in the first team in that position. In 1950-51 he replaced Paddy Blatchford in the No 11 shirt and made 38 League and Cup appearances, scoring ten times. The following season Argyle stormed to the title, with Govan and his fellow winger Gordon Astall scoring their share of Argyle's 107 League goals. The duo soon carved a reputation as one of the best wing combinations outside the top division.

Govan was the classic winger, small, tricky and with the ability to provide pinpoint and varied crosses. Few full-backs ever got the better of him and he was the type of player the crowds loved to see. He adopted Bill Strauss's tactic of drifting in from the wing. Govan recalls how the crowd loved this particular ploy but would bemoan his absence should the ball suddenly be played to where he was expected to be. For a small player, he was also good in the air and a reasonable proportion of his goals came from headers.

When, in 1952-53, Argyle reached the heady heights of fourth place in Division Two, Govan and Astall continued to earn rave reviews. Supporters felt that, at last, the club had the basis of a side that could climb into Division One. To their dismay, in the close season Govan was sold to Second Division Birmingham for £10,000, and Astall followed him soon after. Govan had not asked to go. Manager Jimmy Rae was blamed for breaking up one of Argyle's most successful sides, although the decision was out of his hands.

Govan scored on his Birmingham debut and in 1954-55 he won a Second Division champions medal. Birmingham became the first English city to compete in the Inter City Fairs Cup and drew mighty Inter Milan in the first round. Govan scored both goals in the home leg to seal a famous victory. Birmingham reached the semi-finals before being beaten by Barcelona.

The Blues also reached the 1956 FA Cup final, losing to Manchester City. Being introduced to the Queen ranks as one of Govan's proudest moments. Playing alongside him and Astall that day were former Pilgrim Len Boyd and Johnny Newman, who was later to join Argyle.

Govan was close to winning international honours. Scotland selected him for the squad to face Austria, but the game was just before the Cup final and Birmingham would not release him.

Not content with exciting wing play, Govan also became a prolific scorer. During 1956-57 he scored *five* hat-tricks for Birmingham, a record for a winger and one that is unlikely ever to be broken. Three of those hat-tricks came in the space of ten days.

Having scored 53 goals in 165 League appearances for the Blues, Govan briefly joined Portsmouth before a second spell at Home Park beckoned. It was a timely return, as Argyle won the Division Three title in 1958-59. Govan played for a further two years, covering for regular wingers Peter Anderson and Harry Penk.

After retiring he became manager of the Hyde Park Hotel in Plymouth, while looking after Argyle's third team, which competed in the South Western League. He worked alongside another ex-Argyle player, coach Frank Sloan.

Govan was sacked from this role in unusual circumstances. The third team consisted mainly of youngsters eager to make the grade. Many had full-time jobs and for evening matches the team bus would collect them at various points in the city. Govan and Sloan would treat the youngsters to a cup of tea *en route* to a game and fish and chips on the return journey, claiming expenses from the club. On one occasion Govan added a drink for the bus driver. Chairman Ron Blindell queried the subsequent claim for fourteen portions of fish and chips but fifteen cups of tea. On hearing Govan's explanation, Blindell replied that the club did not fund the driver's refreshments. Govan took a threepenny piece from his pocket and handed it over, adding 'now we're squared up'. This was not to Blindell's liking and Govan was sacked.

After eight years in the pub business, Govan became proprietor of a grocery store in Plymouth and subsequently worked for a local firm, Gleasons, for a further 23 years. Much of his retirement is spent on the golf course. One of his sons, Tommy, signed as an apprentice with Argyle in the 1970s, although he never graced the first team.

Still living in Plymouth, Alex Govan closely follows the fortunes of his former clubs. He is a regular guest of Birmingham City at various functions. A true gentleman, he is always willing to help anyone who takes an interest in the game and, still with a broad Glasgow accent, talks passionately about the game he played so well.

Magic Moment: *Having revealed in an interview that his favourite song was Harry Lauder's 'Keep right on to the end of the road', Govan was overcome with emotion when Birmingham fans adopted it.*

Worst Nightmare: *Govan sat shocked in the dressing room after underdogs Gateshead had defeated Argyle in an FA Cup-tie, scoring with their only chance, after one of the most one-sided games ever seen at Home Park.*

ARGYLE RECORD	Appearances	Goals
Football League	142	35
FA Cup	8	3

No 26. **ERNIE EDDS**
Debut: v Tottenham, 23 November 1946
Final Farewell: v Rotherham, 23 April 1955

Like Govan, Ernie Edds was not blessed with even average height, and at 5ft 7in was one of the smallest centre-forwards in League football. But lack of inches did not prevent him finding the net on a regular basis.

Born in Portsmouth on 19 March 1926, Edds' talent emerged at an early age, playing for his school, St Mary's Road, in his home town. He then played for Portsmouth juniors before Millwall snapped him up on a professional contract, but war broke out before he could play for them. It was Argyle's good fortune that towards the end of the conflict Edds was posted to Crownhill Barracks in Plymouth.

He attracted Argyle's attention through his performances for the 16th Holding Battalion's team that competed in the Plymouth and District League. Manager Jack Tresarden struck a deal with Millwall that saw Edds join the Argyle staff in October 1946. A month later he was selected for his Pilgrims debut, a daunting ordeal in front of a crowd of 41,000 at Tottenham. The 1-2 defeat proved to be his only appearance that season.

With Tadman missing the early part of 1947-48 through injury, Edds was given the occasional outing, which became an extended run when Jimmy Rae was appointed manager part way through that campaign. Edds finished the season top scorer with fourteen goals from only 23 starts. It was largely thanks to Edds notching twelve of Argyle's seventeen goals in the final fifteen matches that relegation was avoided.

Helped by his small stature, Edds was quick on the turn and had the ability to aim his shots wherever he wanted. His nimble feet outwitted many a centre-half, accustomed to marking centre-forwards of similar build.

1948-49 saw him start as first choice No 9, but when Tadman was restored to the side and began to find his scoring boots, Edds was moved firstly to inside-left and then left-wing. He found this switch difficult to adjust to, and when 1949-50 got under way he found himself regularly back in the reserves. After just three first-team appearances, in December 1949 he was transferred to Blackburn Rovers. Argyle seemed delighted to receive a fee of £8,500 for a player who was no longer in the frame.

After a season and a half at Ewood Park, during which time he scored three times in eighteen games, Edds moved back to the South West, joining Torquay on a free transfer. His time at Plainmoor proved to be one of the most productive of his career. His 84 League games yielded 34 goals. Among these was a goal at Home Park in April 1952 that almost spoiled Argyle's party. The Pilgrims had clinched the Division Three (South) title and were applauded onto the field by their opponents and a 30,000 crowd. Edds' goal gave Torquay a 2-0 lead, although Argyle fought back to finish 2-2.

Argyle struggled to replace the departed Alex Govan at outside-left. Tadman, the raw Peter Anderson, and even the ageing Bill Strauss had experimented with the No 11 shirt but found it didn't fit. So, in October 1953, it was to Edds that Argyle turned, bringing him back in a straight swap for Harold Dobbie. Edds did well enough, missing only a few games. But the following season, his last at Home Park, he was used rarely, and in July 1955 he moved to Swindon.

After three games for the Wiltshire side, Edds quit football. He continued living in Swindon and took employment running a Working Men's club. He then became landlord of the New Inn in Swindon before working for the Metal Box Company. Prior to his retirement, he worked at the Membury Service Station on the M4 motorway.

Magic Moment: *Edds scored all three goals in Argyle's 3-2 win at Southampton in April 1948. They earned vital points in the fight against the drop, but the hat-trick – his only one – was seen by family and friends who had travelled from nearby Portsmouth.*

Worst Nightmare: *A blizzard, 50 mph winds and a temperature of 20 degrees Fahrenheit greeted Edds as he ran onto the Brentford pitch for a Division Two game in February 1948.*

ARGYLE RECORD	Appearances	Goals
Football League	85	22
FA Cup	3	–

No 27. **PAT JONES**
Debut: v Coventry, 17 May 1947
Farewell: v Southend, 21 April 1958

Yet another player of jockey-sized proportions, Pat Jones virtually monopolised the left-back position for Argyle over a twelve-year period.

Thanks to World War II, Jones was a late starter, being 26 when he made his Argyle debut. Nevertheless, he played almost 450 games for the club and one can only guess at the likely total had war not delayed his introduction.

Born in Plymouth on 7 September 1920, Jones attended the Laira Green School. When war broke out, he joined the Army and served with the Devonshire Regiment, representing the Combined Services XI at soccer whilst stationed in India. On his release, he returned to Plymouth and played for local sides Plymouth United and Astor Institute.

Jones was one of a number of players from local clubs who were given an opportunity to impress Argyle. A few games with the 'A' team convinced Tresarden to sign him in March 1947. After just seven reserve games Jones was pitched into the final three games of a season in which Argyle had struggled to avoid relegation. It was the start of a run that saw Jones play 279 consecutive League games. During that time he also played in eleven of the twelve FA Cup-ties involving Argyle, missing only a replay at Wolves in January 1950 through injury. That League run ended in November 1953 with a groin injury at Crystal Palace, setting an Argyle record that will surely never be broken. The fact that Jones was a defender makes the record even more praiseworthy. In an age when a full-back's brief was usually no more complex than to stop his winger at any price, injuries were common. Jones carried out his instructions, but with style.

At only 5ft 7in and 10½st, Jones had the asset of quickness off the mark. He would encourage his winger to take him on the outside. He would then invariably match him for speed before executing a perfectly timed and fair tackle. Jones's hunched shoulders, rugged features, and a dour, unsmiling expression doubtless gave him a psychological advantage over many an opponent, yet to see him off the field was to confront an almost frail figure.

At first, he must have wondered whether he had put a hex on the side, as it was not until his tenth game that he enjoyed that winning feeling.

Those nine games had brought two draws, seven defeats, and 26 goals conceded.

Honours came his way in 1952 when he won a Third Division (South) champions medal. Needless to say, he was an ever present, as he was in six of his twelve seasons at Home Park.

His appearance record says everything about Jones. Consistent, reliable and honest seem inadequate adjectives to describe a player who became a Home Park institution. He was not the sort to make headlines, but rarely had a bad game. The crowd loved him, helped of course by the fact that he was a local boy. Older supporters today, if asked to name an all-time great Argyle XI, would invariably include Jones at left-back.

During his time he played against some of the great right-wingers in English football, including Stan Matthews and Tom Finney, and Jones matched them all. His decision to retire in 1958 saw him miss out on another medal, as Argyle claimed the Division Three title a year later. By then he was playing for South Western League side, St Austell.

Naturally, Jones remained in his home city and made a return to Home Park in 1961, when he was appointed to the training staff under manager Ellis Stuttard. He remained in this role until 1964, when he left to pursue other business interests, running a café and grocery store at nearby Challaborough. Jones passed away in December 1990.

Magic Moment: *Jones notched his first goal, a header, for Argyle in December 1955 to secure a 1-1 draw with Sheffield Wednesday. It ended a sequence of 352 first-team appearances without a goal.*

Worst Nightmare: *In January 1951 a 40,000 crowd saw Argyle take on First Division Wolves in a Cup-tie. At 1-1, Jones collided with his bulky captain, Jack Chisholm. Jones left the field with a gashed head that required stitches. He returned sporting a rugby skull-cap. During his absence Wolves had scored the winning goal.*

ARGYLE RECORD	Appearances	Goals
Football League	425	2
FA Cup	16	–

No 28. **PADDY RATCLIFFE**
Debut: v Newcastle, 23 August 1947
Farewell: v Rotherham, 3 December 1955

Pat Jones's full-back partner for much of the early 1950s was Patrick Christopher Ratcliffe, commonly known as 'Paddy'.

Ratcliffe was born in Dublin on New Year's Eve 1919 and played junior soccer in what became the Irish Free State. He was nineteen when war broke out, and, although a national of neutral Ireland, he volunteered for the RAF as an air gunner. During an air-raid on Essen, his bomber was shot down in flames. Ratcliffe, suffering shrapnel wounds in his left leg, parachuted out but was captured and spent two years in a Prisoner of War camp.

In 1945 Ratcliffe returned to Dublin and played for Bohemians before signing for Notts County and, in June 1946, Wolves. He made only two first-team appearances for the Molineux giants before joining Argyle towards the end of 1946-47. Due to an early version of the 'transfer deadline', Ratcliffe could play no part in Argyle's relegation fight.

The following season saw Ratcliffe start as first-choice right-back, but when, within a few weeks, Tresarden was replaced by new manager Jimmy Rae, Ratcliffe was dropped in favour of 34-year-old Bobby Stuart. When Stuart left the club, the No 2 shirt did not revert to Ratcliffe but went to George Silk.

It was not until midway through 1949-50 that Ratcliffe grabbed the right-back shirt for keeps. His game had improved in the reserves and he was now developing into a skilful full-back, willing to join the attack and able to cross the ball to good effect. He was equally adept with either foot, and soon became Argyle's regular penalty taker. He was not a fierce tackler in the mould of Jones or George Silk, and at 5ft 10in and 12st could not match Jones for speed, but in harness together they looked formidable. Ratcliffe's appearance was reminiscent of an Al Capone sidekick, with his shirt collar turned up, lop-sided grin and one-eyed squint perfectly complementing Jones's funereal expression.

After missing only three League games in 1950-51, Ratcliffe was ever-present the following season when Argyle claimed the Division Three (South) title. He continued to give excellent service and, during the club's 1954 tour of the United States, played in eight of the ten games and scored four goals.

One of the more amusing anecdotes surrounding Ratcliffe occurred away from the soccer pitch. He was playing golf with Gordon Astall at Yelverton, which, as locals know, is a moorland course. On one hole, Ratcliffe was delighted to see his shot find the middle of the green. As the pair approached, a moorland pony strolled into the undergrowth with Ratcliffe's ball in its mouth. Cursing in his thick Irish brogue, Ratcliffe gave chase, but golf ball and pony were never seen again.

Back on the soccer front, it was not until 1955-56 that Ratcliffe began to fade from the scene. Utility player George Robertson was given an extended run at right-back. That summer Ratcliffe retired and subsequently emigrated to the United States, where he passed away in 1973.

Magic Moment: *On the North American tour of 1954, Ratcliffe scored a rare goal from open play and was one of eight Argyle players to find the net in a 16-2 win over the Colorado 'All Stars'.*

Worst Nightmare: *As if his wartime adventures were not enough, Ratcliffe suffered an airborne scare on the American tour when the plane from Chicago and Detroit was caught in an electrical storm.*

ARGYLE RECORD	Appearances	Goals
Football League	236	10
FA Cup	10	—

No 29. **MAURICE TADMAN**
Debut: v Newcastle, 23 August 1947
Farewell: Blackburn, 12 February 1955

Paddy Ratcliffe and Maurice Tadman were two of five players to make their Argyle debuts in the opening game of the 1947-48 season. For Tadman, it was a memorable game for more than one reason, as we shall discover later.

Born at Rainham, Essex, on 28 June 1921, Tadman began his soccer career with Bexleyheath and Welling FC who, at that time, acted as a 'nursery' club for Charlton Athletic. As a centre-forward he showed an eye for goal and signed for Charlton in June 1938, joining his elder brother, George, already an established first-team player at The Valley.

War interrupted the Tadmans' soccer careers, but when football resumed towards the end of 1945, Maurice took root in Charlton Athletic's reserve team, scoring 38 goals in the London Combination League. Competition for first-team places was such that, having played just three games, Tadman signed for Argyle in August 1947. The fee was £4,000.

On his debut Tadman scored Argyle's only goal in a 1-6 collapse at Newcastle. A return of seven goals in twenty League and Cup games that season was a fair return. He was on the sidelines for the start of 1948-49, but with the team wondering where their next goal was coming from, he was restored and in his second game scored twice in a 2-2 draw with Chesterfield. He kept his place and finished that season top scorer with fifteen goals.

Twelve months on, Argyle were relegated. Tadman's nine goals have to be seen in the context of a losing team. With the club back in the Third Division, Tadman found a level of football at which he could excel. October and November 1950 saw an extraordinary sequence of seventeen goals in eight matches. His purple patch started with two goals at Torquay. A week later he scored four in a 5-1 triumph over Aldershot. He bagged another four as Argyle thrashed Brighton 6-0, and a week later restricted himself to three in a 3-0 FA Cup win at Gainsborough Trinity. In the one game in which he failed to score, Argyle still won 4-0. Not surprisingly, he again finished as top scorer that season, with 26 goals.

Tadman was an integral part of the side that scored over 100 goals in returning to Division Two. His final tally of 27 goals yet again made him top scorer. Argyle were now seemingly on the up, their supporters dreaming of promotion to Division One. It wasn't to be, but the Pilgrims came mightily close, finishing the 1952-53 season in fourth place. Tadman's reputation meant he was tightly marked, but he still found the net fifteen times, more than any other colleague.

Eleven goals in 1953-54 once again saw him as the club's leading scorer, but it is fair to say that he was never as effective following the departure of wingers Gordon Astall and Alex Govan, who had for seasons past created so many chances for him.

The natural assumption to make on studying Tadman's physique, 6ft tall and 13st, would be that he was a typical bruising forward who was good in the air. In fact, the opposite was true. His heading skills could best be described as average, and he was happiest with the ball at his feet, from where he could take on, and beat, opponents. This skill on the ball was employed on the left wing during the latter part of his career.

Both on and off the field he was a modest man. There were never any histrionics from him as yet another shot found the net. A nod of the head and a few brief handshakes with team-mates, and let's get on with the game. He did not change with time, and many years later, when invited back to Home Park as a guest of the club, he expressed his amazement that he was even remembered by supporters.

The emergence of two local forwards, Neil Langman and Eric Davis, restricted Tadman to seven appearances in 1954-55, which proved to be his last season as an Argyle player. When he left Home Park he had joined an elite corps of players who had scored more than 100 goals for the club. To this day, his tally puts him fifth in the all-time list of Argyle goalscorers.

His playing career was not yet done. He joined Irish League side Belfast Distillery as player-manager, and in his first season scored 41 goals – including the fastest ever hat-trick in Ulster football – which helped the club win the Irish Cup.

On his return to England, he settled back in his native Essex and worked for many years as a management accountant with the Basildon Development Cooperation. He retired in 1986 and remained in Essex until his death in November 1994.

Magic Moment: *Tadman was selected to feature in a national campaign advertising Quaker Oats. Apparently, the product gave Tadman 'match winning fitness and extra winter energy'.*

Worst Nightmare: *Tadman broke his wrist during his Argyle debut. His arm was still in plaster when he made his comeback.*

ARGYLE RECORD	Appearances	Goals
Football League	240	108
FA Cup	13	4

No 30. **GEORGE DEWS**
Debut: v Chesterfield, 1 November 1947
Farewell: v Ipswich, 16 April 1955

Frequently sharing the goalscoring headlines with Maurice Tadman, George Dews was one of the most popular players ever to grace Home Park.

Dews was born in Ossett, Yorkshire, on 5 June 1921. He began his soccer career during the War with Middlesbrough, and was a regular in their First Division side in 1946-47. After 33 games and eight goals, it was surprising that he accepted a move to Argyle, a struggling Second Division club, but a fee of £11,000 brought Dews and his team-mate, Bobby Stuart, to Home Park in October 1947. Apparently the thought of the mild climate in the South West was a factor in Dews's decision. A host of top clubs were chasing Dews, and the decision to sell him did not go down well with the Boro fans.

Although Stuart's Argyle career was short-lived, no one could argue that Dews was not value for money. He proved to be one of the club's most consistent performers over an eight-year period.

There was nothing flashy about Dews's game, but his work-rate was prodigious and, as an inside-forward, he would cover virtually every blade of grass during a game. Wherever the action was, the fair-haired Dews would never be far away, always making himself available to receive a pass to set up another attack, and appearing seconds later to support the forwards. If this gives the impression that speed was another attribute, then this is misleading. Dews was decidedly one paced, perhaps a factor in his seemingly endless stamina. No game better illustrates Dews's contribution to the Argyle cause than his debut at Chesterfield. Dews's performance transformed a losing side. His non-stop running instilled an urgency to the team that had been lacking and also created the type of chances Maurice Tadman craved. Chesterfield fans left the ground wondering why Argyle were languishing near the foot of the table.

Dews could fill in elsewhere if necessary. Should any Argyle player leave the field through injury, Dews was normally the man to plug the gap. Over the years he deputised in both full-back positions and even took over in goal in a match against Rotherham, when Les Major was forced off with a hand injury.

Even-tempered, irrespective of any rough stuff metered out by opponents, Dews would remain calm and unruffled, earning him the nickname 'Gentleman George'.

Despite his many attributes, in his early Argyle years Dews gave few signs of the goalscoring prowess he would come to display. His first three seasons brought just seventeen goals in 103 starts, but in 1950-51 he mustered twenty strikes in 44 League and Cup matches, followed by 25 goals in Argyle's title-winning season.

Curiously, Dews never played in Argyle's final match of any season. There was a good explanation. Dews spent his summers playing for Worcestershire Cricket Club. He played for the county from 1946 until 1961, scoring almost 17,000 runs with a highest score of 145. As a middle order right-handed batsman, he exceeded the magical 1,000 runs in a season on eleven occasions. He was also an outstanding fielder, as his record of 355 catches in 376 games confirms. Some thought him worthy of an England place.

Argyle manager Jimmy Rae was a big fan of Dews, but his successor, Jack Rowley, was not. As is often the case with a change at the top, fresh ideas and fresh faces were the order of the day. Dews, now 34, found himself out of favour. It was nevertheless an unpopular decision with the supporters, when he was allowed to sign for Walsall in June 1955. The move to the Midlands did not really suit Dews. He played only nine games for the Saddlers, scoring once.

He continued his cricket career and also took up employment at the Round Oak Steelworks. Sadly, events in later life have not been kind. He was made redundant from his job when aged 59 and a few years later suffered a brain haemorrhage which has badly affected his health. He currently resides in a nursing home near the family residence in Brierley Hill in the Midlands.

Magic Moment: *In October 1950, Dews netted with the last kick to complete a 7-1 rout of Colchester and ensure that every Argyle forward had scored. Colchester's keeper that day was an ex-Argyle player, George Wright.*

Worst Nightmare: *Dews had a 'goal' disallowed against Cup finalists Leicester in April 1949. His header had bounced down off the bar and over the line. The players were already lining up for the restart when a linesman persuaded the referee that Bill Strauss had been offside. Even the normally placid Dews was livid.*

ARGYLE RECORD	Appearances	Goals
Football League	257	76
FA Cup	14	5

No 31. **GORDON ASTALL**
Debut: v Luton, 14 February 1948
Farewell: v Everton, 10 October 1953

Like George Dews, Gordon Astall made his Pilgrims debut during 1947-48. Unlike Dews, Astall had no previous League experience.

Born at Horwich on 22 September 1927, Astall joined the Royal Marines late in the War upon leaving school. As with Ernie Edds, Astall's wartime service saw him posted to Plymouth and he came to Argyle's attention playing for the Marines in local football. On his release from service in December 1947, he signed a professional contract with the club and debuted two months later.

Playing on the right wing, he quickly settled and held his place for the remainder of the season. He played in 36 League matches in 1948-49, but the following season was a disappointment, with Argyle relegated and veteran Bill Strauss often preferred to Astall in the No 7 shirt.

The emergence of Alex Govan in late 1950 seemed to spur Astall, and suddenly Argyle possessed two wingers able to inject fear into any defence. The two wide-men did, in fact, have differing styles. Whilst Govan was more of a winger in the old style, jinking one way, then the other, Astall relied more on speed. He would rarely dribble past his full-back, preferring to push the ball past him and beat him for pace. Another successful tactic was having right-half Neil Dougall play the ball inside the full-back for Astall to chase. His quickness off the mark earned him the nickname 'Flash'. Unlike Govan, he was also two-footed with a fierce shot which he liked to unleash when he cut inside his marker. Unlike Govan, too, Astall preferred to drive the ball low into the area.

His grounding in the Marines had given Astall a strong physique, which he employed to hurl long throws into the penalty area, no mean feat given the weight of those old-style leather balls.

Astall and Govan were pivotal to Argyle's championship season, 1951-52, with Astall missing only one game and contributing eighteen goals. With the team now pressing for promotion to Division One, Astall's contribution was recognised by selection for the England 'B' side that played France in Le Havre in 1952. England lost 1-7.

By the start of 1953-54, Govan had departed for Birmingham City and in October they came back for Astall, thereby reuniting a wing-combination that had probably never been bettered at Home Park.

Like Govan, Astall had no urge to leave Plymouth, but the move to Birmingham was one he would not regret. With promotion to the First Division, Astall found himself part of Birmingham's Inter Cities Fairs Cup adventures. He was also selected for a Football League representative side.

His best year was 1956. He graced a (losing) FA Cup final and won two full England caps. He even scored on his international baptism, in a 5-1 win in Finland, and retained his place in a 3-1 win in Berlin over the defending World Cup holders. No more caps came his way, but nothing could dilute the memory of having played alongside the likes of Nat Lofthouse, Billy Wright and Duncan Edwards.

His Birmingham career lasted until July 1961, by which time he had scored 57 goals in 235 League appearances. A free transfer took him to Torquay, but after one season an Achilles injury forced his retirement. He remained living in Torquay, taking employment with a firm of bookmakers before working for a stationery firm. He then spent twenty years in the insurance business.

Still living in Torquay, he remains active through his membership of Stover Golf Club as well as being a keen bowls player.

Magic Moment: *At Brighton in April 1952, Argyle had to win to secure promotion. At 2-2, Astall's shot hit the woodwork, rebounded onto the keeper's foot and into the net. It proved to be the winner.*

Worst Nightmare: *After a game at Newport, played in dreadful conditions, Argyle returned to the dressing room to find no hot water. The home team were luckier, so Argyle had to wait for them to finish bathing before being forced to use the same water!*

ARGYLE RECORD	Appearances	Goals
Football League	188	42
FA Cup	6	1

No 32. **NEIL DOUGALL**

Debut: v West Brom, 12 March 1949
Farewell: v Bradford City, 13 December 1958

The man who fed Gordon Astall his diet of passes was Neil Dougall, another Scot who gave Argyle loyal service both on and off the pitch.

It was, perhaps, inevitable that Cornelius Dougall, to give him his actual name, would become a professional footballer, given that both his father William (Falkirk, Bury and Scottish League) and nephew James (Preston, Carlisle, Halifax and Scotland) had both made their mark on the game.

Born in Falkirk on 7 November 1921, Dougall joined Burnley on a semi-professional basis in 1940 but did not make the first team. His career actually flourished in the war. Whilst in the RAF, he was selected for the Air Force Wartime XI, playing alongside such luminaries as Stan Matthews and Stan Mortensen. He also played for the Scottish international wartime side, not to mention guesting for Oldham, Watford, Walsall and Coventry.

No sooner had the War ended than Dougall joined Birmingham City as an inside-forward. He was also chosen for the Scottish side to play England in a 1946 Victory international and the following year won his only full Scotland cap when he finished on the losing side at Wrexham.

Despite his blossoming career, Dougall was still not a full-time professional, as his father had insisted that he complete his apprenticeship with a printing firm. Despite this distraction, Dougall became a regular at St Andrews and in 1947-48 was part of the team that won the Second Division championship. After 93 League matches and fifteen goals for Birmingham, Dougall dropped a division to join Argyle in March 1949 for the weighty sum of £13,000.

He might have had second thoughts after his first full season, when Argyle were relegated. He was constantly fighting back from injuries which affected his form. Having started the season in his familiar inside-forward role, he was switched to right-half, the position in which he is best remembered by Argyle fans.

It was an inspirational switch. The ginger-haired, rugged-faced Scot found that his speed and intelligent use of the ball were well suited to the position. He also packed a mighty shot, and if any criticism can be levelled it is only that his venomous shooting brought him few goals. Dougall displayed commendable versatility and during his time at Home Park he played in every position bar goalkeeper and outside-left.

By the end of 1950-51, manager Jimmy Rae was forging a side with potential, built around the combination of Dougall, Jack Chisholm and Johnny Porteous – generally regarded as the best half-back line in Argyle history. This potential was realised the following year by winning the Third Division (South) title. Such was Dougall's form during this period that many considered him unlucky not to win more Scottish caps.

Dougall continued to give excellent service. Two years after their title success, many of the side had departed, and Dougall and Pat Jones became the last survivors of an immortal team.

By 1956, local lad Johnny Williams was emerging, so Dougall switched to inside- or outside-right. The 1956-57 season was his best in terms of goalscoring with nine, including doubles against Northampton and Swindon.

Ironically it was Dougall who initially replaced Pat Jones at left-back when the dependable defender finally called it a day, and it was wearing No 3 that Dougall played his final games for Argyle in 1958, until the club signed a specialist full-back in Wally Bellett. Despite not playing after Christmas, by May Dougall had earned another champions medal.

By then Dougall had acquired his FA coaching qualifications and was appointed player-coach of Argyle's reserves. When manager Jack Rowley suddenly departed in 1959, the directors appointed former Tottenham player Vic Buckingham to replace him. Buckingham never arrived, however, being lured by a more tempting offer from Sheffield Wednesday, whereupon Dougall and another ex-Pilgrim, George Taylor, were named as chief coach and chief trainer respectively, with joint responsibility for team selection. The following season Dougall was given the title of team manager, with sole responsibility for team affairs.

Although the side consolidated in Division Two and enjoyed a good League Cup run, Dougall, by his own admission, was not cut out for management. He was perhaps too nice a character to come down hard on wayward players. His tenure as manager lasted only six months and in November 1961, yet another Argyle old boy, Ellis Stuttard, replaced him. Dougall remained at the club in the joint capacity of chief coach and chief scout. He also undertook the role of Argyle's public relations officer and together with former player, Bill Strauss, pioneered the club's first serious fund-raising schemes.

When he finally departed the Home Park scene in the early 1970s, Dougall ran a fitness club in Plymouth. From 1973, he ran the Mayflower

Sports Centre, adjacent to Home Park, until his retirement in 1986. He still lives in his adopted city.

Magic Moment: *In a Division Two game at home to Everton in November 1952, Dougall scored a controversial late winner. He thought he was fouled and a whistle was heard. Everton keeper Ted Sagar hesitated, believing a free-kick had been given, but Dougall continued and scored. To general disbelief, the goal stood.*

Worst Nightmare: *Dougall did not share Argyle's title triumph in 1951-52, missing the last weeks of the season due to a spinal injury.*

ARGYLE RECORD	Appearances	Goals
Football League	274	26
FA Cup	15	–

No 33. **JOHN PORTEOUS**
Debut: v Bradford PA, 20 August 1949
Farewell: v Blackburn, 14 January 1956

Alongside Neil Dougall in Argyle's formidable half-back line was yet another Scot, Johnny Porteous.

Born in Motherwell on 5 December 1921, Porteous's best footballing years were lost to him by the outbreak of war when he was only seventeen. He served in the RAF and after demobilisation joined his hometown club, Motherwell, with whom he spent two seasons without breaking into the first team. Two frustrating seasons were spent there without playing a first-team match.

The versatile Porteous did better with Alloa, and in July 1949 Argyle manager Jimmy Rae, on one of his many Scottish 'raids', persuaded Porteous to uproot, his fee being £2,000.

For the opening game of 1949-50, Porteous played right-half, a problem position for Argyle since the departure of Len Boyd to Birmingham. Porteous, the quiet man of the side, displayed tenacity and energy, and soon proved up to the task, though he tasted victory only once in his first eleven games.

Interestingly, his energy on the field was not matched off it. Porteous acquired a habit of falling asleep at every opportunity, blaming the mild South West climate, which was not what he was familiar with back in Scotland.

On the field, Argyle were on the wane. The arrival of Jack Chisholm prompted a reshuffle, with Neil Dougall switching to right-half and

Porteous moving to left-half. The switch helped stem the flow of goals against, but Argyle's real problem was the lack of a regular goal-poacher. A paltry eight goals scored in the final fifteen games deserved, and got, relegation.

But for the next two seasons, Porteous was an integral part of a side that virtually picked itself week after week. Fourth place in 1950-51 was trumped by the championship the following season. The team contained players who regularly made the headlines. The goals of Maurice Tadman, the dominance of 'Jumbo' Chisholm, and the wing-play of Gordon Astall and Alex Govan, captured the public's imagination, but former team-mates pay tribute to Porteous's value – his unfussy, no-nonsense approach, and impressive work-rate. Slight of build and not very tall, he was the ideal half-back, tenacious in the tackle, but also willing to support the attack.

He continued as a first-team regular at left-half, but it was not until late in 1953-54 that the versatility he had shown in Scottish football was put to good use. With Argyle again threatened by relegation, Porteous was moved up to inside-left. Having scored just two goals in his first four seasons at the club, he now bagged three in the final seven games as the drop was narrowly averted.

He continued in this role for much of the following season. To his, and everyone else's surprise, he finished 1954-55 with eight goals, a tally which made him joint top scorer with Eric Davis and Peter Anderson.

With Porteous now approaching his mid-30s, new manager Jack Rowley began to look elsewhere. Porteous's final appearance was, incidentally, made at centre-forward, after which, in March 1956, he joined local rivals Exeter. His departure severed one of the last connections with the title-winning side of five years earlier. Whilst many supporters were sad to see him leave, few could argue that he had not repaid the modest fee Jimmy Rae had spent on him.

A two-year spell at Exeter saw him make a further 40 League appearances, without scoring. He finished his soccer career with Truro City. Employment was gained in Devonport Dockyard and he also worked in Mauritius for a telecommunications company.

Now, of course, retired, Porteous lives in Plymouth, a neighbour to another former team-mate, Tony McShane.

Magic Moment: *With Argyle needing to beat West Ham in April 1954, Porteous scored a late winner. He was carried back to the halfway line by Paddy Ratcliffe and at the end was swept off the pitch by Jack Chisholm. Porteous admitted that he hadn't even seen his match-winner go in.*

Worst Nightmare: *In Argyle's 4-8 defeat at Everton in February 1954, Porteous was overwhelmed by the man he had to mark, inside-forward John Parker, who scored four of Everton's goals.*

ARGYLE RECORD	Appearances	Goals
Football League	215	13
FA Cup	7	–

No 34. **JACK CHISHOLM**
Debut: v Chesterfield, 24 December 1949
Farewell: v Doncaster, 24 April 1954

Completing the great half-back triumvirate with Neil Dougall and Johnny Porteous is Jack Chisholm.

In terms of pure football ability, Chisholm ought never to have made it into the professional ranks. At 6ft 2in tall and weighing 14st, he lacked speed, agility, stamina and ball skills. Added to which, he was bowlegged and had cartilages removed from both knees. But he played for Argyle for five seasons, during which he established himself as one of the most inspirational figures in Argyle history.

'Jumbo' Chisholm was born at Edmonton, London, on 9 October 1924. He started out with nearby Tottenham in October 1942 at the age of seventeen. With Britain at war, service as a guardsman took precedence, although he appeared as a guest for Millwall and Fulham.

After the War, Chisholm resumed his soccer career but found it hard to break into the Spurs side. After only two first-team appearances, in October 1947 he moved to Brentford. With 49 League appearances under his belt, he signed for Sheffield United, staying there for six months in which he made 21 appearances.

In December 1949, Argyle manager Jimmy Rae paid a club record £14,000 to buy the huge stopper. It proved to be a masterstroke, for Chisholm was a born leader. He was an imposing figure who would issue orders with a gruff voice, and woe betide any colleague who, in Chisholm's eyes, did not pull his weight. Not surprisingly, he was immediately appointed team captain.

As a defender, he was dominant in the air and used his sheer physical presence to get the better of opponents. There were times, however, when his physique was a distinct handicap. One example came during a match at Everton in February 1954, when on a snowbound pitch Chisholm kept losing his footing. The fleet-footed Everton forwards ran in eight goals.

The highlight of his time at Argyle was, of course, the 1951-52 Division Three (South) title. Though Argyle possessed some outstanding individual players, few would dispute that it was Chisholm's drive and leadership that gelled them. Chisholm was ever present that season and even scored a rare goal in a 1-3 loss at Northampton.

His off the field exploits also became legendary. To say he enjoyed the social side of football is to understate. He liked a pint or two, and on more than one occasion, so the story goes, was said to enjoy a drink in the nearby Britannia Inn *before* a home game!

Another anecdote concerns Argyle's 1954 tour of North America. Chisholm and the diminutive Pat Jones challenged each other to a mule race. The outcome is not known, but with Chisholm's mount carrying a handicap of at least five stones, one can hazard a guess.

Chisholm also enjoyed tremendous influence within the football club itself. On one occasion, he successfully campaigned of behalf of the players when the directors initially refused to pay a bonus in the event of beating Wolves in an FA Cup-tie. Following his intervention, the board backed down. Not that his bargaining powers were always successful. At that time, the players were on a bonus of £2 per win. Prior to Devon Professional Bowl fixtures against local rivals Torquay and Exeter, Chisholm approached manager Rae and requested his win bonuses in advance, so sure was he of victory. Needless to say, his request was refused.

The most enduring image is of Chisholm sporting the only beard in the whole Football League. Virtually every picture of Chisholm seems to feature him unshaven, and he did not in fact grow his beard until the latter part of his time at Argyle.

By the end of 1953-54, injuries and, perhaps, his life-style, had taken their toll and Chisholm opted to call it a day. A well-deserved benefit game was held on his behalf in May 1955 when Argyle played a combined Spurs-West Brom team.

For a time, Chisholm remained in the South West, pursuing his other love, cricket. He had been a promising fast bowler in his youth, having played for the MCC and in 1947 made one first-class appearance for Middlesex, scoring 12 and 2 with the bat and finishing with bowling figures of 1-15 and 0-18. He also played Minor Counties cricket for Bedfordshire from 1949-51, whilst he was on Argyle's books, and for Devon in 1956. After his retirement from League football he managed Cornish side Helston and played cricket for nearby St Just.

Back in Plymouth, Chisholm made the inevitable, if perhaps, unwise move into the licensing trade, taking over the Harvest Home pub. He was a generous host, which was appreciated by all, except his bank manager, and his venture into the pub trade was short-lived.

Chisholm subsequently returned to the London area to manage Finchley. He became Romford's first professional manager in 1958, taking the club into the Southern League. Even in later life, his maverick approach to life did not diminish. Whilst at Romford his liking for a tipple saw him end up in hospital. After enjoying a liquid lunch, Chisholm returned to his office at Romford's ground where he promptly dozed off. He rested his legs on an electric fire, which happened to be switched on. He awoke to the smell of singed flesh and required treatment to his burnt legs. On another occasion he was invited to appear before local magistrates, being accused of punching a policeman.

In later years, Chisholm ran a betting shop back in his birthplace, Edmonton. On 24 August 1977 he died suddenly at the early age of 53. He is fondly remembered by all who knew him as a loveable rogue who always had a mischievous twinkle in his eye.

To this day, Chisholm's legend at Home Park endures. One of the main sponsor's lounges is named 'The Chisholm Lounge' and in it hangs a magnificent portrait of the great man.

Magic Moment: *A typical act of bravery on his debut endeared Chisholm to the Argyle crowd. He suffered a cut head which required stitches. With no substitutes allowed, the team was down to ten men. But Chisholm later reappeared, his head swathed in bandages.*

Worst Nightmare: *Chisholm's attitude to training was less than enthusiastic. His favourite exercise was to give a vigorous thrashing to a boxing-style punch-bag in the gym. On one occasion, Chisholm was too slow to dodge out of the way and the bag smacked him in the eye.*

ARGYLE RECORD	Appearances	Goals
Football League	175	2
FA Cup	12	—

No 20. Archie Gorman was
a tenacious half-back

No 21. Jimmy Rae both played for
Argyle and later managed the club

No 23. Bill Shortt was a Welsh international goalkeeper

No 28. Paddy Ratcliffe was shot down
over Germany in World War II

No 33. Half-back John Porteous was
the quiet man of the Argyle side

No 34. Jumbo Chisholm (left) disliked training
No 23. Bill Shortt (right) could perhaps have done with some more

No 35. George Robertson
served Argyle in various capacities

Chapter Four

~ *Local Heroes* ~

No 35. **GEORGE ROBERTSON**
Debut: v Colchester, 17 March 1951
Farewell: v Newcastle, 21 December 1963

George Robertson was a star-struck young player who faced the daunting task of replacing legendary Jack Chisholm. It was, perhaps, inevitable that Robertson would make the grade in the game, given that his father, William, had been a professional in pre-war times, having played for Third Lanark, Ayr, Stoke, Manchester United and Reading.

Robertson junior was born at Bainsford near Falkirk on 20 April 1930. During his National Service with the RAF, his club, Gairdoch, wrote to Argyle boss Jimmy Rae, recommending Robertson for a trial. Robertson was based at Salisbury, and played in a Devon Wednesday League game against City Police. He did enough to progress to Argyle's second team.

After the War, having heard no more from Argyle, Robertson returned to Scotland and was set to sign for Stenhousemuir. On learning this, Argyle reminded him that he had signed amateur forms and Argyle had first refusal on his services. Robertson signed a professional contract in January 1950, costing just £10 for a signing-on fee.

He was unfortunate to arrive at a time when Argyle's defence was stable and picked itself. In fact, Robertson made only two first-team appearances in his first three years at Home Park. It was not until 1953-54 that he established himself, missing only one match, but he was used as a utility player, covering for injuries in Argyle's ageing team.

Following Chisholm's retirement, it was Robertson who took over at No 5. At only 5ft 9in, weighing 10½st, he lacked Chisholm's physical presence. Indeed, his thin frame and gaunt features were the antithesis of 'Jumbo'. He was, however, more mobile than his predecessor and – combined with his solid tackling and excellent reading of the game – filled the gap until Peter Langman made his breakthrough from the reserves, whereupon Robertson reverted to right-back or right-half.

It is in the No 2 shirt that he is best remembered by Argyle fans. In that position he played 33 games in the 1958-59 championship side and for four seasons he was rarely out of the side.

Robertson's long service created another record. He was the only player to undertake both Argyle's overseas tours – to the USA in 1954 and Eastern Europe in 1963. He actually played in every game of both tours, from the start too, except for that against Legia Warsaw in 1963, when he came off the bench before what will probably be the largest crowd ever to watch Argyle. Some 100,000 turned up to witness a 2-1 Legia win. True, Argyle were not the main attraction. The match coincided with an international cycle race and was held up on three occasions as the cyclists entered the stadium.

Apart from nine games in 1963-64, that tour proved a fitting swan-song to Robertson's Argyle career. Now approaching his mid-30s, he was offered a new contract, but with little prospect of first-team action he decided that an offer to become groundsman at Plymouth College was too good to miss. He retained his soccer links by becoming a successful player-manager of Falmouth Town, winning several South Western League titles and Cornish Senior Cups, as well as leading the side into the first round proper of the 1967-68 FA Cup, before losing 2-5 at Peterborough.

When Billy Bingham was appointed Argyle manager in 1968, Robertson was brought back to run the third team in the Plymouth and District League. His Argyle links continued into the early 1970s when, under Tony Waiters' youth scheme, the club purchased Elm Cottage to house the club's apprentice professionals. George left his job at Plymouth College and, together with his wife, was given the task of running the hostel and catering for the youngsters.

After Waiters' departure, the youth scheme was phased out and Robertson, in 1983, was made groundsman. His loyal service was rewarded in May 1986, when former Pilgrim Bobby Saxton brought his Blackburn side to Home Park for a testimonial.

Now retired, Robertson remains living in his adopted city.

Magic Moment: *One of Robertson's two Argyle goals came on the last day of 1961-62 against Liverpool, who fielded his cousin, Tommy Leishman. Their keeper was future Argyle star Jim Furnell.*

Worst Nightmare: *Robertson played right-back for the reserves at Luton on the final day of 1948-49. Argyle crashed 0-9, convincing him that his career at Home Park was at a premature end.*

ARGYLE RECORD	Appearances	Goals
Football League	359	2
FA Cup	18	–
League Cup	5	–

No 36. **PETER ANDERSON**
Debut: v Brentford, 11 April 1953
Farewell: v Middlesbrough, 22 September 1962

One of George Robertson's early games deputising for Jack Chisholm came against Brentford in 1952-53. A 20,000 crowd turned up to see the Bees' legendary Tommy Lawton, but a player with other things on his mind was Peter Anderson, who was making his League debut.

A local lad, Anderson was born in Devonport on 11 September 1932 and appeared in the same Plymouth Schoolboys side as his future Argyle colleague, Reg Wyatt. Like many Argyle players of the time, he was plucked from the Plymouth and District League. He had played for Oak Villa and, just seventeen, had represented the Devon County side. He joined the Home Park staff on a part-time basis in 1949.

A nimble winger, Anderson was kept out of the side by the star pairing of Alex Govan and Gordon Astall. He was introduced for the last four games of 1952-53, scoring twice, but even after Govan's departure he could not land a regular spot, as Ernie Edds was chosen ahead of him.

The 1954-55 season saw his first lengthy run. He played 33 matches and finished joint top scorer with eight goals. By then, he was mixing his soccer career with his National Service, which he undertook in the RAF. Demobbed in 1955, Anderson focused on a full-time soccer career. 1955-56 started brightly with four goals in the first six games, but a broken leg against Stoke meant he missed the remainder of that season.

To fill the gap, another winger, Charlie Twissell, had been brought in, and the fully recovered Anderson found it hard to dislodge him. Twissell was not the answer, but the arrival of yet another winger, Harry Penk, seemed to inspire Anderson. The pair forged a useful wing partnership.

At 5ft 6in and just over 9st, Anderson was small enough. But Penk, at 5ft 4in, was even tinier, and together they presented one of the most midget set of wingers in the Football League.

Both quick on their feet, they would often switch flanks to confuse opponents. As well as being skilful with the ball, Anderson could also score goals, many of them spectacular. The 1958-59 championship owed much to the chances created for Wilf Carter and Jimmy Gauld, with Anderson weighing in with seven strikes himself.

His tally that season included his only Argyle hat-trick in an extraordinary 6-4 win at Doncaster. The match had started badly. Anderson, who was only told he was playing twenty minutes before kick-off, missed an early sitter, but he made amends as Argyle, 2-4 behind at one stage, turned the tables.

Penk was eventually transferred to Southampton, but Anderson remained at Argyle for another three seasons, before joining rivals Torquay United in December 1962. He netted them eighteen goals in 77 League matches before dropping down a level to play part-time for Bideford. Another broken leg forced his retirement from the game.

Anderson lived in his native Plymouth, running a florists in Efford and working in Devonport Dockyard for seventeen years. He now enjoys his retirement, pursuing his other sporting interests, golf and bowls.

Magic Moment: *In January 1962, Home Park was packed for a Cup-tie with double-winning Tottenham. There was no giant killing. Spurs won 5-1, but Anderson scored Argyle's only goal.*

Worst Nightmare: *Whilst driving to Plainmoor to conclude his transfer, Anderson's car got stuck in snow. A passing lorry gave him a lift, but snow prevented the Gulls from playing for six more weeks.*

ARGYLE RECORD	Appearances	Goals
Football League	241	41
FA Cup	10	4
League Cup	8	1

No 37. **NEIL LANGMAN**
Debut: v Everton, 27 February 1954
Farewell: v Brentford, 9 November 1957

Like Peter Anderson, Neil Langman also progressed from the ranks of the local leagues.

Born in the village of Bere Alston on 21 February 1932, Langman's rise to the professional ranks is remarkable, considering he barely played at all until he was fifteen, when he joined the local village side 'for something to do on a Saturday afternoon'. Within a year the young centre-forward had been selected for the Devon Under-18s. A move to Tavistock in the Plymouth and District League soon followed, before spending two years of National Service with RAF Fighter Command. He eventually returned to Tavistock, whose player-manager was former Argyle winger Sid Rawlings. By now a prolific scorer, Langman was signed by Argyle manager Jimmy Rae as a part-time pro in September 1953. Elder brother Peter, a centre-half, was already on Argyle's books.

Langman banged 23 goals for Argyle in nine South Western League matches and four in his first five reserve appearances. He was clearly ready for first-team soccer and was thrown in at the deep end for a daunting debut at Everton, replacing the injured Maurice Tadman. It was a match Langman will never forget. He scored two and made another of the Pilgrims four goals on a snowbound pitch. Sadly, Everton scored eight. Langman retained his place and a month later scored his first hat-trick in a 4-0 home win over Derby.

Another example of Langman's deadly aim came during the 1954 American tour. In the second game, he scored six goals in Argyle's 8-4 win over the St Louis All Stars, and finished the tour with thirteen goals from ten appearances.

Despite this early success, Langman remained a part-timer, combining his soccer with an apprenticeship with the South Western Electricity Board. Unable to train regularly with the Argyle squad, he was often seen pounding the streets in his home village. He had little confidence of making the grade as a professional and was once quoted as saying 'I have a good job and intend hanging on to it. If I get really well established in the game, I might consider turning professional, but at the moment that is very doubtful.'

A goal in the opening fixture of 1954-55 helped Langman secure the No 9 shirt, now that Tadman's career was coming to an end. The early promise soon faded, though. The side struggled and Langman found goals elusive, losing his place for a while to another local product, Eric Davis. Ironically, whilst Langman was out of favour, his brother Peter was finally given his first-team opportunity.

The following season, Langman was again in and out, but nevertheless finished top scorer with nine goals, including a hat-trick at home to Liverpool. Despite relegation, Langman agreed to sign as a professional.

In 1956-57 he was back with a vengeance. Joining brother Peter in the side, he scored eighteen times in 34 League and Cup appearances to again finish as leading marksman. Another hat-trick came his way in February 1957 in a 4-1 win at Coventry. He was selected for a Division Three (South) select XI against their northern counterparts, with Langman scoring in a 1-1 draw.

By now few defences could cope with Langman's buffeting style. He was the archetypal battering-ram centre-forward, with hair swept back and rugged features. At 14st, he carried a physical, no-nonsense approach to each game. He once admitted that he could not really play football but was merely in the team to score goals.

Scoring goals is exactly what he continued to do. He recorded a fourth hat-trick for Argyle in September 1957 at Reading, but by this time Wilf Carter had joined the club and was also regularly finding the net. The club decided that at the right price Langman could go, and when Colchester offered £7,000 in November, only a few weeks after Langman had scored against them, he was on his way.

By one of those quirks, the final Argyle appearance of both Langman brothers came in the same match. Peter disappeared into the reserves before joining Weymouth in the Southern League side, while Neil departed with a goalscoring ratio of a goal every two games. He spent three years at Colchester, scoring 49 times in 128 League appearances.

Between 1961 and 1963 he played for Bath City, top scoring in both seasons. He then moved to Barnstaple Town and subsequently played for Falmouth and St Austell in the South Western League.

Langman became a caretaker at Tavistock School, close to his birthplace, and then spent 24 years as a warden at the Devon and Cornwall Police Headquarters at Middlemoor, Exeter, before retiring in December 1997. He now lives at Tiverton in Devon.

Magic Moment: *In October 1954 Langman was involved in a freak goal at Home Park. He clashed with Fulham keeper Frank Elliott, who, prostrate and nursing a broken wrist, threw the ball over his head into his own net.*

Worst Nightmare: *In January 1955, Langman missed a chance to level in an FA Cup-tie with Newcastle. He flung himself at Keith Thomas's cross two yards out. Langman ended up in the back of the net, but the ball bounced clear off keeper Ronnie Simpson's knee.*

ARGYLE RECORD	Appearances	Goals
Football League	97	49
FA Cup	3	1

No 38. **JOHNNY WILLIAMS**
Debut: v Blackburn, 10 September 1955
Farewell v Crystal Palace, 11 April 1956

Another powerful player in the mould of Neil Langman, Johnny Williams was often considered to be a 'local' but hailed originally from Bristol.

Born on 16 August 1935, Williams moved to Plymouth from his birthplace, when his father got a job at the *Western Evening Herald* newspaper. It was during his early education at Tamar School that the young Williams began his soccer career with Virginia House.

After leaving school, he gained an apprenticeship at Devonport Dockyard as an electrical fitter and continued his amateur football career with firstly, Co-op Welfare, and then Dockyard side EEM Department.

His father felt his son worthy of a trial at Argyle and approached ex-Argyle star Bill Strauss, who was by then working on the administrative side at Home Park. Strauss alerted manager Jack Rowley, and Williams was soon playing for the club's South Western League and reserve sides.

He was given his first-team debut early in 1955-56 at inside-forward. Still an amateur, Williams found himself in and out of an evolving team, and played a few times at centre-forward. It was wearing No 9 that he scored his first goal for the club, in only his third appearance, before an Anfield crowd of 35,000. Liverpool beat the Pilgrims 4-1.

A switch to right-half, in which position he is best remembered, happened almost by accident. The Argyle third team had reached the final of the South Western League Cup. Faced with a glut of injuries, the club asked Williams to play in the half-back line. His performance transformed his future prospects.

1956 saw the start of his Army National Service. Other players had found this a disruption to their soccer careers, but Williams saw it as an opportunity to broaden his experience. He continued to play for Argyle and also benefited by selection for the Army side – where he found himself alongside Bobby Charlton, Cliff Jones and Gerry Hitchens – then being coached by England manager Walter Winterbottom.

By this time, Williams was beginning to make a real impression. His all-round game was well suited to the half-back role where his strong tackling and powerful running were allied to his flair for attacking from deep. The feature of his game that is best remembered, however, is his ballistic shooting.

Once over the halfway line, an attempt on goal was a distinct possibility. Williams was not afraid to try his luck from anywhere within 40 yards of goal, and was often on target. Many a spectator behind the goal – forced to take swift evasive action whenever his aim was awry – will vouch for the venom of his shooting. Naturally, these long-range efforts excited the crowd and roars of encouragement would greet another Williams venture into opposing territory. His final tally of 55 Argyle goals contained its share of long-range specials.

Honours finally came Williams' way when he won a Third Division champions medal in 1958-59. His seven goals that season included a double strike in a 8-3 win over Mansfield. By this time another John Williams had joined the club and to differentiate between the two, records referred to our subject as J S Williams.

J S seldom missed a match and for three consecutive seasons in the early 1960s he was ever present. Bigger clubs were taking notice but whereas in the past Argyle would offload if the price was right, a daunting £40,000 transfer fee was slapped on him to deter interested parties. Many observers felt Williams good enough to merit international honours, which he could only get in the top division. It was not to be. He continued to give sterling service until the mid-1960s, contributing to Argyle's run to the League Cup semi-finals in 1964-65 by scoring past Gordon Banks in the first leg defeat by Leicester.

With an eye to the future, Williams had invested in a garage business in Blandford Road, Plymouth. Derek Ufton had arrived as Argyle manager for the start of 1965-66 and by the end of that season Williams had fallen out of favour. Languishing in the reserves, in December 1966 Williams joined Bristol Rovers, though he remained living and training in Plymouth. Two years at Eastville produced ten goals in 66 (plus three substitute) appearances.

When Billy Bingham replaced Ufton, Williams was tempted back as reserve-team coach, but both men lost their jobs during 1969-70. Williams joined Bodmin Town as player-manager, then Falmouth Town, where he played his part in that club's remarkable record of completing three successive Western League seasons without a defeat.

After hanging up his boots, Williams concentrated on expanding his business interests. In due course he purchased two garages in Plymouth, which he still runs today.

Magic Moment: *One of Williams' most spectacular goals came at Anfield in December 1961 when he despatched a 30-yard volley past one of his former Army colleagues, Bert Slater.*

Worst Nightmare: *With a number of First Division clubs taking an interest in him, Williams handed in a transfer request to Argyle which was immediately declined.*

ARGYLE RECORD	Appearances	Goals
Football League	41(+1 sub)	48
FA Cup	19	1
League Cup	17	6

No 39. **REG WYATT**
Debut: v Blackburn, 14 January 1956
Farewell: v Coventry, 22 August 1964

Another player to break into the Argyle side soon after Johnny Williams was Plymothian Reg Wyatt.

Born on 18 September 1932, Wyatt was selected for Plymouth Schoolboys as an inside-forward. He then went on to play for local sides Oak Villa and Astor Institute, before joining Argyle on a part-time basis in 1950, combining his playing career with learning a trade as a central heating engineer. He spent six years at the club before being given his first-team opportunity.

He commenced his Army National Service in 1955 and actually made his Argyle debut while serving. His first game was at left-back but relegation lay in store and by the end of that campaign Wyatt had reverted to his preferred inside-forward position. He even scored a rare goal in a 1-7 reverse at Bury.

After National Service it was not long before Wyatt had impressed Argyle sufficiently to be offered full-time professional terms. He featured rarely in 1956-57 until the latter stages, when he replaced the injured Peter Langman at centre-half. Wyatt, a quiet, unassuming character with an eternally receding hairline, quickly took to his new role. At 6ft 1in, he had the height to combat aerial threats, but also had the skill to play himself out of trouble. Such was his consistency that he missed only one game the following season. Langman, back to fitness, had to be content with reserve-team football and was subsequently released.

1958-59 saw Wyatt gain his only honour during his Pilgrims career, a Third Division championship medal, although following a shock 2-4 home defeat by Accrington Stanley he lost his No 5 shirt to Gordon Fincham. Wyatt was restored to the side at left-back for the final few games and was able to share in the glory of winning the title. It provided his fondest memories of his time at Home Park, particularly when, having clinched the title with a 1-1 draw at Accrington, crowds of supporters lined the city streets to greet their heroes on their return. Four days later, a Home Park crowd of 26,000 attended the final game against Bradford City.

In Division Two, Wyatt was in and out, and when he was in he never knew where. Sometimes it was at centre-half, sometimes at right-back. It was at No 2 that he mostly played in 1960-61, switching on occasions to centre-half if Fincham was absent.

Wyatt's first-team appearances dwindled with the years. The end of his career appeared to be in sight until, with Argyle battling relegation in 1963-64, new manager Andy Beattie called upon his experience at centre-half for the final eighteen games. The ploy worked, with Argyle escaping the drop by one place.

The opening game of 1964-65 proved to be Wyatt's last League outing for the club and in October 1964 he signed for Torquay, helping them to promotion from Division Three in 1965-66. He also discovered his scoring boots at Plainmoor, scoring six times in 80 appearances

On retirement from football, Wyatt returned to his previous trade with the Department of the Environment, where he remained for 25 years. His soccer career also continued for a while with Cornish side Wadebridge Town.

He has lived in the same house in Plymouth for some 40 years, a property that he used to rent from Argyle in his playing days, before purchasing it outright. His nimble footwork has also come in useful during his later life, with Mr & Mrs Wyatt having won a number of local dancing competitions.

Magic Moment: *Wyatt scored his second and last goal of his Argyle career during the 1958-59 championship season. It clinched a vital 3-1 win over Bournemouth in front of a crowd of 24,000.*

Worst Nightmare: *Argyle's run to Round 4 of the first League Cup in 1960-61 was almost scuppered by Wyatt. His own-goal at home to Birmingham was overturned when Argyle replied with three goals.*

ARGYLE RECORD	Appearances	Goals
Football League	202	2
FA Cup	8	–
League Cup	7	–

No 40. **WILF CARTER**

Debut: v Shrewsbury, 24 August 1957
Farewell: v Swansea, 31 March 1964

Joining Reg Wyatt in Argyle's side for the 1957-58 season's opening game was new signing Wilf Carter.

Born at Wednesfield on 4 October 1933, Carter had joined West Brom in January 1951, straight from school, and debuted at the age of eighteen. Unable to command a regular place at the Hawthorns, he made just 57 appearances, scoring twelve goals, in six years at the club. It was hardly a record to leave Argyle fans drooling when he signed in March 1957 for a modest fee of £2,500. Strangely, it appears he was promised regular first-team action.

As it turned out, Jack Rowley's new inside-forward proved to be one of the best buys in Argyle history, and he became one of the most prolific scorers the club had seen.

Carter did not take long to make his mark, scoring twice in his third game in a 4-2 win over Aldershot. After Neil Langman was sold to Colchester, Carter partnered a number of forwards for the rest of that 1957-58 season, none for any great length of time. Not that it seemed to matter to Carter. From mid-November onwards he couldn't stop scoring. A double strike in a 6-2 FA Cup victory over Watford set in train a fifteen-game spell that saw him hit the net on nineteen occasions. These included hat-tricks against Coventry, Queens Park Rangers and Dorchester in the FA Cup. In the blink of an eye he was transformed from an under-achiever at West Brom to a goal-machine at Argyle. Albion fans studying press reports must have concluded that Argyle had two Carters on their books. Significantly, on the two occasions Wilf was absent, the side failed to score. Not surprisingly, he finished that first season top scorer by a huge margin, and it was thanks mainly to his goals that Argyle finished third in Division Three (South).

The Pilgrims started the following season, the first in a unified Division Three (comprising the top twelve from the old South and North sections) as one of the favourites for promotion. This optimism was soon justified, with the side losing only twice before Christmas. Carter now had a productive ally in the shape of Jimmy Gauld. Between them they scored 47 League and Cup goals. Carter's contribution was 25, including a hat-trick at Mansfield and a number of penalties. These were often awarded for fouls against Gauld, who liked to burst into the penalty area.

With the Third Division championship secured, speculation centred on whether Carter could be as prolific at a higher level, now that his strike partner, Gauld, had departed. Carter's reputation was sure to have preceded him, and he could expect close attention from Second Division defenders. These fears proved unfounded as Carter notched up another 22 goals, including a hat-trick against Charlton. Yet again his goals had made all the difference, for Argyle just avoided relegation.

Many an opposing manager must have spent hours devising ways to combat Carter, but, analysing his game, it was difficult to pick out any particular strength or pinpoint the source of his goals. At 5ft 9in and 11st, he was of average build and not particularly good in the air. But he possessed tremendous acceleration and reflexes and was always prepared to make an attempt on goal, even from the narrowest of angles. He was, simply, one of those strikers that appear now and again who have an ability to snap up half-chances with regularity.

December 1960 saw one of the craziest months in Argyle history. The side followed up a surprise 3-3 draw at Aston Villa in the third round, first leg, of the League Cup, by crashing 0-9 at Stoke in the League. Two days later, Argyle were holding Villa to a scoreless draw after 90 minutes, but with extra-time scheduled a waterlogged pitch caused the tie to be abandoned. On Boxing Day, Argyle and Charlton served up ten goals at the Valley, but sadly six of them went to Charlton. Carter was not among the Argyle scorers but, with the corresponding fixture due to be played at Home Park the following day, he made amends. In another goal feast, Argyle reversed the result, winning 6-4, with Carter netting five to set a new Argyle scoring record which still stands.

Charlton seemed to inspire Carter. Over his career he played against the Addicks on fifteen occasions and scored no fewer than 25 goals against them. No wonder that, following his hat-trick against them the previous season, Charlton had tried to buy him, deterred only by Argyle's asking price of £20,000. Carter finished 1960-61 in his customary position as Argyle's top marksman with 28 strikes.

Fifth in Division Two was Argyle's finishing position in 1961-62, with Carter maintaining his record of reaching twenty goals in each season as an Argyle player. He started 1962-63 with four in the first two games, before suffering a relative goal drought. The barren spell was interrupted by a hat-trick against, yes, Charlton, and Carter finished with fourteen goals for the campaign.

The following year finally showed signs that Carter was beginning to lose his sharpness. Argyle failed to win any of their first eleven fixtures. The team was switched around and Carter found himself shunted to left-back for a while. It was a position he had flirted with during his West Brom days but, nevertheless, it seemed one of the quirkier tactical changes of the time.

Although relegation was avoided, Carter was one of a number of players released, thus concluding a memorable Argyle career that had seen him climb to second place, behind Sammy Black, in the list of all-time Argyle goalscorers. Like many before him, Carter joined Exeter City, but the Midas touch had deserted him and in two mediocre seasons at St James Park he scored only six times in 48 games.

He continued playing for a further four seasons with Southern League Bath City before becoming manager of Salisbury Town. After two years in that job he turned his back on football to work for an engineering firm in Bath before taking a job as a security officer for the Ministry of Defence.

Now retired, Carter still lives in the Bath area but is still fondly remembered as one of the greatest goalscorers in Argyle history. And all for £2,500!

Magic Moment: *In a League Cup replay against Villa in February 1961, Carter's penalty was saved by keeper Nigel Sims. The referee ordered a retake. This time Carter prodded the ball forward from the spot for Johnny Newman to rush up and blast the ball home.*

Worst Nightmare: *In a home match with Southend in April 1958, Carter 'scored' after the ball had come off two defenders, but he was given offside. Argyle lost 2-3, which cost them promotion. The referee so incensed the crowd that he abandoned his hotel in Plymouth and took refuge in Torquay.*

ARGYLE RECORD	Appearances	Goals
Football League	253	134
FA Cup	11	10
League Cup	10	4

No 41. **JIMMY GAULD**
Debut: v Crystal Palace, 26 October 1957
Farewell: v Bradford City, 29 April 1959

Wilf Carter's goal bonanza was boosted by a number of penalties, thanks mainly to the efforts of Jimmy Gauld, a maverick character both on and off the field whose name will remain etched in soccer history for the wrong reasons.

Born on 9 May 1929 in Aberdeen, the young Gauld attended Gordon's College, a Scottish public school, before joining his home-town club Aberdeen, with whom he was selected for the Scotland Youth side. The Dons did not take to him, so he turned to Waterford in the Irish Free State. A record 46 goals in 28 games saw him selected for the Irish Free State League in representative matches against the English and North of Ireland League select XIs. He was also selected for the RAF representative side during his National Service.

Naturally, such a prolific goalscoring record attracted the big clubs and in May 1955 a fee of £4,000 took him to First Division Charlton. A return of 21 goals in 47 games persuaded Everton to buy him in October 1956. Gauld's time on Merseyside as not so successful, yielding only seven goals in 23 League appearances. Nevertheless it was a surprise when Jack Rowley persuaded Gauld to drop into Division Three (South). The transfer was completed on the Friday evening before his debut and discussions lasted only twenty minutes. The deciding factor was, apparently, Argyle's agreement that Gauld could hold down a job as well as playing, something he had also done at his other clubs.

His first season at Argyle saw him ensconced in his favourite inside-forward role. Although the club finished third, Gauld's personal contribution of six goals in 22 League and Cup appearances was disappointing for a player with First Division experience, and gave no indication of the fireworks ahead.

Following the amalgamation of the old Third and Fourth Divisions, Argyle stormed to the new Third Division title. Gauld and Carter formed a prolific partnership that contributed 43 of the 67 League goals scored by Argyle that season. Gauld's 21 League goals included a hat-trick against Swindon Town. A week later he scored in an 8-3 victory over Mansfield Town. Ironically, he would later play for both of those defeated sides.

No one who saw Gauld play would deny that his style was unique. Argyle fans had never seen, nor are ever likely to see again, a player who would exploit such unorthodox methods to the full. Close control was Gauld's forté, and he often took on and beat several defenders. His dribbling was hardly conventional. A broad physique measuring 5ft 10in and weighing 12st meant he did not possess a turn of speed or a deft body swerve. Instead he used to simply run with the ball straight at, and usually through, opponents. These runs often commenced around the halfway line as he set off on the most direct route to goal. Once momentum was gained his bulk made him difficult to halt within the laws of the game, and it is easy to see why desperate defending often resulted in a penalty being awarded. He often retained control of the ball under the fiercest of challenges, using various parts of his anatomy – chest, midriff, thigh and knee – to maintain possession.

One match in particular typifies the Gauld style. Swindon Town were on the receiving end at Home Park in October 1958. Gauld had already scored himself and won a penalty which Carter had converted when, with the minutes ticking away and the game all square, he collected the ball on the halfway line. He set off on one of his typical electrifying bursts. Several defenders were left in his wake as he uncorked a shot which Swindon keeper Sam Burton failed to hold, leaving Gauld to net the rebound.

There were times when Gauld got carried away and continued on a run when team-mates were better placed to receive a pass, but the Home Park crowd loved him for what he was, and were quick to forgive when he took the wrong option.

Having been on the receiving end of Gauld's magic, it was no surprise when Swindon bid for him. To the dismay of the Argyle faithful, after only two seasons with the club, he was allowed to go. Fifteen months at

Swindon produced fourteen goals in 40 League games, after which he moved back to his native Scotland to join St Johnstone. Never one to settle, Gauld signed for Mansfield for a fee of £4,000, but after only four games suffered a broken leg which effectively put paid to his playing career.

In the spring of 1964 Gauld's life took a dramatic turn. On Sunday, 12 April *The People* newspaper exposed details of three Sheffield Wednesday players 'fixing' a match between Wednesday and Ipswich. The trio had each won £100 by betting on their own team to lose.

Rumours of match-fixing had been rife for some time and this proved to be the tip of the iceberg. Gauld appeared to be heavily implicated, revealing that other Third and Fourth Division matches had been 'fixed' that same day. Eleven players from various clubs were charged and most, including Gauld, were suspended from soccer for life. Criminal charges followed and on 29 January 1965 ten players were convicted at Nottingham Assizes. Gauld received the heaviest sentence, four years in jail and £5,000 costs. The other nine also received jail sentences of between four and fifteen months.

With any involvement in football out of the question, Gauld has since pursued a number of business interests and has also lived in France.

Magic Moment: *At home to QPR on Boxing Day 1958, desperate defending saw Gauld's shorts ripped away. Freshly attired, he scored twice, his second after beating four defenders on the by-line.*

Worst Nightmare: *Gauld's involvement in the match-fixing scandal of the early 1960s led to a jail sentence.*

ARGYLE RECORD	Appearances	Goals
Football League	64	25
FA Cup	7	3

No 42. **JOHN NEWMAN**
Debut: v Middlesbrough, 16 January 1960
Farewell: v Millwall, 28 October 1967

In terms of playing styles, there could be no more contrasting performers than Jimmy Gauld and Johnny Newman. Whilst Gauld was a head down, all-action forward, Newman was a cultured defender.

Although born in Hereford on 13 December 1933, Newman won junior honours as a Welsh international. He graduated from schoolboy football with Hereford 'Lads' Club to play for Hereford United reserves at the age of only fifteen.

Hereford were a non-League club in those days, and young Newman had ambition. He joined the Birmingham City groundstaff in July 1949 and captained the club's nursery side, St Andrew's Athletic. He was awarded a professional contract in March 1951 and enjoyed two first-team outings, albeit in Festival of Britain friendlies against Airdrie and Dinamo Yugoslavia. He had to wait almost a year before making his League debut at home to Coventry in March 1952.

A record of 65 League and Cup appearances without scoring in six and a half years at St Andrews is mitigated by the fact that this was a golden period for City. He played seventeen games during 1954-55 when Birmingham won the Division Two championship, and was part of their side beaten by Manchester City in the 1956 FA Cup final. Injury deprived Roy Warhurst of his regular half-back slot and Newman was drafted in to replace him. Newman kept his place for Birmingham's adventures in the Fairs Cup, playing at Inter Milan and Dinamo Zagreb.

The lure of regular first-team action saw Newman sign for Leicester in November 1957. He was appointed club captain and helped steer the Foxes clear of relegation.

It was, therefore, something of a surprise when Newman was persuaded to sign for Plymouth Argyle at a time when, still only 27, he was at his peak. In an attempt to stave off the drop, Argyle signed Newman along with George Kirby and Jimmy McAnearney, and all three made their Argyle debuts in the same match. Rowley had been so desperate to sign Newman that on one occasion the player arrived home to find Rowley extolling the virtues of the South West to Mrs Newman.

With Newman in the side, relegation was avoided, he was made skipper, and the team gradually turned results around. Newman's top-level experience was soon evident. He was employed mainly in his favoured left-half position, but was equally proficient on the right side or at centre-half. He gained the respect of his fellow players through his well-groomed appearance and calm and assured manner both on and off the pitch. As a player, he read the game intelligently, was always comfortable in possession, and was a fine passer. Although only 5ft 10in, he was a useful target at set pieces, from which he would score the occasional goal. Recognition of Newman's consistency came at the end of the 1965-66 season when he was awarded the inaugural Argyle 'Player of the Year' award.

One of the highlights of his career came in September 1966, when Home Park hosted a match between the Football League and the Irish

League. A 35,000 crowd, still basking in England's World Cup triumph a few weeks earlier, turned out for a memorable evening which saw community singing and a parade of the Jules Rimet trophy. Newman was chosen as substitute for a Football League side that included six of England's World Cup winning eleven, and easily defeated their Irish counterparts 12-0.

1967-68 started badly for Argyle and signalled the end of Newman's distinguished career at Home Park. In November he and Alan Banks moved to Exeter for a combined fee of £8,000. Yet again, Newman was instrumental in pulling a side away from the foot of the table, for Exeter were in grave danger of having to seek re-election.

When Exeter boss Frank Broome was dismissed in February 1969, Newman was given temporary charge of the team. He had been groomed for the job for some time and the only real surprise was that it took the club two months to confirm his appointment on a permanent basis. He continued as a player-manager but picked himself less and less. His final League match came in September 1971 at the age of 37, by which time he had exceeded 500 League appearances.

Newman remained as Exeter manager until December 1976 and throughout this period earned himself the respect of fans, players and media with his honest and conscientious approach to the job. When he departed to take over as manager of Grimsby, he had taken Exeter to the top of the table and laid the foundations for his successor, Bobby Saxton, to achieve promotion.

He failed to steer Grimsby clear of relegation but two years later led them to the Fourth Division championship. Newman's name was back in the spotlight and he moved to First Division Derby as assistant to Colin Addison. When Addison left, Newman took charge for six months before he was popularly appointed manager of his home town club, Hereford.

After four years in that post, he moved to assist Bobby Saxton at York and John Barnwell at Notts County, before becoming youth development officer at Mansfield, under ex-Argyle player George Foster. Recently, Newman has been involved with non-league Burton Albion. He is still active in the game and occasionally coaches Worcester City.

Magic Moment: *Newman netted a rare goal against Northampton in the 1964-65 League Cup, earning a semi-final against Leicester.*

Worst Nightmare: *Newman captained Argyle to the worst defeat in their history, a 0-9 thrashing by Stoke City in December 1960.*

ARGYLE RECORD	Appearances	Goals
Football League	298	9
FA Cup	10	–
League Cup	20	2

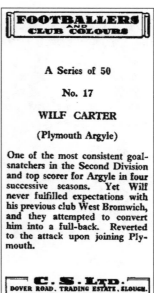

No 40. Wilf Carter still holds the record for scoring most Argyle goals in one game (5)

No 42. Johnny Newman was voted Argyle's first ever Player of the Year

No 45. Frank Lord, much-travelled striker

No. 49 John Hore, Argyle player then manager

Chapter Five

~ *The Swinging Sixties* ~

No 43. **GEORGE KIRBY**
Debut: v Middlesbrough, 16 January 1960
Farewell: v Derby, 15 September 1962

Making his debut alongside Johnny Newman was striker George Kirby, who led a nomadic existence for much of his soccer career, both on and off the field.

Liverpudlian Kirby was born on 20 December 1933 and signed as a professional for Everton in June 1952. His first-team opportunities were limited. After debuting in 1955, he made just 26 appearances, scoring nine goals in almost seven years. Kirby fared little better in nine months with Sheffield Wednesday, where he was limited to three games and one goal.

Meanwhile, Second Division Argyle were desperately seeking an attacking partner for Wilf Carter. Neil Dougall and George Taylor had been given joint responsibility for team affairs, and were aware that a lack of goals was the main reason Argyle were down among the deadmen. Although Carter mustered 22 goals that season, the next highest scorer was right-half Johnny Williams with just eight. The big, brave Kirby might be the answer, and he signed for Argyle in January 1960, along with Owls team-mate Jimmy McAnearney.

Things didn't go to plan at first. Kirby failed to score in his first fourteen games and supporters were tut-tutting about the wisdom of buying a striker who could not score. To their credit, Dougall and Taylor kept faith with Kirby, and sighs of relief filled Home Park in April when he got off the mark in a 3-1 win over Swansea. Kirby was instantly transformed, harrying the Swansea defence and having a hand in Argyle's two other goals. Six wins from the last eight games saw the drop avoided.

Like any striker, Kirby's confidence was up when scoring goals. A goal in the opening game of 1960-61 gave him a boost. The planned formidable partnership of Carter and Kirby was now a reality. Carter's goal-rate did not slacken, and Kirby was now matching him. He scored his first League hat-trick in a 5-1 home trouncing of Portsmouth in September 1960 and a week later scored two more as Argyle repeated the score at Huddersfield. Kirby's final goal tally that season was eighteen, within touching distance of Carter's 24.

Kirby was the perfect foil for Carter. A six-footer weighing 12st, he was brave and fearless, unafraid of physical challenge. He was also quick and mobile for his size. Although not considered a 'dirty' player, he could certainly look after himself.

1961-62 again saw the Kirby-Carter partnership bear fruit. They mustered 35 League goals between them to help Argyle reach the heady heights of fifth in Division Two. Kirby was now a wanted man, and in September 1962 Argyle manager Ellis Stuttard accepted an offer from Southampton of £17,000. Shortly after signing for the Saints, Kirby scored a four-minute hat-trick.

In March 1964 he signed for Coventry, and then spent time with Swansea and Walsall. His next move saw him become one of the first British imports to the North American Soccer League. Kirby became a firm favourite with the New York Generals, and his 47 NASL appearances produced 23 goals.

A brief spell with Brentford in 1968 ended a Football League career which had brought him more than 120 goals. In the summer of 1969 he was appointed as assistant trainer at Halifax and two years later took up his first managerial appointment, at Watford. In 1973 he went walkabout, taking managerial posts in countries as diverse as Kuwait and Iceland.

He returned home to Halifax, of all places, managing the club from November 1978 to June 1981 and becoming a paid director and chief executive. Further stints abroad, in Indonesia and Saudi Arabia, preceded a spell as scout for Queens Park Rangers in the late 1990s.

Kirby's health took a downturn and on 24 March 2000 he died of cancer. His death was reported in the Plymouth press, prompting letters from Argyle supporters who remembered Kirby's swashbuckling play at Home Park.

Magic Moment: *Kirby broke his scoring duck at home to Swansea. Having missed three chances, he was on target with a header from Newman's free-kick. Kirby thought his effort was going over the bar.*

Worst Nightmare: *Argyle chairman Ron Blindell was reported to the League for confronting a linesman who hadn't told the ref that Kirby had been struck in the face. Southampton vice-chairman John Barber claimed Kirby initiated the 'rough stuff'.*

ARGYLE RECORD	Appearances	Goals
Football League	93	38
FA Cup	3	–
League Cup	8	1

No 44. **MIKE TREBILCOCK**
Debut: v Southampton, 12 April 1962
Farewell: v Derby, 27 December 1965

The man who eventually assumed George Kirby's forward role was Cornish youngster Mike Trebilcock (pronounced 'Trebillcoe'), who would achieve brief fame on a greater stage than Home Park.

Born in the Cornish village of Gunnislake on 29 November 1944, Trebilcock took up employment as a pipe layer while playing for Tavistock, then Wadebridge Town, with whom he turned in rave performances in the South Western League. After joining Argyle he netted seven times in six South Western League games. Promotion to the reserve team brought him a return of ten goals in eighteen appearances.

Manager Ellis Stuttard pitched Trebilcock into the first team and he responded to his debut by scoring the winner. He played in the final six games of the season and was chosen in a fifteen-man Argyle squad to tour Poland and East Germany in May 1963. In front of huge crowds he played in three of the four games, scoring in the final match against East German side S C Turbine.

His early promise seemed hidden the following season as he played only six times without finding the net. Trebilcock's situation was reminiscent of the great Ray Bowden, 30 years earlier. Both were Cornish-born players who had come from local soccer. As with Bowden, critics claimed Trebilcock was too small to prosper as a forward in the hurly-burly of League football. Certainly, at 5ft 7in and just over 10st the dark, curly-haired youngster was never likely to be a swashbuckling striker in the George Kirby mould. But, perhaps significantly, when Frank Lord appeared on the scene to bear the brunt of blood-and-guts defending, Trebilcock's career blossomed as an inside-forward.

It was unfortunate that for most of Trebilcock's time at Home Park the side were trapped in the lower reaches of Division Two. There were frequent changes of management as the board strived for a solution. Ellis Stuttard was briefly replaced by Andy Beattie, before Malcolm Allison arrived for the first of his two spells as manager. Allison's modernistic approach to tactics and coaching suited Trebilcock. He was given almost a free rein to display his skills and finished that season as top scorer with seventeen League and Cup goals. He also played in every round of Argyle's march to the League Cup semi-finals, scoring in the semi-final first leg defeat at Leicester.

The start of 1965-66 saw yet another incumbent in the Home Park hot seat. Allison had gone to Manchester City and Derek Ufton had replaced him. The change did not affect the team's fortunes and Trebilcock kept up his good form, bagging a hat-trick in a 6-1 win against Birmingham in early September.

What was frustrating about Trebilcock was his inconsistency. On his day, he was a handful for anyone, possessing a crisp shot and a clinical finish, yet at other times one would hardly know he was on the pitch.

Such a lull towards the end of the year saw him dropped. Out of the blue, Everton manager Harry Catterick contacted Argyle with a view to buying Trebilcock. Catterick insisted that the deal be concluded quickly and without a whiff to the press. When Ufton was given the details he suspected a hoax, particularly in light of Trebilcock's dismal form. Once convinced otherwise, secretary Graham Little was despatched to Trebilcock's home with appropriate papers, only to find him out. Little sat in his car until late in the evening to await the player's return. After agreeing to sign, Trebilcock was despatched on a train to Liverpool the next morning with Argyle receiving a fee of £20,000. By the end of the campaign, no other Argyle player had reached Trebilcock's total of eleven goals, so he top-scored by playing only half a season.

At Everton, an injury to England international Fred Pickering saw Trebilcock pitched into the 1966 FA Cup semi-final against Manchester United. Everton won, Pickering declared himself fit for the final, but Catterick would not gamble on him. Trebilcock found himself marching out at Wembley for the Cup final against Sheffield Wednesday.

Catterick's caution seemed to have backfired when Wednesday took a two-goal lead. But cometh the hour, cometh the man. In a five-minute spell Trebilcock scored twice with first-time shots. Derek Temple then scored a third to complete the comeback of the season. The virtual unknown from a small Cornish village was the centre of attention and a great future was predicted.

In fact, Everton fans came to accept that Trebilcock was a one-match wonder. He struggled to adapt to top-flight football, and in January 1968, having played just fourteen games for the club, he left for Portsmouth in a £35,000 transfer. Now sporting a Mexican droopy moustache, he did better for Pompey, netting 33 times in 99 League starts before returning to the South West in July 1972 to briefly join Torquay.

In 1974, he was offered a coaching role at Australian side Western Suburbs. He remains living in Australia, where he has worked as a delivery driver as well as continuing to coach.

Magic Moment: *After the 1967 Cup final, a pub in Trebilcock's home village of Gunnislake created the 'Trebilcock Bar' in his honour.*

Worst Nightmare: *His final game for Everton saw Trebilcock almost completely anonymous. On a quagmire of a pitch, he was the only player at the end of the game to still have clean shorts.*

ARGYLE RECORD	Appearances	Goals
Football League	71	27
FA Cup	2	1
League Cup	8	1

No 45. **FRANK LORD**
Debut: v Norwich, 23 November 1964
Final Farewell: v Barrow, 9 November 1968

There could not be two more contrasting players than the nimble, fleet-footed Mike Trebilcock and the bustling Frank Lord. Grace, style and finesse are three words that would not be used when describing Lord's play. He was more akin to George Kirby. Indeed, his career followed a similar path as he served a number of lower League clubs before embarking on a successful coaching career abroad.

Born in Oldham on 13 March 1936, Lord's first club was Rochdale, with whom he spent seven years and scored 54 goals in 122 League games. His goal-ratio improved at Crewe: 68 League goals in 108 games made him a cult figure. He recorded four hat-tricks in 1961-62 and would achieve that feat eight times for Crewe, creating a club record which he still holds.

Following the sale of Kirby, Argyle had struggled to fill the gap. Trebilcock was out of form; Alex Jackson, Kirby's replacement, was out with a broken leg; and Wilf Carter was but a shadow of his former self. Lord's scoring feats made him the ideal candidate to lead the attack and he joined Argyle in November 1963. He was immediately handed the No 9 shirt and led the attack with vigour. His eight goals in that first season were enough to make him top scorer, such a meagre total underlining the scoring drought facing the team.

It was Lord's gauche style that stirred up feeling during his time at Home Park. Powerfully built, his physical approach often riled defenders, leading to errors and chances for his colleagues. Some Argyle fans questioned his style, but there is no doubt that it was preferable to have him playing for you than against. He was particularly strong in the air, and scored his share of bullet headers.

1964-65 saw him top the scoring charts at Home Park with Mike Trebilcock, both finishing with seventeen League and Cup goals. Lord's tally included six in as many matches in the League Cup, and all three in the 3-1 defeat of Stoke in a fourth round replay. Shortly after, however he broke a bone in his left leg which kept him out for two months.

When Derek Ufton took charge in 1965-66, Lord endured a lean spell and lost his place. There was no shortage of interested buyers, and in February 1966 he moved to Stockport. Eighteen goals in only 27 matches brought another move, this time to Blackburn. Chesterfield was next on his travels, but in October 1967 he found himself back at Home Park as player-coach under Billy Bingham. Coaching took precedence over playing, but Lord was drafted in from time to time to cover for injuries.

Thereafter he became a footballing nomad. He coached at Crystal Palace before heading for Cape Town – which has been his base for much of the time since – interspersed with various other coaching appointments. He won the South Africa Manager of the Year award in 1977 (his prize being a return trip to England), before being appointed manager of Hereford in December 1979, a post he held until September 1982. Jobs in Malaysia and South Africa followed, and it was while in Malaysia that he applied unsuccessfully for the vacant Argyle manager's position.

He was appointed assistant manager at Lincoln in 1994, before taking a position of football coordinator, and briefly caretaker manager, at Wigan. This was his last involvement in football and he has now moved back to South Africa.

Magic Moment: *One of Lord's finest goals was the first of his League Cup hat-trick against Stoke in November 1964. He headed in from Nicky Jennings' cross.*

Worst nightmare: *Lord pleaded with Malcolm Allison to play in the second leg of the League Cup semi-final against Leicester, despite being out for six weeks. Allison agreed but Lord took a knock on his weak leg and was a passenger thereafter.*

ARGYLE RECORD	Appearances	Goals
Football League	75	25
FA Cup	1	–
League Cup	9	6

No 46. **NICKY JENNINGS**
Debut: v Bury, 1 February 1964
Farewell: v Rotherham, 7 January 1967

Nicky Jennings broke into the Argyle side around the same time as Frank Lord. Jennings was a tricky left-winger who, for an all too short period, formed with Barrie Jones one of the most effective wing partnerships in recent Argyle history.

Born in the Somerset town of Wellington on 18 January 1946, Jennings joined Argyle in 1963. After thirteen reserve matches, he made his first-team debut shortly after his eighteenth birthday.

Initial impressions were that he was unlikely to withstand the rigours of Second Division football. He looked even younger than he actually was, and the thought of his thin legs and frail body being subjected to bone-crunching tackles was not one to dwell on.

Jennings soon showed, however, that his skill could triumph over his physical deficiencies. He exhibited the classic wing-man's capabilities of close ball control, excellent dribbling, and the ability to beat his marker and deliver a well-flighted cross. Despite his inexperience, Jennings held his place for the remainder of a relegation-haunted season.

The following year saw the arrival of record transfer Barrie Jones, to replace injury victim Dave Corbett. Jones, an international, naturally attracted greater attention from both the media and opposition. This was to Jennings' benefit, and he proved just as capable of unlocking defences as his more illustrious colleague.

Jones and Jennings played together for just two and a half seasons, and for much of that time Argyle lacked an in-form target man to capitalise on their steady supply of crosses. It was not until Mike Bickle burst on to the scene that the club seemed to unearth the right combination.

Jennings wing-play had made him a crowd favourite, but it was not a view shared by manager Derek Ufton. Inexplicably, Jennings did not seem to figure in his plans for the club. Within the space of two months early in 1967, both he and Jones had departed, much to the fury of Pilgrim followers. Jennings was sold to Portsmouth for £25,000 in January, and to prove the fans' theory that he was one who 'got away', he gave seven years productive service to Pompey, playing over 200 games and scoring almost 50 goals. He was subsequently joined at Portsmouth by two other Argyle 'old boys', Mike Trebilcock and Norman Piper.

Another former team-mate, Johnny Newman, then signed Jennings for Exeter. In his second game for the Grecians, a home League Cup-tie with Swansea, he scored the only hat-trick of his career. He became a regular in the Exeter side for two seasons and missed only three games during the promotion campaign of 1976-77. A succession of injuries preceded Jennings' retirement from the professional game in May 1978.

To pay tribute to a career that had spanned fifteen years and more than 400 games, a testimonial against League champions Nottingham Forest was staged for Jennings' benefit in February 1979.

He coached several Wessex League clubs before working in various capacities at Wimborne Town. In 1992 he was their assistant manager when they won the FA Vase at Wembley. Jennings now works as a welfare officer with the Dorset Probation Service.

Magic Moment: *A home game with Ipswich in February 1966 was played on a quagmire. At one stage Jennings was dripping in mud. He was about to don a fresh shirt when the ball came his way. He raced after it bare chested, his clean shirt flapping in his hand.*

Worst Nightmare: *No sooner had Jennings established himself in the Exeter side than a broken arm kept him out for six months.*

ARGYLE RECORD	Appearances	Goals
Football League	98	11
FA Cup	4	1
League Cup	7	–

No 47. **BARRIE JONES**
Debut: v Ipswich, 12 September 1964
Farewell: v Crystal Palace, 4 February 1967

Complementing Nicky Jennings' left-wing trickery was his opposite number on the right, Barrie Jones. Born in Swansea on 10 October 1941, Jones won schoolboy and youth caps for Wales. He soon broke into Swansea's first team, making his debut in 1959-60. Selection for the Welsh Under-23s against their Irish and English counterparts soon followed, with Jones scoring in both games. He progressed to a further six Under-23 caps and it was little surprise when he made the full Welsh side, thereby becoming one of the few players to have gained international honours for his country at every level.

His time with Swansea Town saw him play 166 League games, scoring 23 goals, and winning seven full caps. He was part of the Swansea side that reached the FA Cup semi-final in 1964 before losing to Preston North End.

With Malcolm Allison at the helm at Home Park, Argyle's policy was to develop young players or recruit from non-league circles. The exception was Jones. Allison tabled bids of £30,000 and £40,000, both rejected, before Argyle committed themselves to a final offer of £45,000. The deal was done, creating not only a club record fee for Argyle but also, at that time, a British record fee for a winger.

This astronomical figure, in Argyle terms anyway, created high expectations of the new recruit. Not since Bill Shortt in the 1950s had Argyle counted a current international player in their ranks.

There were times when Jones looked every inch an international. One such occasion came in a Division Two match at Swindon in March 1965. Jones's marker was young John Trollope, who would go on to make almost 800 appearances for the Wiltshire side. The blond winger gave the raw Trollope a hiding. Time and again he skipped past the full-back to deliver dangerous crosses. Jones scored twice himself that day and made the other goal for Mike Trebilcock.

Keeping possession of the ball was the key to Jones's game. With the ball at his feet he was capable of tearing any defence apart, but without it he would often be left isolated. A former team-mate, John Tedesco, recalls how Jones would frustrate Allison, who wanted him as an out and out winger. But Jones would regularly cut inside his full-back and bring the ball into midfield. To make his point, Allison would keep Jones in for extra training, encouraging him to take on Argyle full-back Mike Reeves, with Jones instructed to beat the defender on the outside. It is not surprising, perhaps, that Jones spent the latter part of his career in a midfield role.

His two goals against Swindon were an exception, for Jones was more of a goal-maker than goal-taker as his final modest tally for Argyle signifies. His three seasons at Home Park were spent in the lower reaches of the Second Division but success came his way when the Greens reached the 1965 League Cup semi-final. He was among several players missing through injury for the first leg at Leicester, but returned for the second, where a goalless draw could not overturn a 2-3 deficit. During his time at Plymouth he was largely overlooked by the Welsh selectors, winning only one cap, against Denmark in 1965.

In March 1967 Jones returned to Wales to play for Cardiff City. Opinion was divided amongst Argyle supporters as to whether the club had received value from its record signing, especially as the £25,000 fee represented a loss of £20,000 on the player. But the move proved to be a wise one for Jones, who was now in the shop-window for international selection. He took his total of Welsh caps to fifteen and also won three Welsh Cup-winners medals with the Bluebirds, which granted entry into the European Cup-Winners' Cup.

In 1967-68 Cardiff fought their way to the semi-finals, thanks in part to Jones's home goal against Moscow Torpedo in the quarter-final. A crowd of 71,000 saw Cardiff achieve a 1-1 semi-final draw at Hamburg, but Cardiff lost the home leg 2-3.

Jones played 107 League games for Cardiff scoring eighteen goals before injury ended his top-class career in 1971. He played for Yeovil before restricting himself to charity games while running his own building firm. More recently he has become a sportsmaster at two private schools in the Swansea area.

Magic Moment: *Jones scored his first international goal against Scotland at Hampden Park in front of 56,000 spectators.*

Worst Nightmare: *Jones's League career was terminated by a badly broken leg whilst playing for Cardiff at Blackpool.*

ARGYLE RECORD	Appearances	Goals
Football League	98	9
FA Cup	5	3
League Cup	7	—

No 48. **NORMAN PIPER**
Debut: v Ipswich, 16 January 1965
Farewell: v Shrewsbury, 18 April 1970

The mid-1960s saw Argyle blessed with an array of skilful players such as Nicky Jennings and Barrie Jones. The name of Norman Piper can also be added to that list.

Born at North Tawton on 8 January 1948, Piper played for Devon side Hatherleigh before signing for Argyle as an apprentice in October 1963. Within six months he found himself playing in the reserves, easily coping with the transition from village soccer to the Football Combination. It was clear from an early stage that Argyle had found a talent worth nurturing, a view that was widely held, as Piper's selection for the England Youth side confirmed.

It was Malcolm Allison who gave Piper his full debut, sixteen months after joining the club. Argyle were going through an awful patch, having taken just one point from six games. With regular No 11, Nicky Jennings, injured, Allison drafted in the slightly built, fresh-faced youngster.

Piper played eleven more games that season, including the first leg of Argyle's League Cup semi-final at Leicester. Sometimes he was fielded at full-back, for even at that early stage he possessed an astute footballing brain that saw him adapt to any position. Early in 1965-66 Piper was switched by new manager Derek Ufton from full-back to his favoured midfield role.

From that point and for the next five seasons, Piper was rarely out of the side. He was equally at home anywhere across the midfield line, although his creative talents were used to best effect from a central position, where he passed intelligently, found space with astute runs, and always made himself available to receive a pass. Sadly for Piper, his years at Home Park coincided with the team struggling from one season to the next. Many fans considered Piper a bright star in a dark sky, although his game was also felt to be too advanced for less gifted team-mates, negating his value rather than stimulating theirs.

But Piper's silky skills made him a crowd favourite and at the end of 1966-67 he was awarded the Player of the Year trophy. The start of the new season saw him, aged nineteen, become Argyle's youngest ever captain. He was unable, however, to bring sufficient influence to bear and the Greens found themselves relegated.

He was ever present in 1968-69, when the club finished fifth in Division Three. Piper's consistency was rewarded by ex-England star Jimmy Armfield, who selected him for an FA Select squad to undertake an eleven-match tour of New Zealand and the Far East. Playing alongside First Division stars such as Bruce Rioch, Tony Hateley and George Eastham provided Piper with valuable experience, despite the weakness of the opposition. Piper played in six matches and scored seven goals, which inevitably increased speculation about his future.

Inconsistency blighted Argyle's chances in 1969-70 and they slumped to sixteenth by the end. Above the dross, Piper shone like a beacon. No game typified his ability more than the Boxing Day clash with local rivals Torquay. The Gulls arrived on the back of a run of ten unbeaten games. Argyle's solitary point from their previous four outings gave little hint of what was to come. Piper was supreme, dictating play, scoring two goals himself and setting up numerous other chances from midfield, with centre-forward Mike Bickle netting four times in a 6-0 rout.

On 8 April 1970, Home Park hosted an Under-23 international between England and Bulgaria. With Piper being selected, a crowd of 28,000 turned out to see the local hero parade his skills alongside the likes of Peter Shilton and Tony Currie. Cynics retorted that the selection of a home player by Sir Alf Ramsey was merely a gesture in order to boost the attendance. There may have been an element of truth to this, but Piper was not overawed by the occasion and did enough to earn three other Under-23 caps after he left Plymouth.

As it transpired, that was to be Piper's last game at Home Park, as Argyle finished the season with four away fixtures. That summer he signed for Portsmouth for £40,000, with fans of both clubs feeling that

Pompey had secured him on the cheap. Piper was a stalwart at Fratton Park for seven years, in which time he made over 300 appearances

Admitting that his earlier tour with the FA had given him a taste for travel, in 1977 Piper plied his trade in the USA with Fort Lauderdale. Two seasons in the NASL saw him score eight goals in 45 matches before he moved to Indoor League soccer with Wichita Wings.

After his playing days he turned to coaching. He had a spell in Canada before returning to Kansas. Recently he has moved to California but still returns to Britain and is a regular guest of Portsmouth reunions.

Magic Moment: *Against Birmingham in September 1965, Piper split the Blues' defence with a back-heeled pass to Nicky Jennings, who crossed for Frank Lord to head a superb goal. Argyle won 6-1.*

Worst Nightmare: *Argyle played a friendly at Holsworthy to open new changing facilities. This was close to the Piper family home and he was made captain. He led the side out, first to applause, then laughter from spectators. The rest of the side had stayed back in the dressing room.*

ARGYLE RECORD	Appearances	Goals
Football League	215	35
FA Cup	9	1
League Cup	9	1

No 49. **JOHN HORE**

Debut: v Northampton, 20 April 1965
Farewell: v Blackburn, 21 October 1975

Johnny Hore was another local player who broke into the Argyle first team around the same time as Norman Piper. Cornishman Hore, who was born at Foxhole near St Austell on 10 February 1947, first came to the attention of Argyle whilst playing for East Cornwall Schools and signed for the club as an apprentice in 1962.

At the tail end of 1963-64 he was given three outings in the reserves as a half-back. The following season he was a second-team regular, which proved an excellent grounding. The Football Combination included the likes of Arsenal, Chelsea and Spurs whose reserve teams contained seasoned pros who had either been dropped or were recovering match fitness after injury. Before the season was through, with little to lose, Malcolm Allison even handed Hore his first-team debut at left-back at Northampton.

That summer Allison was replaced by Derek Ufton, who selected Hore for his first game in charge. One substitute per team was now permitted, and Hore created a small piece of Argyle history by becoming its first playing No 12 when he replaced the injured Frank Lord during a match at Charlton on 31 August 1965. It was not long before Hore was given an extended run, proving equally comfortable at left- or right-half.

From November 1966, and for the next eight years, it was rare to see Argyle take the field without Hore somewhere in the line up. He was also appointed captain during the early 1970s. It is a testament to his value that a succession of Argyle managers considered Hore vital to their plans. He was never spectacular, lacked pace, and goals were rare. Yet he would do the simple things well, often covering team-mates, nullifying attacks by his solid tackling and then distributing short passes to retain possession. If the opposition had a star player who required close attention, Hore was the man to do it. It is not surprising to learn that he modelled his game on his boyhood idol, Dave MacKay. Although Hore's contribution often went unnoticed, it is difficult to remember him having a poor game.

Part of his charm was his appearance, for Hore seemed to have discovered eternal youth. His ruddy complexion, short curly hair and boyish looks contrasted with the long locks and sideburns, shirt outside the shorts image of footballers of that time. Even when new lightweight boots became all the rage, Hore preferred the old style, ankle-high rugby boots. Add to this his broad Cornish accent and friendly smile and it was easy to mentally transport Hore back to an Argyle side of the 1930s.

Whilst much of Hore's Argyle career was spent in midfield, he was used as a full-back in his later years. The period under Tony Waiters' management was certainly Hore's most productive. He played in every round of the 1973-74 League Cup run and made 33 appearances when winning promotion the following season. Eight games into that campaign, only five points were in the bag and relegation seemed more likely than promotion. Hore was one of several players to stand down and it was not until late November that he was recalled, taking over at right-back from the suspended Peter Darke. Determined to keep his place, Hore played some of the best football of his career, finishing on the losing side only four more times that season. These were magical times for the player. Shortly after promotion was secured, Bob Paisley brought a near full-strength Liverpool side to Devon for his testimonial.

By March 1976 Hore was deemed to be surplus to requirements at Home Park. He joined Exeter City and, mainly at full-back, played 221 games for The Grecians without scoring, missing only two matches in over four years. From 1980 he managed Bideford Town to two Western

League championships. Despite this record, it surprised many when, following the departure of Bobby Moncur as Argyle manager early in 1983-84, the directors turned to Hore to take over. After all, he was inexperienced at League level. But momentous events awaited. Hore's tenth game in charge was a first round FA Cup-tie at Southend. That goalless draw precipitated the club's extraordinary charge to the semi-finals, where they lost by a single goal to Graham Taylor's Watford.

Such was the fervour surrounding the cup run that it masked a dreadful League campaign. It needed seven points from the last four games to lift Argyle clear of the trap-door. The poor form continued into the following season, and after just one win in the first ten games, Hore – so recently a hero – was sacked, replaced by Dave Smith.

He returned to Exeter as a coach and was appointed caretaker manager following the dismissal of Jim Iley, but was passed over for the full-time post in favour of Colin Appleton. He returned to management with Western League side Torrington, before concentrating on his own health club business, which he still operates from premises in the centre of Exeter. It was a far cry from his intended post-soccer career as restaurateur, to which end he had studied catering during his time at Argyle.

Hore's experience is now being harnessed as manager of Barnstaple in the Western League. He still looks no older than he did as a player.

Magic Moment: *Hore marked Pele in Argyle's friendly with Santos in March 1973. At the end of the game he exchanged shirts with the great man and proudly keeps that famous No 10 shirt to this day.*

Worst Nightmare: *On Boxing Day 1967, at home to QPR, Hore's 'tackle' on Rodney Marsh was deemed a penalty. It was converted for the only goal of the game. The decision sparked a pitch invasion.*

ARGYLE RECORD	Appearances		Goals
Football League	393	(+7)	17
FA Cup	17		–
League Cup	23		–

No 50. **MIKE BICKLE**

Debut: v Southampton, 11 December 1965
Farewell: v Rochdale, 27 September 1971

Unlike Johnny Hore, Mike Bickle did not follow the traditional route through the apprentice ranks, instead relying on his raw goalscoring instincts to make the transition from local leagues. Bickle owes much to Derek Ufton, for it was he who plucked him from non-league soccer at the relatively late age of 21.

Plymothian Bickle, born on 25 January 1944, had been a Co-op milkman. Ufton, assistant to Malcolm Allison, spotted Bickle through his prolific goalscoring exploits with St Austell and for his works side, Co-op Welfare in the Devon Wednesday League. An earlier recommendation to Allison had fallen on deaf ears, perhaps because Argyle had a surplus of centre-forwards at that time. After Ufton replaced Allison he stepped in to sign his man.

Six games for the reserves produced eight goals and was enough for Ufton to throw the No 9 shirt to Bickle. A goal on his debut justified his selection, and even Ted Bates, manager of opponents Southampton, was impressed by Argyle's debutant.

Bickle was a raw talent, but he loved scoring goals and the standard of the opposition mattered little. His attitude was that if there was a chance of a goal, he would take it. He was strongly built, though only 5ft 9in, and his courage was beyond question. He would often dive in without fear of his own, or his opponents', welfare and in consequence his career was blighted by injury.

That first season saw him score nine goals in seventeen games, adding for good measure a hat-trick against hapless Corby Town in the FA Cup. It was as a result of Bickle's form that his predecessor in the No 9 shirt, Frank Lord, was allowed to leave.

In each of the next four seasons at Home Park, Bickle finished top scorer, achieving hero status with the fans. With few exceptions, most Plymouth-bred players have enjoyed an affinity with the crowd and Bickle was no exception. With long sideburns and a Brylcreamed quiff, he could have belonged to a 1960s skiffle group, but his goal celebration – one arm held aloft above a gap-toothed smile – became a familiar sight at grounds around the country.

Bickle twice scored four goals in a match. The first came in his second season as Argyle demolished Cardiff 7-1; the second was in the Boxing Day derby with Torquay in 1969, when the Pilgrims won 6-0. Not only was Bickle an asset on the field. A succession of managers have paid tribute to him, describing him as one of the nicest people in the game, a willing worker both in games and in training.

1967-68 saw Argyle suffer relegation from Division Two. Bickle missed the opening fourteen games through injury, during which time Argyle collected only six points and scored nine goals. One can only speculate as to what difference Bickle would have made, for his return sparked an upturn in form that might have brought safety – had it started sooner.

The 1969-70 season was Bickle's best in terms of his personal goal tally – eighteen – but the following season was disrupted by injury. Even when he was fit, the scoring exploits of Keith Allen, Jimmy Hinch and Don Hutchins saw him dumped into the reserves.

At the start of 1971-72 former colleague Andy Nelson, manager of Gillingham, tabled a bid of £7,000 for Bickle's services. The offer was accepted and he found himself on the move to Kent. As often happens, a new club cannot guarantee continuation of good form, and though Bickle gave wholehearted commitment to his new team, the goals did not flow. He had managed just seven in 32 League games before his career was brought to a premature and abrupt end.

Gillingham were playing an evening fixture at Stockport. At a Gills' corner-kick, Bickle and team-mate David Galvin went for the ball and clashed heads. Galvin required eight stitches but had come out lucky. Bickle had taken the full force of the collision and was rushed to hospital. When he regained consciousness he found himself paralysed from the chest down. Full feeling was gradually restored but the prognosis was not good. He had broken a bone in his neck that connected to the spinal cord, and further damage would result in permanent disability. Bickle's career in professional football was at an end.

Bickle did not bow out easily. He pleaded with Nelson for a chance, but the manager bowed to medical opinion and refused. By way of consolation, Nelson promised Bickle a memorable farewell and arranged a testimonial at Home Park in May 1973 between Argyle and Manchester City managed, ironically, by Malcolm Allison. A large crowd turned out to pay tribute to one of the most popular players to have served the club.

Bickle returned to live in Plymouth. He took up employment in Devonport Dockyard, where he remains to this day.

Magic moment: *To exemplify his unquenchable spirit, Bickle's last two goals of his foursome against Cardiff in October 1966 came in injury-time.*

Worst Nightmare: *Bickle was denied the opportunity, because of his neck injury, to play any part in his own testimonial match.*

ARGYLE RECORD	Appearances	Goals
Football League	171 (+10)	71
FA Cup	7 (+1)	3
League Cup	6 (+1)	–

No 51. **STEVE DAVEY**
Debut: v Blackburn, 19 November 1966
Farewell: v Gillingham, 21 September 1974

Steve Davey, like Mike Bickle before him, was another local lad who made his mark at Home Park.

Born in Plymouth on 5 September 1948, Davey attended Frederick Street and Valletort schools. When not playing himself he would watch Argyle. Unable to afford the admission, the young, enterprising Davey would climb a tree outside the ground at the Barn Park End and imagine himself running onto the Home Park pitch in Argyle green. He was selected for both Plymouth and Devon Schools and it was no surprise when in July 1964 he was taken on as an apprentice by Argyle.

Used mainly as an inside-forward, Davey progressed through the Argyle ranks and was given his first-team debut by Derek Ufton, as a replacement for the injured Barrie Jones. International honours came his way with selection for the England Youth squad in a tournament in Turkey dubbed 'The Little World Cup'. Davey played in two games alongside some future 'greats' of the game, including Peter Shilton, Trevor Brooking and Brian Kidd.

With Argyle labouring and, eventually, suffering relegation at the end of 1967-68, Davey was not sure of a regular place until the following season when, in Division Three, he netted eleven goals in 37 starts.

1970-71 saw Davey display previously unknown versatility when he was used at right-back. It was not a role he cherished but the form of Derek Rickard and Don Hutchins in attack made it difficult for him to depose them. He adapted well to his defensive duties where his speed, close control, and good passing encouraged him to overlap into forward positions.

The situation whereby Davey never knew whether he was in or out, and, if playing, where, continued for a couple of seasons. It took the arrival of new manager Tony Waiters for Davey to take wing. Waiters' first full season was undoubtedly Davey's best in Argyle colours. He would have been ever present but for suspension – following his expulsion in an infamous Sunday game at Port Vale in March 1974 – and struck up a partnership with young Paul Mariner. Mariner outscored Davey in the League, but Davey's overall total of nineteen made him leading scorer, a figure boosted by seven goals in six League Cup-ties which helped carry Argyle to the semi-finals.

The first leg at home to Manchester City on a muddy, grassless pitch proved memorable for Davey, who found himself in opposition to one of his idols, Denis Law. Davey also scored the goal which gave Argyle a half-time lead, when seizing on a mistake by City's Willie Donachie.

The inclusion of another forward, Billy Rafferty, saw Waiters start 1974-75 with an experimental three-pronged attack, but after only six games the plan was abandoned. Davey was the man left out, partly, he believes, through his generosity in allowing Rafferty to take a penalty to complete his hat-trick against Tranmere. Waiters, ever the professional, berated Davey, the regular penalty taker, for putting sentiment above the welfare of the team. The relationship between player and manager soured, and Davey found himself in the reserves. This provoked uproar from supporters, who had taken to Davey since his League Cup scoring exploits, but it made no difference. Argyle secured promotion without him.

With few prospects at Home Park, in August 1975 Davey joined Hereford, managed by his former Argyle colleague John Sillett. Sillett saw Davey as vital to his promotion plans and offered a deal based on payment by results, which was valued at around £10,000. In Davey's first season at Edgar Street, Hereford clinched the Division Three title, helped by the partnership of Davey and Dixie McNeil. Between them, they scored 53 League goals with Davey contributing eighteen. At the end of that season Davey returned to Home Park with Hereford for a well-deserved testimonial.

Two successive relegations saw Hereford back in Division Four. It was time for Davey to move on, and after 32 goals in over 100 appearances for Hereford, he joined Portsmouth for a small fee. He spent three years with Pompey, who used his experience mainly in a sweeper role. His 83 League appearances, plus ten as substitute, saw him add eight goals to his scoring record. His final League club was Exeter, for whom he played twenty League and Cup games without scoring.

At non-League level, Davey played until 1984 with Bideford, Liskeard, Saltash, and St Blazey. He returned to live in Plymouth and started his own upholstery business. In recent years, he has taken over the ownership of a residential home in the city.

The Davey family has many football connections. His wife is the sister of another Argyle favourite, Fred Binney, and both Davey's sons were on Argyle's books as youngsters. One of them, Damien, is physio at Exeter City, having held the same post at Torquay.

Magic Moment: *During Argyle's 1973-74 League Cup run, Davey scored a beauty at Birmingham. Furnell punted the ball upfield, Paul Mariner flicked it on, and Davey volleyed home from 30 yards.*

Worst Nightmare: *Near the end of Argyle's first leg League Cup semi-final with Manchester City, Davey dislocated his shoulder whilst diving for the ball and was forced to miss the crucial second leg.*

ARGYLE RECORD	Appearances	Goals
Football League	213 (+11)	47
FA Cup	8	1
League Cup	16	7

No 58. Jim Furnell, Argyle's evergreen keeper of the 1970s.

No 58. Furnell follows out skipper Mike Green (No 71.) after clinching promotion

No 63. Ernie Machin, midfield general   No 65. Brian Johnson, dashing winger

No 66. Paul Mariner is sandwiched between two Hull City defenders

No 67. Colin Randell swings at the ball and Billy Rafferty takes evasive action

No 69. Billy Rafferty, goalscoring partner to Paul Mariner

Chapter Six

~ *Bingham's Boys* ~

No 52. **PAT DUNNE**
Debut: v Huddersfield, 25 February 1967
Farewell: v Rochdale, 2 November 1970

Unlike Steve Davey, Pat Dunne had already experienced top-flight soccer before coming to Argyle. Born on 9 February 1943, Dubliner Dunne was already well known from his years as Manchester United's first-choice goalkeeper.

Having represented Dublin Schools and Irish Schoolboys, Dunne graduated to win an FAI Cup winners medal with Shamrock Rovers. In May 1964, Matt Busby persuaded him come over to join his older brother, Tony Dunne, who was also on United's books. Pat's fee was £10,500.

Injuries to regular keepers Harry Gregg and Dave Gaskell permitted Dunne an early debut, ironically against Everton, with whom he had trialled some years earlier. United stayed undefeated in Dunne's first fifteen games, winning all but two, the perfect springboard for winning the 1964-65 championship. Dunne played 37 games that season. As well as making the FA Cup semi-finals, United also reached the last four of the Inter Cities Fairs Cup. What was good for Man U was good for his country, and Dunne earned one Under-23 and five full Republic of Ireland caps.

Dunne's star faded quickly. After two games the following season he was ousted by Gregg and thereafter was never more than an understudy at Old Trafford. His prospects were further blighted by the signing of Alex Stepney, and in February 1967, after 66 appearances for United in all competitions, Dunne joined Argyle for £5,000.

A big name, bought cheaply, was warmly welcomed by the Argyle faithful. Since the departure of Dave MacLaren, none of his successors had impressed at Home Park and, with Argyle staring relegation in the face, Dunne's arrival came not a moment too soon.

Things did not go according to plan. In contrast to his baptism with Manchester United, it was not until Dunne's eighth game for Argyle that he finished on the winning side, though five unbeaten games late on saw Argyle climb to safety. Dunne retained links with Shamrock Rovers, and that summer Argyle allowed him to tour the USA with the Dublin club.

Argyle's fortunes dived during Dunne's first full season at Home Park, 1967-68. Argyle ended with the wooden spoon, though no blame could be attached to the goalkeeper. A miserly strike-rate of 37 goals from 42 games highlighted where the real problem lay. Dunne missed only one match and were it not for his heroics week in, week out, matters would have been worse.

The fearless Dunne possessed sharp reflexes and was an excellent shot-stopper. At 5ft 11in, he would be considered a small goalkeeper by today's standards, though not necessarily by those of his time. But if criticism can be levelled against him it was his occasional vulnerability on crosses, which meant he did not always dominate the penalty area as he should.

Despite relegation, the Home Park crowd recognised his efforts and voted Dunne the Player of the Year. He was also called into the Ireland squad on a number of occasions, but never again made the starting line up.

The following season saw Dunne sustain his excellent form. He was ever present as Argyle finished fifth in Division Three under Billy Bingham. 1969-70 saw early hopes of promotion fade after Christmas, and Dunne briefly lost his place to young Martin Clamp, though he was soon recalled.

Towards the end of 1970, Jim Furnell signed for Argyle from Rotherham. His arrival mirrored that of Dunne, almost four years earlier. Furnell also boasted First Division experience and, like Dunne, signed for Argyle for a modest fee. Furnell was installed as No 1 and within weeks, Dunne, still only 27, returned to Shamrock Rovers, for whom he gave several years service. He actually continued playing into his 50s. In the early 1990s he was still turning out in the United Churches Premier League, with his side winning the 1992-93 championship.

Magic Moment: *At Fulham in October 1970 Dunne pulled off a string of saves. A newspaper stated he 'kept Argyle in the game with saves that the goalkeeper had no right to be anywhere near'.*

Worst Nightmare: *When Dunne conceded the only goal at Barrow in November 1968 the scorer was – the referee! A shot from George McLean was going wide when it struck the foot of the man in black, Ivan Robinson, and flew into the Argyle net with Dunne stranded.*

ARGYLE RECORD	Appearances	Goals
Football League	152	–
FA Cup	5	–
League Cup	7	–

No 53. **BOBBY SAXTON**
Debut: v Preston, 3 February 1968
Farewell: v Orient, 13 September 1975

Another name inexorably linked to Steve Davey, owing to that infamous 'Black Sunday' fixture, is Bobby Saxton.

Born at Balby near Doncaster on 6 September 1943, Saxton epitomised the gritty, determined Yorkshire spirit, qualities that have served him during his post-playing days, when he has become a successful manager and coach. He began with Gainsborough youth team before moving to Denaby United in the Midland League. The tough-tackling defender was signed by Derby County in February 1962.

By 1964, his leadership qualities were rewarded with the club captaincy. Saxton went on to make 94 League appearances for the Rams, plus two as substitute, scoring a solitary goal. But with the arrival of Brian Clough as manager, and the emergence of Roy McFarland at centre-half, Saxton was out in the cold.

At Home Park, new manager Billy Bingham had introduced several players to try to stave off relegation. Saxton seemed the ideal man to shore up a leaky defence and he signed in February 1968 for a fee of £12,000. Bingham had whittled away at the original asking price of £20,000, completing the deal at 1.30 in the morning. The new signing only half paid off. Although the goals-against column improved, the goals scored didn't, with the result that Argyle finished bottom of Division Two.

The following season Saxton established himself as a popular figure with his never-say-die attitude, but before the curtain rose on 1969-70 disaster struck. He was involved in a road accident that left him with a broken leg. It was not a clean break, complications arose, and he was forced to miss the whole season.

That summer, 1970, Saxton was permitted by Brian Clough to train at Derby. The two men enjoyed a mutual respect and Clough would join Saxton in training rather than see his former captain exercise alone. Ellis Stuttard, who had replaced Bingham, was sufficiently convinced of Saxton's recovery to install him in the side for the new season as skipper. Stuttard's faith was rewarded. Saxton played in every game and seemed as good as new.

Argyle fans were also pleased to see him back at the heart of the defence. It was the Saxton of old, tackling hard, marshalling his defence, cajoling team-mates with his high-pitched voice and, occasionally, berating officials. He played and looked tough. His boxer's nose, the recipient of many a bruising encounter, gave the impression that he had just gone ten rounds. There were times when he took the law into his own hands, but, whether through guile or a quiet word with the referee, he would usually get away with it. When he became the third Argyle player dismissed at Port Vale in March 1972, it was the first time he had ever received marching orders.

After such a successful comeback, the following season was something of an anti-climax, and the arrival of Dave Provan saw Saxton restricted to just thirteen starts. 1972-73 saw him in an unfamiliar midfield role, where he was asked to add bite, but with the arrival of Tony Waiters as manager, he reverted to his customary stopper position. Waiters saw him as the natural leader of the side and Saxton became the driving force behind Argyle's League Cup campaign of 1973-74 and promotion-winning side of the following season.

Saxton had only a taste of Division Two football. After three appearances he was sold to Exeter for £4,000, becoming the linch-pin of the side that gained promotion from Division Four in 1976-77. By December manager Johnny Newman had moved to Grimsby, leaving Saxton as his natural successor. His enthusiasm and knowledge of the game soon made him a name to watch.

To the dismay of Exeter fans, Saxton returned to Home Park as manager in January 1979, replacing Malcolm Allison. Not only did he leave Exeter rudderless, he also brought with him Exeter's backroom staff, including his chief scout, Jim Furnell.

Whilst results at Argyle were not spectacular under Saxton's reign, shrewd signings (David Kemp, John Sims, and Geoff Crudgington) enhanced his standing, and when he was invited to take over from Howard Kendall at Blackburn 1981, the financial terms made it impossible to refuse. He spent almost six years at Ewood Park before moving in one capacity or another to York City, Newcastle, Manchester City and Blackpool. In recent years he has become a familiar figure as Peter Reid's sidekick at Sunderland. A recent fly-on-the-wall TV documentary at Sunderland showed that Saxton had lost none of his enthusiasm and passion, as demonstrated by the overworked 'bleeps'.

Magic Moment: *In an attempt to prove his fitness following his broken leg, Saxton played in a practice match. An Argyle team-mate, on the other side, complained about Saxton's tough tackling.*

Worst Nightmare: *When complications arose following Saxton's broken leg, there were fears that he may have to quit football.*

ARGYLE RECORD	Appearances		Goals
Football League	224	(+7)	7
FA Cup	11		–
League Cup	11	(+3)	–

No 54. **DAVE BURNSIDE**

Debut: v Hull, 16 March 1968
Farewell: v Rotherham, 1 May 1971

Billy Bingham's next signing for Argyle, after Bobby Saxton, was Dave Burnside, one of the most skilful players ever to grace Home Park.

Burnside, middle name 'Gort', was born at Kingswood in Bristol on 10 December 1939. He played for Bristol Schoolboys and England Youth. Surprisingly, neither Rovers nor City snapped him up and it was West Brom who signed him. The Hawthorns crowd knew of Burnside's ability before he had played a game, as he had regularly been invited to display his ball-juggling skills as half-time entertainment.

Burnside debuted for the Throstles in February 1957 and went on to make 127 League appearances, scoring 39 goals. In 1960 he also hit the headlines by winning a competition organised by *The Sunday Despatch*. Contestants had to play keepy-uppy with their heads, no feet. Burnside won with a remarkable tally of 495, the runner up scoring a 'mere' 286.

In September 1962, a fee of £18,000 took Burnside to Southampton, where he scored a creditable 22 times in 61 League games. Moving to Crystal Palace in December 1964, he netted twice on his debut in a 4-2 win over Portsmouth and, in time, was appointed captain. Next stop was Wolves. The deal was completed on 6 September 1966, the day before Wolves were to play Palace, Burnside wore No 8 and had the cheek to score Wolves' goal in a 1-1 draw. After eighteen months at Molineux, Burnside's next port of call was Argyle, Billy Bingham paying £7,000 for his services.

At the time of his arrival in March 1968, the club were staring into the abyss. A 2-0 away win on Burnside's debut proved to be a flash in the pan. He tasted victory just once more that season and the club finished rock bottom.

It was in 1968-69 that Argyle saw the best of Dave Burnside. Not only was he skilful: he played with intelligence, able to find team-mates with cunning passes, and break from midfield with his strong running. He liked to play without shin-pads and with socks rolled down, and was the sort of player who, on taking possession of the ball, injected a sense of expectancy in the crowd.

Having started the season in midfield, Bingham experimented by switching Burnside to centre-forward, a position to which no player was able to lay claim. The experiment paid off, with Burnside bringing other forwards into the game and showing that he possessed an eye for goal. At the end of a season in which he missed only four League games and scored nine goals, he was named as Argyle's 'Player of the Year'.

The following season was not so good. Burnside started only fifteen League games, and many observers felt that his choice to commute daily from his family home in Bristol was taking its toll. 1970-71 saw Burnside regain a regular berth. Reverting to midfield, he scored five times in 36 League appearances. These included a strike at Rotherham in the final game, which, it transpired, was his last League appearance for the club.

In December 1971, following a period in the reserves, Burnside joined Bristol City. This seemed a perfect arrangement, given his domestic circumstances, but the move did not work out, and after one game he signed for Gillingham. After thirteen games for the Gills, Burnside called time on his League career. He returned to his Bristol base to manage Bath City.

That was the start of a coaching career which proved even more successful than his playing days. He has worked with Walsall, with the FA in a range of capacities, and was also manager of the Oxford University side for a spell. In recent years, Burnside has returned to Bristol City, where he now holds the position of director of the club's youth academy.

Magic Moment: *During his early years, Burnside was paid £25 to entertain the West Brom crowd with his ball-juggling act, earning more than the club's star international player, Bobby Robson.*

Worst Nightmare: *Burnside had to make daily pre-motorway journeys to and from Plymouth from his Bristol home.*

ARGYLE RECORD	Appearances	Goals
Football League	105	15
FA Cup	3	1
League Cup	5	1

No 55. **COLIN SULLIVAN**
Debut: v Rotherham, 19 March 1968
Farewell: v York, 6 May 1974

A young player who benefited from Dave Burnside's considerable experience was Saltash born full-back, Colin Sullivan.

Born on 24 June 1951, Sullivan came from a talented footballing family. His brothers, Keith and Phil, followed him to Home Park, but made it only to the reserves and were eventually released.

Colin was the exception. Having been recommended to Argyle by another Saltash-born full-back, Mike Reeves, his rise through the ranks was rapid. The 1967-68 season saw him play ten Western League games for what was effectively the Argyle third team, before he was promoted to the reserves. After just eight Football Combination appearances, Sullivan was tossed by Billy Bingham into his League debut, at left-back, in a tough clash with Rotherham. At sixteen years, eight months and 23 days, he had become the youngest player ever to represent Argyle in a first-team fixture, a record that was to stand until the late 1990s when it was broken by Lee Phillips.

Young Sullivan quickly settled into the side, displaying a strong tackle, good positional sense and the ability to overlap and cross with his left foot. These qualities would serve him well in a career that eventually spanned almost twenty years. It should be remembered that, at first, Sullivan was not even on a professional contract, but he kept his place for the rest of the season and joined the fully paid ranks in July 1968. It was of little surprise that international honours soon followed. Sullivan was selected for the England Youth squad that competed in a European tournament in Germany.

The thrill of breaking into Argyle's first team was tempered by the fact that they finished bottom. The following season saw Sullivan in and out of the side, but from the beginning of 1969-70 he was almost a permanent fixture until the arrival of the experienced Allan Harris put his place under threat.

Although quiet and unassuming, Sullivan was determined and ambitious to compete at the highest level. It was not long before he proved himself to be one of the best attacking full-backs in the lower divisions. 1972-73 was one of his best seasons. He was consistency personified, an ever present in League and Cup, and played in the memorable friendly against Pele's Santos.

Bigger clubs were beginning to covet the small, youthful looking defender and took notice whenever he faced more exalted company. Such an opportunity arose in October 1973 when Home Park was again chosen for an England Under-23 international, this time against Poland. As with Norman Piper some years earlier, Sullivan was picked for England, partly to generate local interest, partly on merit. Playing alongside big names like Trevor Francis, Charlie George and Steve Perryman, Sullivan took the event in his stride and did well enough to earn a second cap against Denmark later in the season. It was now only a matter of time before Argyle bowed to a tempting offer to buy him.

The arrival of Tony Waiters and the run to the League Cup semi-finals kept Sullivan's name to the fore. At the end of 1973-74 he was sold to Norwich for an initial £50,000, with a further £20,000 if and when he played a certain number of games. If that suggested lack of confidence in Sullivan's ability to cope with First Division football, the fears were unfounded. He was soon a regular in the Canaries' No 3 shirt, and was part of the side that lost to Aston Villa in the 1974-75 League Cup final. Sullivan played 154 League games for Norwich (including substitutions), scoring three goals, before a £60,000 fee took him to Cardiff City in February 1979. In December 1981 he moved to Hereford but four months later signed for Portsmouth, where he remained for three years, playing 94 games, and was an ever present in the side that won the Third Division title in 1982-83. His final League club was Swansea, where full-back partners included another ex-Pilgrim, Colin Randell.

Sullivan retired from League soccer in 1985 and took up residence in Locks Heath, near Southampton, where he still lives. He played briefly for the local side and worked as a postman before concentrating on his own market gardening business, which he still operates.

Magic Moment: *Sullivan scored a rare goal at home to Halifax in September 1969. It was a 20-yard blaster with his rarely used right foot and it won Argyle the points, 1-0.*

Worst Nightmare: *Sullivan once turned up for a reserve match at Reading 40 minutes after kick-off.*

ARGYLE RECORD	Appearances		Goals
Football League	225	(+5)	7
FA Cup	12		–
League Cup	14		–

No 56. **DON HUTCHINS**
Debut: v Tranmere, 30 August 1969
Farewell: v Bradford City, 18 April 1972

Don Hutchins was another predominantly left-footed player to join Argyle during the late 1960s. Born in Middlesbrough on 8 May 1948, he was selected for the school teams of both Middlesbrough and the North Riding of Yorkshire. On leaving school he combined employment as an invoice clerk with amateur appearances for Middlesbrough's junior sides, but, to his disappointment, he was released by his home-town club and joined nearby Stockton Juniors. There, his displays as a dashing left-winger attracted a number of scouts from bigger clubs.

Coventry, Derby and Norwich were among those vying for his signature, but it was Leicester City scout George Carr who persuaded Hutchins to attend trials at Filbert Street. He signed in February 1966 and was soon in City's reserves, competing in the Football Combination against Argyle's reserve side. Hutchins marked his card against Chelsea's reserves, collecting the ball on the halfway line, beating four defenders, and driving the ball into the top corner. Leicester, incidentally, won that game 10-1. Before long he was also experiencing the glamorous side of football, being part of the Leicester team that won an international Under-20 tournament in Holland.

An injury to experienced winger Mike Stringfellow gave Hutchins his League debut, when Leicester manager Matt Gillies selected him to play at Burnley in April 1967. He made a handful of other first-team appearances too, but it was a reserve match against Argyle at Filbert Street that brought to him to the attention of Billy Bingham. The original asking price of £8,000 was finally reduced to £5,000 and the deal was concluded in July 1969.

Hutchins' first season at Home Park was not a source of banner headlines. The club already possessed a capable left-winger in Aiden Maher and Hutchins was restricted to thirteen appearances. The disillusioned youngster asked to leave. The Argyle board acquiesced, but with no firm offers on the table Hutchins stayed to fight for his place.

Though left out of the opening game of 1970-71, Hutchins replaced Maher for the second game and maintained a level of performance that made it difficult for Maher to get back in. Not since Nicky Jennings a few years earlier had Argyle possessed an out and out winger capable of getting the crowd on its feet. The slightly built flank-man with the tumble of curly hair was capable of shattering a full-back's confidence with his speed and trickery. Once near the by-line, he could deliver pinpoint crosses, though he often cut inside to deliver a shot on goal. These were often on target, and resulted in Hutchins becoming Argyle's top scorer for the season with eleven goals.

With Bingham departed, the new managerial duo of Stuttard and Edwards played a big part in Hutchins' development. The following season saw him repeat his tally of eleven goals. In the summer of 1972 Blackburn make a bid for his services. In contrast to his early days, Hutchins was quite settled at Home Park, even though the club were enduring one of their darker periods in Division Three. Nevertheless, the deal went through.

Two years at Rovers saw Hutchins appear in 40 League games, scoring six times. At one stage he was advised that Tony Waiters was hankering for his return to Argyle. Perhaps Hutchins would have welcomed a return, but it never materialised. Instead, he linked up with his former Argyle coach, Bryan Edwards, at Bradford City. Hutchins became one of Bradford's most popular players of recent times, logging more than 250 appearances in seven years at the club, scoring 44 League goals.

A series of injuries precipitated his retirement from full-time soccer in 1980. He played briefly for Scarborough in the Northern Premier League side but soon gave up the game.

Still living in the Bradford area, Hutchins has for many years worked for a paint distribution company, most recently as regional sales manager for the north of England. His retains his connections with Bradford City. Along with a number of other former players, he assists on matchdays with corporate hospitality at Valley Parade.

Magic Moment: *Against Aston Villa in Division Three in October 1971, Hutchins scored through team-mate Keith Allen's legs to put Argyle one up. He later netted a second as Argyle won 3-1 to go top of the table.*

Worst Nightmare: *When Hutchins let team-mate Peta Bala'c borrow his car, the young keeper crashed it into a Plymouth city-centre roundabout.*

ARGYLE RECORD	Appearances		Goals
Football League	94	(+1)	23
FA Cup	2		–
League Cup	2		–

No 57. **DEREK RICKARD**
Debut: v Halifax, 13 December 1969
Farewell: v Charlton, 16 April 1974

A player to benefit from Don Hutchins regular stream of crosses was Derek Rickard, who almost slipped through the Argyle net.

Born in Plymouth on 1 October 1947, Rickard signed for the Pilgrims at fifteen as an amateur, but after five games in the reserves in 1965-66 he was released. Taking employment in the Dockyard as a joiner, he played for Torpoint and St Austell, where he developed into a prolific goalscorer.

It was fortunate for Rickard that former manager Ellis Stuttard was still chief scout at Argyle. Stuttard was a believer in giving local talent a chance, and it was he who invited Rickard back for a second chance. Rickard was put straight into the reserves at the beginning of 1969-70. Whereas Rickard had struggled three years previously, a sackful of goals since had boosted his confidence.

A reserve match against Chelsea, when he scored both goals in Argyle's victory, proved decisive. When Rickard was omitted for a reserve midweek fixture four days later, it was evident that his first-team baptism was imminent. By now Stuttard had taken over the hot seat from Billy Bingham and, as Mike Bickle was going through a lean patch, Rickard got his chance.

It was not the dream start he would have wished. Argyle lost 0-2. Nevertheless, Stuttard's faith was soon repaid. Rickard proved the catalyst in Argyle's revival. Results improved, Bickle began to find the net, abetted by the busy and skilful Rickard – who kept his place for the rest of the season – scored nine goals himself, and bagged a hat-trick against Shrewsbury. Argyle climbed to sixteenth and Rickard's displays earned him the Argyle Player of the Year award.

Injuries wrecked Rickard's next two seasons. 1970-71 saw him notch nine goals by the end of January, before he was crocked, and cruel luck followed again in 1971-72. In only eighteen games he found the net on fourteen occasions (including nine goals in seven games around Christmas), before his injury jinx struck again. He only returned for the final game of the season, inevitably scoring, to confirm his position at the top of Argyle's scoring charts.

There was no secret to Rickard's game. He was full of running, his fair head appearing everywhere. For a player of average height he was deceptively good in the air, and on the ground was an opportunist, unafraid of attempting half-chances. Pele's Santos fell victim to Rickard's heading ability, a deft touch producing a goal in that famous 1973 friendly.

The arrival of Tony Waiters sparked the beginning of the end of Rickard's time at Home Park. New starlets like Paul Mariner and Brian Johnson – together with a resurgent Steve Davey – saw Rickard pushed to the fringes of the team. In July 1974 he departed for Bournemouth, along with Neil Hague, in a joint-transfer valued at £15,000. Rickard made only 22 League starts at Dean Court (plus ten as substitute), scoring six times, and the Cherries suffered instant relegation. That was his finale. A League career that had begun at the advanced age of 22 was at an end six years later. Rickard returned to his original job in the Dockyard and played part-time with Falmouth and Saltash.

He built up a newsagency in the city which he sold in 1998, and he is now working as a delivery driver for the local *Evening Herald* newspaper. He has also found himself involved with the Weston Mill club in various capacities.

Magic Moment: *At Leeds in the FA Cup fourth round in February 1973, Rickard's header levelled the scores. Sadly, the First Division side scored again, but Rickard had given them a huge fright.*

Worst Nightmare: *Having established himself as an Argyle first-team regular, Rickard fractured his cheekbone in February 1971.*

ARGYLE RECORD	Appearances		Goals
Football League	101	(+9)	41
FA Cup	6	(+1)	1
League Cup	1	(+2)	–

No 58. JIM FURNELL
Debut: v Gillingham, 7 November 1970
Farewell: v Carlisle, 24 April 1976

Jim Furnell played a major part in Argyle's success of the mid-1970s. He was born in Manchester on 23 November 1937 but when he was three his family moved to nearby Clitheroe. He undertook his secondary education at Clitheroe Royal Grammar School. When interviewed by a youth employment officer, Furnell said, straight-faced, that he wanted to be a professional footballer. The officer was a friend of Burnley manager Frank Hill, who offered Furnell work as an office boy at Turf Moor, while training and learning the ropes.

No sooner had Furnell arrived than Hill left, but his successor, Alan Brown, was no less impressed, offering the young keeper a professional contract as soon as he was seventeen. Furnell faced stiff competition for the No 1 jersey, with internationals Colin McDonald (England) and Adam Blacklaw (Scotland) both at the club. In consequence, Furnell spent five years in Burnley's reserves, making his League debut against a Blackpool side that included Tony Waiters. He played just once more, Burnley losing 3-4 to Chelsea in 1960-61 with Jimmy Greaves scoring three. The Clarets had fielded a side containing ten reserves and were fined £1,000 for their pains. In these restricted circumstances, in February 1962 Furnell jumped at the opportunity to join Liverpool for £18,000.

Despite Liverpool riding high in Division Two, manager Bill Shankly dropped popular keeper Bert Slater, and Furnell played the final thirteen games of the season. He let nobody down and the Reds duly clinched the Division Two crown. Furnell started 1962-63 as first choice, but a broken finger closed the door at Anfield. Tommy Lawrence took full advantage and displayed such form that Furnell never regained his place.

In November 1963, Billy Wright gave Furnell another chance at Arsenal. The £15,000 signing quickly established himself as the Gunners' No 1, making his debut against Blackpool, whose keeper was still Tony Waiters. Furnell went on to play 167 League and Cup games for Arsenal, including the 1968 League Cup final defeat by Leeds.

Shortly after that Wembley defeat Furnell lost his place to Bob Wilson, never regained it, and by September was sold for £8,000 to Tommy Docherty's Rotherham. He played 76 games, but when Docherty was replaced by former Pilgrim Jimmy McAnearney, the youthful Roy Tunks was preferred in goal.

On a cold November evening at Scunthorpe, Argyle manager Ellis Stuttard watched Furnell in Rotherham's reserves. Argyle's keeper, Pat Dunne, was out of sorts, and a one-month loan was quickly arranged. Furnell was pitched into a struggling Argyle side and his experience and ability was soon evident. No sooner had the loan period expired than Furnell signed a permanent contract.

Furnell was now 33, and the modest £2,500 fee reflected the fact that Argyle could expect no more than two years' service. As it transpired, it proved to be one of the bargain-buys of all time. Once in the side, Furnell stayed in, and was voted Player of the Year.

His run continued until midway through the following season, when a bout of flu saw him step down in favour of Peta Bala'c. Furnell couldn't get back in, but bided his time helping and advising his young replacement. That summer Furnell qualified as a coach, a skill he would put to good use over the years.

Bala'c held his place until November 1972, when seven goals flew past him at Oldham. Furnell was subsequently restored, beginning a second lease of life in the twilight of his career. The man who brought Furnell back was none other than Tony Waiters, under whom results improved. Argyle finished eighth.

While Argyle's League form stuttered in 1973-74, this could be attributed in part to the distraction of a League Cup run which saw the Pilgrims reach the last four. Furnell was in thick of that run, particularly in the third round at his former club, Burnley, when his save to deny Ray Hankin defied belief.

Waiters' side built on that cup run the following year, gaining promotion. Furnell was by now one of the most popular players in Argyle's history. Approaching his late-30s, he was the oldest player in the League, and ever present in that promotion season.

The tall, slim greying keeper still possessed tremendous agility as well as displaying bravery and coolness under pressure. Over 6ft tall, his handling and domination of his area – a facet of his game that had drawn criticism during his earlier career – made it difficult to imagine a better keeper in the lower divisions. Furnell carried his superstitious ways to rare heights. He insisted on a hot bath an hour before kick-off and on being the first player kitted up. He always put on his right boot first, ran out on to the pitch second in line, and placed his cap and gloves in the left side of the goal.

Unfortunately for Furnell, the new Division Two campaign started with Milija Aleksic in goal, and Furnell played in only the final thirteen matches. This signalled the end of a distinguished playing career, but Furnell remained at Home Park as sponsorship manager, which he combined with coaching. It also allowed him to pursue his other love, cricket, and he was a regular for local side Roborough.

In May 1977 he was awarded a testimonial, when an All Star team, including former Argyle star, Paul Mariner, visited Home Park. Furnell's later career was mostly spent with former team-mate Bobby Saxton. When Saxton was in charge at Exeter, Furnell was appointed chief scout, and following Saxton's return to Argyle in January 1979, Furnell also returned as reserve-team manager. Both men then linked up at Blackburn. In recent years Furnell put his experience to good use as the FA's Academy Director for the North West.

Magic Moment: *With Argyle 2-1 up in an FA Cup-tie with Crystal Palace in December 1974, the visitors were awarded a last-gasp penalty. Terry Venables struck the kick to Furnell's right, but he flung himself to parry and grasp the ball at the second attempt.*

Worst Nightmare: *When Leeds scored the only goal in the 1968 League Cup final, Arsenal's Furnell claimed he was impeded by two Leeds players and was unable to prevent Terry Cooper from scoring.*

ARGYLE RECORD	Appearances	Goals
Football League	183	–
FA Cup	12	–
League Cup	11	–

No 59. JIMMY HINCH
Debut: v Swansea, 13 February 1971
Farewell: v Brighton, 8 September 1973

Joining Jim Furnell in the ranks of six-footers at Argyle was Jimmy Hinch, a player who divides supporters over his merits as much as any other Pilgrim, before or since.

Born in Sheffield on 8 November 1947, 22-year-old Hinch was playing for Welsh League club Porthmadoc when spotted by Tranmere manager Jackie Wright, who bought him for a small fee in March 1970. Hinch went straight into Rovers' forward line and soon adjusted to the demands placed upon him, scoring ten goals in 39 (plus three as substitute) appearances. He had been on Tranmere's books less than a year when Ellis Stuttard brought him to Home Park by offering a straight swap with out of favour centre-half Fred Molyneux.

Hinch's style could not have contrasted more with that of the man he replaced, the injured Mike Bickle. Whereas Bickle was direct and forceful, the 6ft 2in Hinch was more of a target man, playing with his back to goal, keeping possession and laying the ball off to team-mates. Needless to say, he was a threat in the air, but defenders also had to cope with the ungainly flailing of his arms and legs. Spectators doubted he knew what he was going to do when the ball was played to him, and there were times when a football appeared an alien object to him, so laughable was his ball-control. Then, moments later, he would take possession again, bring the ball under control, and lay off a superb pass. Inevitably, Hinch was capable of spectacular goals and hilarious misses.

It was this inconsistency that split supporter opinion down the middle. Was he a redoubtable striker who could give the best defenders a run for their money, or, at best, a gangly non-league forward who made schoolboy errors and wasted the easiest of chances? A League career in which he scored over 60 goals in more than 200 games suggests modest accomplishment, but whatever his shortcomings, a sequence of experienced managers wanted him in their side. During his time at Argyle, Hinch was rarely out of the starting line up, and scored his quota of vital goals.

His first season at Argyle brought him six goals in eighteen games. The return of Derek Rickard part way through 1971-72 at last gave Hinch a forward partner to capitalise on his flicks and knock-downs. Their partnership was flourishing when injury put paid to Rickard's season. Hinch's twelve goals during that campaign put him second to Rickard's fourteen in the scoring charts.

Ten more goals arrived the following season, when Hinch missed just one game, and the opening fixtures of 1973-74 – with Tony Waiters in charge – saw Hinch once again in possession of the No 9 shirt. But two quick defeats prompted Waiters to throw caution to the wind and give youth its chance. An evening game against Rochdale saw Hinch replaced by young Paul Mariner, and the rest is history.

Hinch never featured again and shortly moved to Hereford. He did the rounds with York City, Southport, Sheffield Wednesday and Barnsley, before finding himself, aged 30, on the soccer scrap-heap. Like many other 'pro's' in fear of the knackers' yard, Hinch crossed the Atlantic to join the NASL, where he combined playing with coaching. He took to the lifestyle and remained living in the USA after he retired from football.

These days he enjoys a comfortable life in Santa Ana, California, where he runs a real estate and insurance business under the name of 'James A Hinch'.

Magic Moment: *The opening match of 1971-72 at Villa Park saw Hinch rise to head in from Les Latcham's free-kick. His effort was not enough, as Argyle went down to a 1-3 defeat.*

Worst Nightmare: *Those Argyle fans unimpressed with Hinch would sing 'Jesus Christ Superstar' but with the lyrics adapted to 'Jimmy Hinch, Superstar, how many goals have you missed so far?'*

Argyle record	Appearances	Goals
Football League	102 (+5)	28
FA Cup	5	1
League Cup	4	1

No 60. **DAVE PROVAN**
Debut: v Preston, 6 March 1971
Farewell: v Port Vale, 12 October 1974

The 6ft 2in David Provan, an experienced Scottish international, provided stability to the Argyle defence in the early 1970s.

Although born (on 11 March 1941) and raised in Falkirk, Provan admits that as a youngster he was a Stirling Albion fan. After leaving school he worked in an iron foundry and played for local side Bonnyvale Star, whilst attending Ibrox weekly for training. In a reversal of normal practice, it was the player who approached the club about signing, but Rangers agreed to take him on.

Provan debuted in 1959 at Hearts, but was forced, in the main, to be content with reserve-team football. Only when Eric Caldow broke a leg playing for Scotland at Wembley in 1963 did he get a look in. With Provan in their side Rangers won the Scottish 'treble' in 1964 and finished runners-up to Bayern Munich in the 1966-67 European Cup-Winners' Cup. Despite twice suffering a broken leg, Provan's twelve-year Ibrox career saw him play 262 games in all competitions, scoring eleven goals. His final honours tally included one Scottish championship, three Scottish Cups, two League Cups, not to mention five full Scottish caps.

In 1970 Willie Waddell's new regime showed the door to a number of players. Provan was one of them, and in June of that year he joined Crystal Palace. He had played for Palace just once when, in February 1971, Ellis Stuttard brought him to Home Park on loan. Provan insisted that he remain living in London as his daughter was a patient at Great Ormond Street hospital. During the week, Provan trained with Palace, travelling down to Plymouth on matchdays.

Relegation was avoided and Provan, playing in central defence, made his move permanent in time for the following season. Despite commuting from London, the long-legged defender confirmed the adage that there is no substitute for experience. His leadership qualities shone through and his determination was an inspiration to everyone. Only suspension robbed him of being ever present that season and his value to the team was recognised by the Player of the Year award. He also became a reliable penalty taker and eight of his ten goals for Argyle came from spot-kicks.

The 1972-73 season again saw Provan in fine form. He missed just two games, through suspension. After Tony Waiters succeeded Stuttard as manager, arrangements were made for Provan to make his home in Plymouth. He was also appointed captain. During that season he reverted to right-back and it was wearing No 2 that he played in Argyle's 3-2 victory over the elite Brazilian side, Santos, who included Pele in their side. Provan was given the task of marking another famous Brazilian, Edu, and with speed not one of Provan's gifts he was given a testing time by the flying winger. At a post-match reception Provan was presenting his opponent with a commemorative plate when a team-mate slyly commented that it was the closest Provan had got to Edu all evening!

1973-74 was not so memorable. Provan missed much of Argyle's storming League Cup run, although he was restored for the FA Cup third-round tie at Manchester United. The following season proved to be Provan's last at Home Park, and consisted of only a brief spell at left-back in place of the injured Phil Burrows.

By this time, Provan had taken up coaching, and it was no surprise when his subsequent career took that route. After leaving Argyle, he moved back to Scotland, joining St Mirren as part-time player-coach under Alex Ferguson, with whom he had played at Rangers. Provan worked in a pub during the day and assisted with the coaching in the evenings. When Ferguson moved to Aberdeen, many expected Provan to follow, but Fergie was reluctant to import a dual-Rangers connection to Pittodrie, and Provan remained in Glasgow. For a time he was Rangers' chief scout, and later was recruited by former Argyle colleague Johnny Hore, who was then Argyle manager, to scout for the club in Scotland.

After working as a rep for a whisky firm, Provan became reserve-team coach at Partick Thistle under Bertie Auld. A return to Ibrox followed as youth-team coach before Provan was appointed manager of Albion Rovers, whom he led to the Scottish Second Division title.

Since 1992 Provan has worked for the Scottish Football Association and is now Youth Development Officer with Inverclyde Council. He retains his links with Rangers by acting as a matchday host at Ibrox. Despite suffering a heart attack in recent years, Provan remains active, not only through his coaching but by playing golf off an impressive nine handicap. He retains fond memories of his time with Argyle.

Magic Moment: *Provan led a Plymouth Argyle team onto the field against Santos in front a capacity crowd of 38,000.*

Worst Nightmare: *Dubbed 'Black Sunday' by Argyle supporters, Provan was one of three Greens sent off at Port Vale in March 1974. Steve Davey was ordered off in the first half, and late in the second Provan followed after clashing with Ray Williams. When Provan saw Bobby Saxton enter the changing room he asked if the game was over. Having also been expelled, Saxton's reply is unprintable.*

ARGYLE RECORD	Appearances		Goals
Football League	128	(+1)	10
FA Cup	5		—
League Cup	4		—

No 61. **NEIL HAGUE**

Debut v Bristol Rovers, 27 November 1971
Farewell: v Wrexham, 20 April 1974

Neil Hague was one of Dave Provan's defensive partners during their time at Argyle. Born at Thurcroft in Yorkshire on 1 December 1949,

Hague signed professionally for Rotherham on his seventeenth birthday. His early promise was rewarded with England Youth caps, and Tommy Docherty gave him his Rotherham debut at Millwall in November 1967.

Very much a utility player in those days, Hague played in virtually every position for Rotherham and scored vital goals. He had a particular taste for Argyle and in five games against the Pilgrims scored four goals. Hague's Rotherham career spanned 145 League games, including eleven as substitute and produced 23 goals. His final game for the Millers was at Millmoor against Argyle, and Hague had special reasons to remember it.

The Yorkshire side, defending an unbeaten run of twelve games, went two goals up, only to see the Pilgrims storm into the lead. Hague was introduced as a 75th-minute substitute, and with five minutes remaining Rotherham levelled. In the dying seconds Hague planted a header past his former Rotherham team-mate, Jim Furnell, to win the game 4-3.

Argyle boss Ellis Stuttard had already been keeping tabs on the Yorkshireman and 24 hours after his stunning effort had sunk Argyle a fee of £15,000 brought him to Home Park. Hague immediately partnered Provan in central defence and played in every remaining fixture of that campaign.

The following season, 1972-73, was Hague's best in Argyle colours. He missed only two matches and went about his defensive duties in a sound, quietly effective manner. As a defender, he would mark his opponent tightly, and also showed composure on the ball. Mainly left-footed, he could be relied upon to use the ball efficiently.

But Hague was also valuable at set pieces. Whenever a corner or free-kick was won, the barrel chested Hague, long hair flopping, would stroll up to add his aerial power to the attack. He was a threat to any defence and his impressive tally of twelve League and Cup goals that season, mostly headers, saw him finish second top scorer behind Alan Welsh. Hague's all-round contribution was fittingly rewarded with the Argyle Player of the Year award.

He missed the start of 1973-74 through injury, but once fit was recalled by new manager Tony Waiters. These were heady times as the famous League Cup run gathered momentum. Hague played in all bar the first round, and also took part in the FA Cup-tie at Old Trafford. During these matches he found himself pitted against top-name strikers, but was seldom found wanting.

Yet behind the Cup euphoria, League results were grim, and in the end of season clear-out Hague was one of a number of players who departed, a £15,000 fee taking him and Derek Rickard to Bournemouth in a joint transfer. Hague was ever present for the Cherries in 1975-76 and went on to play a total of 89 League games for them, scoring seven goals, before a free transfer in June 1976 saw him join Huddersfield, for whom he scored twice in 25 League matches. His last British club was Darlington, where he stayed two years, played 80 times, and scored four goals. Then he was off to the USA, where he was reunited with his former Bournemouth boss, Harry Redknapp, at Phoenix Fire. He had spells with two other American sides, Columbus and Los Angeles, and for a time he also ran soccer camps in California.

In 1981 Hague returned to Yorkshire, where he started his own building business. Three years later he moved back to Plymouth and has lived in the vicinity ever since, running his own property development firm.

To this day he keeps remarkably fit, running fitness classes as well as competing in the Plymouth half-marathon. He also still turns out for the ex-Argyle side in charity games.

Magic Moment: *Hague scored a vital goal against First Division Burnley three minutes from time to give underdogs Argyle a shock away win in the third round of the 1973-74 League Cup.*

Worst Nightmare: *In the first leg of the League Cup semi-final against Manchester City, Hague seemed sure to score with a close-range header, but was denied by keeper Keith MacRae's reflex save.*

ARGYLE RECORD	Appearances		Goals
Football League	98	(+1)	15
FA Cup	7		1
League Cup	7		1

No 62. **PETER MIDDLETON**
Debut: v Shrewsbury, 16 September 1972
Farewell: v Shrewsbury, 16 September 1972

A new face joined Neil Hague on a sunny Saturday afternoon in September 1972 for a Third Division home fixture against Shrewsbury. Apart from this being Peter Middleton's Argyle debut, the match seemed little more than a run of the mill fixture. As it transpired, it proved to be Middleton's only game for the Pilgrims in what became one of the most tragic tales in Argyle's history.

Middleton was born in the Yorkshire village of Rawmarsh on 13 September 1948. In time he was chosen for Yorkshire Schoolboys and went on to win two England Schools caps. Everton and Wolves were among the big clubs chasing his signature, but he chose to join his favourite team, Sheffield Wednesday, as an apprentice in September 1965. The Owls' manager at that time was Alan Brown, later to be chief coach at Argyle. He groomed Middleton's talent, picking him for the reserves when he was just sixteen.

Although Peter never made Wednesday's first team, he was part of the squad that reached the 1966 FA Cup final. When Alan Brown left for Sunderland, Middleton was one of a number of players put up for transfer and in June 1968 he joined Fourth Division Bradford City. In 1973 the Bantams would also sign his younger brother, John, who went on to play almost 200 games for the club.

Peter was a midfield regular at Valley Parade, scoring 25 goals in 127 (plus four as substitute) League appearances. He impressed sufficiently to be poised to sign for Bolton. The swap for two Bolton players fell through when they declined to join Bradford. A £20,000 deal was then agreed, which also fell through, at which point Argyle manager Ellis Stuttard stepped in and brought Middleton to Home Park in a straight exchange for Ronnie Brown.

Middleton's debut was crowned by a spectacular goal. He wriggled past a posse of Shrewsbury defenders before firing past Ken Mulhearn from outside the penalty area. It was Argyle's first goal in a 3-0 win, but it was Middleton's performance that wrote the headlines the following day. One newspaper described him as Argyle's answer to George Best, no doubt prompted by Middleton's similar appearance to the Irish superstar, with his long flowing locks and intricate dribbling skills.

Following the game, Middleton returned to Yorkshire to join his family. Argyle were due to play at Blackburn on the Wednesday, and Middleton rang the club from a telephone box to be told travel arrangements. Leaving the box to cross the road he was struck by a car and was rushed unconscious to a Bradford hospital.

Such were the extent of Middleton's back injuries that surgeons were less concerned about his playing career than whether he would ever walk again. He was given the choice of complex surgery that risked the possibility of permanent damage, or a long period of rest, coupled with more conventional treatment. Middleton opted for the latter. He spent months immobile on his back and more months before he was given the green light to resume light training. He set a target date in his mind, the start of the new season, eleven months from his injury, to make his comeback and spent the summer endlessly toiling away to regain his fitness. He came through the rigours of pre-season training and the signs of a comeback were encouraging.

An early season reserve game saw him score two goals before taking a knock on his back. Medical advice was to quit physical contact sport. Middleton refused to heed the advice, believing that prolonged rest would extend his career. Though he continued to report to Home Park for light exercise, manager Tony Waiters sensed the strain on the player. He advised Middleton to stay away from the ground, fearing that the day-to-day banter of team-mates would leave him even more depressed.

As the months passed it became clearer that Argyle fans were unlikely ever again to see Middleton in a green shirt. Back home in Yorkshire, he had undertaken a milk round in order to support his wife and two young children, but hope burned eternal of resuming his playing career.

At the start of 1975-76 he made another comeback attempt with non-league Stafford Rangers but a slight knock on his back forced him from the field. In September 1975 to conceded to the inevitable and announced his retirement. Both the PFA and Argyle were supportive. The PFA arranged for him to undertake a sales course, and Argyle organised a testimonial with Tommy Docherty's star-studded Manchester United at Home Park in December of that year.

Unbeknown to all but a few, the shattering events of the past three years had affected Middleton's state of mind. He failed to attend his own testimonial, leaving his father to come on to the pitch to accept the applause of the crowd. The club issued a statement that Middleton was suffering from appendicitis but the truth was worse. His mental scars ran deep, and in April 1977 Peter Middleton took his own life, his body being found in his car.

Magic Moment: *Peter Middleton's stunning debut goal for Argyle against Shrewsbury will never be forgotten by those who saw it.*

Worst Nightmare: *After years of treatment and training, Peter Middleton had no choice but to retire from football at the age of 27.*

ARGYLE RECORD	Appearances	Goals
Football League	1	1

No 63. **ERNIE MACHIN**
Debut: v Watford, 23 December 1972
Farewell: v Cambridge, 1 May 1974

The sad tale of Peter Middleton left unanswered the nagging question about how his flair might have benefited from the midfield guile of Ernie

Machin, undoubtedly one of the classiest players ever to wear an Argyle shirt.

Machin was born at Little Holton, near Bolton, on 26 April 1944 and set out on his soccer career at Lancashire Combination side, Nelson. Although several League clubs took an interest, he was persuaded by Coventry City manager Jimmy Hill to become his first signing for the club. Hill had been keeping tabs on Machin for some time, but, after watching one of his less productive performances for Nelson, Hill was questioned by his chairman. 'Machin played poorly,' Hill replied. The chairman assumed that Hill's interest had cooled, but the bearded one added, 'but I like the sparkle and colour of his eyes.' Hill clearly saw something special in the youngster and the decision to sign him in March 1962 proved well founded.

Machin had to wait more than a year before making his League debut against Millwall in April 1963. Knee problems kept him out for most of 1964-65, costing him a place in the England Under-23 squad, before he bounced back, and he was eventually appointed captain in the absence of George Curtis.

Machin's time at Coventry saw the club rise from the Third to the First Division and in the process he laid claim to be one of the top midfield players in the country, although his fragile knees bothered him for many years. They were the cause of him losing his place to another future Pilgrim, John Craven.

One of Machin's later matches for Coventry provoked legal ramifications that were to have an important impact on the game as we know it today. Machin had been sent off in a match but was cleared of a suspension by an FA Disciplinary Committee which had viewed television evidence. Curiously, the same committee watching the same match observed another Machin offence that had gone unpunished. They duly imposed a suspension for that misdemeanour instead. Backed by the PFA, Machin took the matter to the High Court, which ruled that he had been suspended without charge, and without any opportunity to offer a defence. They found this to be against the principles of natural justice and the case led to the establishment of the disciplinary points system.

Machin had reached a total of 280 matches for Coventry when in December 1972 he was signed for Argyle by Tony Waiters, who described him as 'a model professional'. The fee was £35,000.

His signing, on a three-year contract, was something of a coup for Argyle. Here was a highly experienced player who had played at the top level. Moreover, Machin was only 28 and at the peak of his game. He soon lived up to his reputation. He was a class act, invariably controlling the midfield, making probing runs, making intelligent use of the ball, and generally making the game look easy.

His influence soon had an impact on results. Before Machin's arrival, the Pilgrims had won only six games up to Christmas, with relegation to Division Four a distinct possibility. The arrival of Waiters and Machin sparked an improvement, and the side lost only five more games to finish in a respectable eighth place.

The following season began with Argyle harbouring hopes of promotion, but inconsistency plagued the side. Machin was the exception. As Waiters' captain he prompted and probed from midfield, but often found his less able colleagues on a different wavelength, unable to respond to his quick thinking.

In the League Cup, if not the League, Argyle were inspired, outplaying teams from higher divisions to march all the way to the semi-finals. Ernie Machin's class was a telling factor in that run, none more so than in the 3-0 fourth round victory at First Division QPR, where he masterminded play against a Rangers midfield that included Terry Venables and Gerry Francis.

To the grief of Argyle fans, Machin, overwhelmingly voted as Player of the Year, departed at the end of that season for Brighton in a deal worth £30,000. He had become disenchanted at Plymouth and was impatient for success. Bearing in mind that, following his departure, Argyle gained promotion, it could be argued that he was not missed. Still, one cannot but wonder how much more dominant the Greens would have been with his presence.

Machin was immediately installed as captain at Brighton and almost led them to promotion in 1975-76. After 64 games for the Seagulls, he lost his place to the up and coming Brian Horton and was eventually released at his own request. He briefly returned to Coventry as youth-team coach before leaving football to work for Massey Ferguson. He has since been employed by Courtaulds and now works as a driver for a firm in Coventry where he still lives.

Magic Moment: *As a display of Machin's popularity at Coventry, the club arranged a testimonial on his behalf after he had left, with the Sky Blues taking on Aston Villa in May 1973.*

Worst Nightmare: *Machin, though skilful, also had a reputation of being able to look after himself. In an FA Cup-tie against Brentford in November 1973 he was involved in a mass brawl and had his shirt ripped. He escaped punishment, but his assailant was sent off.*

ARGYLE RECORD	Appearances	Goals
Football League	57	6
FA Cup	5	–
League Cup	7	1

No 70. Mr Consistency, full-back Phil Burrows

No 71. Mike Green led Argyle to promotion

No 72. Hugh McAuley, Argyle's tricky, ball-playing winger

No 74. Brian Hall (right) has a crack at goal, watched by No 64. (left) Alan Rogers

No 75. Full-back John Uzzell in the thick of it against Blackburn

No 76. Guitar-playing, goalpoaching Fred Binney leans into a shot

Chapter Seven

~ *Waiters' Wonders* ~

No 64. **ALAN ROGERS**
Debut: v Chesterfield, 25 August 1973
Farewell: v Chester, 24 April 1979

One of the young players to benefit from Ernie Machin's vast experience was Alan Rogers. A Plymothian by birth, on 6 December 1954, he was a pupil at the city's Public Secondary School and was taken on by Argyle as an apprentice in 1970.

He soon became a regular in the Reserve side, and, being a predominantly left-footed player was equally adept as a full-back or winger. Having successfully come through his two-year apprentice period, he signed as a full time professional in July 1972 and in that following season was always knocking on the door of first-team selection and missed only four Football Combination matches.

Rogers debuted in the opening game of 1973-74, when he came on as substitute for Neil Hague. His first start came two weeks later when he – together with two other untried lads, Paul Mariner and Brian Johnson – was part of the team that whipped Rochdale 5-0. Whilst the victory margin was huge, it was fulfilment of Waiters' innovative approach. He insisted that every Argyle side from the first team down played to the same style, thereby making it easier, tactically, for any player to slot into the side.

After his impressive introduction, Rogers made the left-wing slot his own for much of the season, fending off the challenge of the experienced Harry Burrows. The highlight of that first season was, of course, the League Cup run that ended only at the penultimate hurdle. Rogers, tall for a winger, but lean and fast, was far from overawed by the prospect of pitting his skills against high-calibre full-backs. This was particularly true in the semi-final home leg against Manchester City. On a pitch that could be best described as a mudbath, and totally unsuited to Rogers' normal preference for running at defenders, he inflicted damage on the City defence with his range of left-footed crosses. One of these indirectly led to Argyle's only goal, as Willie Donachie miscontrolled one of Rogers' crosses and Steve Davey nipped in to score.

A more familiar sight was of Rogers, with his mane of ginger hair, tormenting his opponent before skipping outside him to deliver a cross.

His skinny frame looked unsuitable for the rigours of League football and he did incur his share of injuries.

Rogers had his ginger locks to thank during an FA Cup-tie at Dartford in November 1974. On a dark wintry afternoon, Argyle were kitted out in their normal green and black striped shirts with black shorts. With the non-leaguers' floodlights operating at candle-power, the players could hardly make out one another in the gathering gloom. Colin Randell, who scored twice that day, recalls the introduction of Rogers as a welcome sight as he could at least pick out his hair against the backdrop.

The euphoria of Rogers' debut season soon passed. Injury wrecked his opportunities in the 1974-75 promotion campaign. To compound matters, another left winger – Hugh McAuley from Liverpool – had displaced him and was turning on the style. It was not until August 1976 that Rogers returned to first-team action, and even then he was used sparingly. Waiters did not help Rogers' cause by abandoning his earlier preference for two playing wingers.

It was under Waiters' successor, Mike Kelly, that Rogers was fully rehabilitated, and although Kelly's reign was short, Malcolm Allison continued to utilise Rogers as a wide-man before converting him to full-back for the latter part of 1978. By Rogers' own admission, the switch didn't work. As an attacking full-back he was fine, but his tackling wasn't up to it. He was put back on the flank, and did so well that in July 1979 Portsmouth manager Frank Burrows spent £15,000 to take Rogers to Fratton Park, where he again teamed up with Steve Davey and Billy Rafferty.

Rogers scored on his Pompey debut – a League Cup-tie with Swindon – and went on to play 154 League matches, plus seven as substitute, and score fifteen goals. The timing of his move was perfect. Portsmouth won promotion twice in three years, including the Division Three championship in 1982-83, when Rogers teamed up with another former Pilgrim, Colin Sullivan.

In March 1984 Rogers became the late Bobby Moore's first signing for Southend, where he spent two and a half years, adding another 84 League appearances and four goals to his record. In August 1986 he was reunited with his old boss, Frank Burrows, who had taken charge at Cardiff. Rogers played just one season for the Bluebirds before retiring from League soccer and returning to live in Plymouth. He was able to boast that after he left Home Park he never lost to Argyle when in opposition.

He continued his soccer career with Saltash United and, for one match, Falmouth. Remarkably, he was called up by Argyle when in his mid-30s. Gordon Nisbet was in charge of Argyle's Western League side and was short of players for a match against Frome Town. Rogers accepted the call and scored twice in a 5-0 win.

For many years, Rogers and his wife have run the Swinton Hotel in Plymouth. Now a keen golfer, Rogers makes the occasional appearance for the ex-Argyle side in charity matches where his cultured left foot still performs wonders.

Magic Moment: *Rogers scored on his full Argyle debut in that 5-0 win over Rochdale. Ernie Machin rolled a short free-kick, and Rogers let fly with a sweet left-foot shot into the net.*

Worst Nightmare: *Rogers' early career was interrupted when he broke his leg in a car accident. The injury required the insertion of a pin and kept him out of action for almost two years.*

ARGYLE RECORD	Appearances	Goals
Football League	107 (+10)	5
FA Cup	7 (+4)	–
League Cup	7	–

No 65. **BRIAN JOHNSON**
Debut: v Torquay, 29 August 1973
Farewell v Rotherham, 2 May 1981

For a time, one of Alan Rogers' wing partners at Argyle was Brian Johnson, although the advent of more cautious tactics during the 1970s – with 4-4-2 and 4-4-3 formations the norm – meant that they rarely played in the same side.

Often regarded as a Plymothian, Johnson was in fact born in Isleworth, London on 21 October 1955. He speaks with a rich London accent, despite the fact that when he was fourteen his family moved to Plymouth.

He played for the Railway Nomads junior side and soon earned a place in the Plymouth Schoolboys team. His early talent saw him break into the Nomads senior side, competing in the Devon Wednesday League, where one of his team-mates was former Argyle stalwart George Robertson. It was Robertson who recommended the youngster to Argyle, for whom he signed apprentice terms in 1972.

While an apprentice, Johnson was almost put off the prospect of League soccer after a trip to York with the first team. He had been taken along as thirteenth man to provide cover and also to give him a taste of what was, for him, the big time. During the game he sat on the bench alongside Tony Waiters. On the pitch, Argyle striker Jimmy Hinch was felled by an opponent's head-butt. He got to his feet and retaliated with gusto, and the two traded blows, kicks and assorted profanities as they retreated to the halfway line. Waiters turned to the ashen-faced Johnson to say, 'That son, is what playing in the Third Division is all about.'

It was not long before Johnson had forced his way into the reserves, and he finished 1972-73 as the stiffs' top scorer with six goals from 28 games. In August 1973 he signed as a pro and was shortly given his first-team debut in a League Cup-tie.

Two weeks later, after the first team had got off to a stuttering start, Waiters thrust three of his starlets – Johnson, Rogers and Mariner – into the first team for the evening visit of Rochdale. The exuberant young-sters stole the show in a stunning 5-0 victory, although the result proved to be a ray of sunshine in a darkening sky.

Johnson, known as 'Ted', due to his liking for chunky sweaters – a well-known trait of local TV fishing expert Ted Tuckerman – was no sooner in the side than out. He was again omitted for the first two months of the 1974-75 season, but with results again looking ominous, Waiters threw caution to the wind by recalling Johnson on the right, with his new recruit from Liverpool, Hugh McAuley, on the left, in a do-or-die 4-2-4 formation.

For a while the plan worked. McAuley was the more dashing of the two, more orthodox, small and tricky. Johnson was tall for a wide player, slightly round shouldered, and did not give the appearance of speed. He was, however blessed with deceptively close control and was difficult to dislodge when in possession. With the ball at his feet, confronted by his marker, he invariably looked blank and bereft of ideas. When the full-back was least expecting it, Johnson would push the ball ahead and use his rangy stride to whip in a dangerous cross. His scoring record was also better than McAuley's, and he was not afraid to try his luck, with either foot, from any angle.

It was Waiters, above all other Argyle managers Johnson served under, who did most to nourish his talent. After Waiters' resignation, the twin-winger policy was dropped by Mike Kelly in favour of a more conven-tional, albeit cautious approach. Johnson was the winger to step down, so that an extra midfielder could be accommodated. After the euphoria of promotion and a regular place in Division Two football, Johnson now returned to the anonymity of the reserves.

In time he was back, starting 1978-79 on the more unfamiliar left wing. When he lost his place to Rogers, he was loaned out to Torquay

United, where he scored twice in five matches. After his return to Home Park he found himself in favour with Bobby Saxton, though asked to play more as a wide midfield player, with defensive responsibilities, rather than a winger.

Over the next two seasons Johnson had periods when he was in and periods when he was out, which did not help his confidence, but worse was to follow. During a reserve game at Bristol Rovers in the early part of 1981-82 he collided with his own goalkeeper, Neil Hards. Johnson was out cold, but recovered to play the second half in a daze, even scoring late on. The following day, hospital x-rays showed the extent of his injuries. A piece of bone was jutting into the retina of his eye and his cheekbone was fractured. Another knock could have induced permanent blindness. He was whisked to the operating theatre where his jawbone was wired up, as it still is today.

Johnson resumed training four weeks later and in September 1981, to aid his recovery, was loaned to Torquay for a second time. During his second game for Torquay he headed the ball and felt a searing pain. Further examination revealed damage to both eyes, and in fear of the consequences he had little option but to retire from the game.

It was obviously a bitter blow to a player who was still only 26. Football had been his life, and to this day he says he would have risked blindness in one eye if it had meant being able to continue playing. To reward his loyalty and provide him with some financial stability, the club arranged a testimonial on his behalf, with Aston Villa visiting Home Park in August 1983, although Johnson himself was unable to play any active part.

After leaving the game, Johnson obtained a civilian role at Plympton Police Station in Plymouth before becoming a driver for a tile company. For many years he has worked for a financial company in the city.

He even returned to football, coaching various youth sides at the Plymstock club in Plymouth and nurturing youngsters through to the club's senior side in the Devon League. He became coach and manager of the seniors until his resignation in September 2000.

Magic Moment: *At Bury in October 1974, Johnson followed Waiters' instructions to exploit keeper John Forrest's small stature. Johnson chipped him. The ball rebounded off the bar onto Forrest's head and into the net. It was the only goal, but was it an own-goal?*

Worst Nightmare: *Johnson, for a while, became Argyle's regular penalty taker. On one occasion he blasted a spot-kick not only over the bar, but also over the Barn*

Park end of the ground and into the adjoining zoo. The ball was later recovered from the hippo pen.

ARGYLE RECORD	Appearances	Goals
Football league	186 (+11)	41
FA Cup	10	1
League Cup	16 (+2)	1

No 66. PAUL MARINER

Debut: v Rochdale, 11 September 1973
Farewell: v Cardiff, 16 October 1976

As we have read, Brian Johnson and Paul Mariner debuted in the same match. Seven thousand spectators were there to witness – unbeknown to them at the time – the first game of a player who went on to represent his country and become the best known Argyle player of modern times, and arguably of all time. It is a testament to his fame that even those with little interest in Plymouth Argyle still associate his name with the club.

Mariner was born in Bolton on 22 May 1953 and he was captain of his primary school team, Horwich County. His early promise appeared to be going to waste when, on leaving school, he undertook an engineering apprenticeship. At seventeen he took up the game again, playing for Chorley side St Gregory's, and signing a year later for Chorley Town in the Lancashire League.

It was Argyle's northern scout, Verdi Godwin, who passed on the word. Mariner was invited down to Devon and played in end of season friendlies against Penzance, Porthleven and St Austell. Though Mariner hit the net a few times, he was so raw that it was touch and go whether Argyle would persist with their interest. It was Godwin who virtually pressed the club into signing him, with a fee of £6,000 proving, in the long term, a superb investment.

1973-74 started badly with one point from three games. For the fourth, against Rochdale, Tony Waiters introduced Mariner, Brian Johnson and Alan Rogers. Mariner scored two of Argyle's five goals, and, which was just as important, looked good when he wasn't scoring. His manager was quick to praise his contribution, while keeping his young star's feet on the ground. 'Reputations are not made in one game,' Waiters said, but for team-mate Rogers there was no doubt where Mariner was headed: 'It was obvious from that first game that he had what it takes to reach the top,' he recalls. 'He had bags of confidence, but at the same time was a lovely lad and did not let success go to his head.'

Four days later Mariner was on the scoresheet again, notching Argyle's goal in a 1-1 draw at Southport, but his doubts about whether he would make the grade as a professional footballer were not easily dispelled. Today he is quick to praise the support he received from all the Argyle coaching staff.

Mariner was soon making a name for himself as a prodigious talent, not only as a goalscorer, but also for his all-round game. In his first season at Home Park he finished with fourteen League goals, though he contributed only one in Argyle's League Cup run. He lifted the Argyle Player of the Year award and Pilgrims fans were already resigned to the fact that Mariner was destined for higher things.

In March that season Bill Rafferty arrived from Blackpool and partnered Mariner up front. The duo played three times together and failed to muster a goal between them when injury curtailed Rafferty's season. This apparent failure gave no hint of what was to follow. The 1974-75 season saw Rafferty back to full fitness and now something clicked. Despite obvious similarities between them, they created havoc week in, week out. Both were mobile, skilful on the ball, and good in the air. They developed a telepathic understanding on the pitch and became close pals off it. In tandem they scored 47 League and Cup goals, without which Argyle would not have gained promotion from Division Three. Although Mariner scored fewer (21 goals) than Rafferty (26), it was Mariner who attracted star billing, becoming the first Argyle player to win successive Player of the Year trophies.

The prospect of the deadly duo scything through Division Two defences was intoxicating, and they delivered what they promised. Their reputation preceded them and ensured ruthless attention from forewarned defences. But the goals continued to flow, with Mariner this time coming out on top with sixteen strikes. By now a stream of managers and scouts were attending every Argyle match, and there was only one player they had come to see. Rumours abounded, with just about every First Division club mentioned at one time or another as seeking Mariner's signature. But he saw out the 1975-76 season and to the surprise of many also began the next.

Mariner was going to cost big bucks, and by September 1976 the interested parties had been whittled down to three. Talks were held with West Brom manager Johnny Giles, but it was Ron Greenwood's West Ham who seemed favourites to sign him. Competition for the young striker's signature had pushed up the fee to £200,000. Transfer forms taking him to Upton Park had even been signed, but at that stage Mariner had not finalised his personal terms, and behind the scenes Ipswich had not given up hope of getting their man. Their scout, Bobby Ferguson, and manager Bobby Robson had watched him many times. Mariner met Robson, liked what he heard – not least about the rural lifestyle in East Anglia – and the deal was done. Mariner was snatched from under the noses of the Hammers.

The money-plus-player deal, valued at £220,000, was a record for both clubs. In exchange for Mariner, Argyle received cash plus two players, Terry Austin and John Peddelty. Whilst the cash was welcome, there was limited value from the new recruits. Peddelty was forced to retire from the game through injury after only 34 appearances and Austin, although no slouch, had the thankless task of trying to fill Mariner's No 9 shirt.

It is Bobby Robson who best sums up Mariner's qualities. 'I was looking for a centre-forward and Paul fitted the bill. He was strong, good in the air, could hold the ball up well and score goals. Just as importantly he was popular in the dressing room, worked hard in training and gave me no trouble at all. In fact, the only thing he never did that I told him, was to get his hair cut! He was not a good player, he was a great player.'

Fittingly, Mariner wound up his Argyle career with a goal in his farewell match. Six days later he was an Ipswich player and thereafter that flowing long hair, so familiar to Argyle supporters, became a regular sight to the nation's millions of armchair fans whenever Ipswich were featured on TV, which was often.

Mariner scored on his Ipswich debut, a 7-0 defeat of, ironically, West Brom and went on to score ten goals in 28 matches, helping the East Anglian side to third in the League. He quickly adapted to the pace and demands of the First Division and only six months after signing for Ipswich won his first England cap as a substitute in a 5-0 thrashing of Luxembourg in a World Cup qualifier. Two months later he played in all three Home International fixtures, although England lost to both Scotland and Wales at Wembley. In October 1977 he scored his first England goal in the return fixture in Luxembourg. Come the end of that season he was Ipswich's top scorer, banging in seven goals in an FA Cup run that went all the way to heaven. Although Mariner did not score in the final against Arsenal, he had a fine game and hit the bar. Roger Osborne's goal clinched victory for Ipswich.

Robson had built one of the top sides in the country, regularly finishing in the top five. This, in turn, led to regular qualification for Europe. Ipswich became veteran campaigners on the Continental stage, but the big prize eluded them until 1981, when victories over the likes of St Etienne (with Mariner scoring a hat-trick) and Cologne saw them reach the two-legged UEFA Cup final against Dutch side AZ 67 Alkmaar. With Mariner scoring in the 3-0 home leg, the trophy seemed all but secure. Alkmaar had other ideas, but winning 4-2 in Holland was not enough and the silverware went back to Portman Road.

At the close of that season Mariner was voted third in the PFA Player of the Year awards, beaten only by his Ipswich team-mates, John Wark and Frans Thijssen.

Back in the League, Mariner was proving to be a consistent performer, and was recalled to the England side for the 1980 Home Internationals. From that point on, he became a regular choice for his country, playing in the 1980 European Championships in Italy and becoming a national hero when, in November 1981, he scored the only goal against Hungary to clinch England's qualification for the 1982 World Cup in Spain. He played in all five of England's matches in those finals, scoring against France and Czechoslovakia, but England bowed out unbeaten after the second stage.

His Portman Road career eventually took him to 96 League goals in 260 appearances, but in February 1984, following a wage dispute, he moved to Arsenal for £150,000. Now 31, he had lost some pace but remained one of the best headers of a ball in the game. He won his last two England caps as a Gunner, for whom he scored seventeen goals in 60 (plus ten sub) appearances.

In July 1986, with younger players coming through at Highbury, a free transfer took Mariner to Portsmouth, where he spent two seasons. This proved to be his League swansong, and he bowed out with 35 caps for his country and fourteen goals. He played a bit in Malta and in the USA, and then took up coaching in Japan before returning to the States. Since 1996 he has been director of coaching at the Juventus Soccer Club in Scottsdale, Arizona, and is now head coach of the Paradise Valley club, where he monitors the skills of more than 1,000 youngsters.

In July 2000, Mariner brought a few of his teams to the UK to play in a tournament and made a nostalgic return to Home Park, and yes the hair is longer than ever! The Mariner name even lives on at Argyle, where Paul's young son, George, has been selected to attend the club's School of Excellence.

In 1999, supporters of each Football League club in England were invited to nominate that club's greatest ever player. Not surprisingly, Paul Mariner was the overwhelming nomination of Argyle fans, a fitting tribute to his enduring popularity. How fitting then, that in a city with a rich naval heritage, someone called Mariner should become one of its most famous sons.

Magic Moment: *Mariner was carried shoulder high from the pitch after scoring the only goal against Colchester in April 1975. The victory secured Argyle's promotion from Division Three.*

Worst Nightmare: *Argyle were drawn at home to Everton in a 1975 FA Cuptie. It was the first time Mariner had faced a top side and the hype was intense. But a late injury ruled him out. There had been no hint of this and his omission stunned the 38,000 crowd into silence.*

ARGYLE RECORD	Appearances	Goals
Football League	134 (+1)	56
FA Cup	8	3
League Cup	12	1

No 67. **COLIN RANDELL**
Debut: v Port Vale, 27 October 1973
Final Farewell: v Millwall, 15 May 1982

With Paul Mariner going on to touch the heights, many also felt that Colin Randell deserved a bigger stage on which to display his not inconsiderable talent.

Born at Skewen in Glamorgan on 12 December 1952, Randell earned Welsh schoolboy and youth caps, and signed professionally for Coventry City in May 1970. Despite Randell's ability to play in defence or midfield, he failed to break into a first team graced by the skills of Ernie Machin, later to become a team-mate at Home Park.

Randell was released on a free transfer and Tony Waiters brought him to Plymouth in September 1973. His debut was made as a substitute, but four days later he was in from the start in a League Cup-tie at Burnley. The prospect could hardly have been more daunting. Not only was Randell totally inexperienced, but his opponents were at that time third in the top division. If that were not enough, he was told to play at right-back, marking Burnley's Welsh international winger, Leighton James.

Randell was awesome, nullifying the threat of James as well as clearing a shot off the line. His calm and assured performance typified the style which he was to display for the rest of his career. He stayed in the side for the remainder of the season, mostly at right-back but occasionally in midfield, and played in both legs of the League Cup semi-final.

Ironically, when Machin left Home Park, it was Randell who eventually fulfilled a similar play-making role. Almost everything Randell did had a touch of class. He was a stylish performer who always had time on the ball. He had the knack of slowing the game and spraying the ball around with pinpoint accuracy. Although his goalscoring record was not great, he created numerous chances for others with his defence-splitting passes. One example of this came in the FA Cup-tie with Everton in January 1975. It was Randell's incisive pass that set up Barrie Vassallo to score Argyle's only goal in a 1-3 defeat.

That defeat was immaterial, as within weeks Argyle had won promotion from Division Three. Randell's performances brought him a Welsh Under-23 cap to add to his earlier international honours. It was later revealed that he had been playing for three months with an Achilles injury. So sore was the tendon that it was put into plaster after each game and not removed until the Friday. Supporters were astonished at the sight of Randell arriving for a game and hobbling into the dressing room. Cortisone injections kept him going and eased him through the pain barrier, but two games in as many days at Easter took its toll and he was forced to miss the next four matches.

Randell continued to do himself justice in Division Two, but the arrival of midfielders Brian Hall and Doug Collins – both with top division experience – for the start of 1976-77 briefly pushed Randell out of the side. It was not long before he was recalled at full-back and appointed temporary captain in the absence of John Craven.

Randell was Waiters' man. The new manager, Mike Kelly, was not so enamoured, and in September 1977 sold him to Exeter for a bargain £10,000. With one-time colleague Bobby Saxton as manager, he remained with Argyle's great rivals until July 1979, notching six goals in 88 League and Cup appearances. When Saxton took up the reins at Home Park he brought Randell back with him. It was certainly good business for Exeter as they received £60,000, a handsome profit on their original investment.

When Saxton departed to manage Blackburn, his successor Bobby Moncur continued to rely on Randell as his midfield linch-pin. Other than Kelly, most managers seemed to rate him, and it was perhaps no surprise when in August 1982 Saxton asked to take him to Ewood Park. The agreed fee was £40,000. Saxton and Randell enjoyed mutual respect, so much so that Randell accepted Saxton's request without even discussing wages.

For three years Randell was a regular at Blackburn. But it was in his native South Wales that he finished his League career, joining Swansea in July 1985 before retiring with more than 400 appearances under his belt for various clubs. He became player-manager of Briton Ferry Athletic in the Welsh League. Randell remains living in Swansea to this day. Having worked as a fitness instructor with the South Wales Police Force for many years, he now acts as the head of their Physical Education and Personal Safety Department.

Magic Moment: *During half-time at Bolton in March 1977, Randell received a phone call saying his wife had given birth in Plymouth to a daughter, Eve. Randell had been injured in midweek at Blackburn and did not play at Bolton. The squad had remained in the north and Randell had not been allowed to return home.*

Worst Nightmare: *During 'Black Sunday' at Port Vale in March 1974, when three Argyle players were sent off, Randell was at one point the only defender. It was so bizarre that he burst out laughing.*

ARGYLE RECORD	Appearances		Goals
Football League	247	(+2)	17
FA Cup	11		2
League Cup	22		–

No 68. **GEORGE FOSTER**
Debut: v Hereford, 20 February 1974
Farewell: v Wimbledon, 20 October 1981

George Foster was heralded a star of the future, being a prolific scorer in schoolboy soccer and becoming the youngest ever player to represent Plymouth Schoolboys.

Born in Plymouth on 26 September 1956, the fair-haired Foster was considered one of the hottest prospects in town and was inevitably taken on as an Argyle apprentice. When just fifteen he forced his way into the reserves and seemed to justify his golden boy tag by scoring in his first two Football Combination matches. Although not particularly tall, he was sturdy for his age – and he needed to be when coming up against battle-hardened defenders like Arsenal's Peter Simpson and Norwich's Duncan Forbes.

Once Argyle's League Cup run was over, and there was no more at stake in the League, Tony Waiters gave Foster a taste of the first team as a substitute. Foster was still only seventeen and had not yet signed a full professional contract. That had to wait till he was eighteen, by which time Mariner and Rafferty were knocking in the goals, Argyle were pushing for promotion, and there was no room for young Foster at all. The following season, 1975-76, was much the same, although he was more or less a regular on the substitutes' bench.

Foster's first lengthy first-team run came near the end of 1976-77. He had been loaned out to Torquay and three goals in six games did his confidence a power of good. Mike Kelly had replaced Tony Waiters and Argyle were struggling. Foster was drafted in but carried the weight of expectation on his shoulders. Two goals in two games could not be maintained indefinitely, and he, like others, seemed to wither on the vine. The fans, frustrated by the team's poor form, which eventually brought relegation, began to target wonder-boy in particular.

One incident early in 1977-78 sparked a change in Foster's fortunes and, with hindsight, also changed the course of his career. Argyle were playing Birmingham in the pre-season Anglo-Scottish Cup. Foster was on the bench, and when centre-half John Peddelty took a knock, Foster prepared to come on. Kelly's intention was to play Foster in midfield and move John Delve into defence. But Foster, who had regularly played in defence during training, pleaded with Kelly to play him at the back instead. Kelly agreed and Foster did well.

As Peddelty had no chance of being fit for Argyle's next game, a League Cup-tie at Exeter, Foster felt confident he would play. But, the day before, he learned that Dave Sutton would play instead. By his own admission, Foster was something of a youthful hothead and he burst into Kelly's office to confront the manager. The air turned so blue that Foster was sure he had burned his boats at Argyle. But he was mistaken. Kelly changed his mind and Foster played in the No 5 shirt for the game.

His performances were transformed. His relative lack of pace, a burden during his days as an attacker, was no longer such a factor. He was strong in the tackle, good in the air, and read the game instinctively. Foster and John Craven formed a rock-solid defensive partnership and Foster played every match thereafter that season.

He continued to be the mainstay of the back four until shortly after Bobby Saxton arrived as manager. At home to Oxford in February 1979 Foster broke his leg, was out for the season, and became a national celebrity. His pet Boxer 'Sadie' had coincidentally broken a paw while playing with a ball in the garden. A national tabloid got hold of the story and Foster and Sadie were pictured together in plaster!

Foster was fit to start the new campaign, and as an inspirational skipper was ever present for the next two seasons. But with the appointment of Bobby Moncur in the hot seat in 1981, Argyle got off to their worst ever start, drawing two and losing nine of the opening eleven games. Changes were inevitable and Foster was one of those to lose his place. Rather than stagnate in the reserves, he went on loan to Exeter, where he shored up a leaky defence for the rest of that season.

It proved to be the end of Foster's Argyle career, with Lindsay Smith and Chris Harrison establishing themselves and Mike Ham waiting in the wings. In June 1982 Foster moved to Derby County, where he stayed for one season, making 30 appearances, before joining Mansfield a year later, thus starting a long association with the Stags. Foster went on to play 373 League matches for Mansfield without scoring and was eventually appointed player-manager. He continued to marshal his side from central defence until his mid-30s. Despite an ever-expanding waistline, Foster's experience and capacity to read the game made him an effective defender. He won no fewer than three Player of the Year awards at Mansfield. It is strange to think that such a prolific youthful goalscorer ended up playing more than 600 League games and scored only nine times.

After leaving Mansfield, Foster continued to pass on his experience with Telford United, Doncaster Rovers, Chesterfield, and Birmingham City, where became the recruitment officer for their soccer academy and took charge of the club's under-18s.

Two scouting posts followed, with Newcastle and Northern Ireland, before he was appointed Lincoln's director of coaching. Ironically it was a last-minute defeat at Plymouth in January 2001 – after Lincoln had dominated the game – that played a part in his downfall. Not long afterwards, Foster and Imps manager Phil Stant were dismissed.

Since then, Foster has acted as chief scout for Wolves, a job he enjoys, and one which takes him abroad for much of the time.

Magic Moment: *As a measure of how he won over the Argyle fans, Foster was proud to receive the 1977-78 Player of the Year award.*

Worst Nightmare: *When Foster broke his leg against Oxford in February 1979, he exacerbated the damage by kicking the ball after he had suffered the injury.*

ARGYLE RECORD	Appearances	Goals
Football League	201 (+11)	6
FA Cup	10	–
League Cup	19	–

No 69. **BILLY RAFFERTY**
Debut: v Watford, 16 March 1974
Farewell: v Fulham, 19 April 1976

If George Foster had persevered with his original position of centre-forward, fate may have decreed that Foster and Billy Rafferty forged a dynamic Argyle partnership. It was not to be, and Rafferty is now inexorably linked with Paul Mariner as the modern equivalent of Jack Leslie and Sammy Black.

Rafferty served no fewer than eight English League clubs, which suggests that the epithet 'journeyman' fits perfectly. Supporters of his other clubs may well agree with this sentiment; Argyle fans most certainly would not.

Glaswegian Rafferty was born on 30 December 1950. At school he played for Port Glasgow Rangers and afterwards trained to be a draughtsman. He was spotted playing by Coventry City's Scotland scout, Dan Morris, and was taken on as an apprentice. He played on the losing Coventry side in the 1968 FA Youth Cup final and signed professional terms in July of that year. His first-team debut did not come until April 1970, but subsequent appearances were few and after 27 games and three goals, he moved to Blackpool in an exchange deal involving Tommy Hutchison.

Eighteen months at Blackpool were marred by cartilage problems which limited him to 35 appearances and nine goals. More significantly, as it turned out, Rafferty worked with first-team coach Tony Waiters, soon destined to become manager at Home Park.

In 1973-74 Waiters was supervising a losing Argyle side, notwithstanding its League Cup exploits. New blood was essential and, turning a blind eye to his knee problems, Waiters signed Rafferty in March 1974 for a fee of £25,000.

Paul Mariner was, by then, already established, but their early games together gave little hint of what was to follow. Rafferty's first two matches in Argyle colours did not have Mariner alongside him. And when Mariner did return neither managed a goal before Rafferty's season was cut short by persistent knee problems. The need for cartilage surgery ruled him out for the campaign.

Whatever happened under the surgeon's knife seemed to create a new player. The new season saw a fit Rafferty display the form of which Waiters knew he was capable. Following a 0-1 defeat at Preston in the curtain raiser, Rafferty scored in the next four games, including a hat-trick against Tranmere. He and Mariner seemed to enjoy a telepathic understanding and soon formed one of the most feared front pairings in the lower divisions.

This lethal combination seemed improbable in many respects. They were similar players, both strongly built, good in the air and able to hold the ball up, but neither could be described as a classic goal-poacher. Yet they had the knack of being in the right place for each other. Rafferty was a particularly strong, tireless runner, whose mobility along the front line created space for others. As if to prove his fitness, Rafferty played in every match that season. The duo scored 43 League goals, with Rafferty's tally of 23 being raised by three FA Cup goals. These included both in a 2-0 FA Cup win over his former side, Blackpool, to set up an appetising tie against First Division Everton.

Argyle lost that match but won the more important prize, promotion from Division Three. Pilgrims' fans relished the prospect of their new heroes laying about them in a higher division. Rafferty's impact was acknowledged by the *Daily Express*'s award of Third Division Player of the Year.

Space was at a premium in Division Two. Whilst the ratio of goals was down on the promotion year, the pair still notched 30 between them, with Mariner edging out Rafferty 16-14 in their personal duel. For the last match, at Carlisle, there was little at stake and Rafferty was omitted. But the significance of dropping him was soon to become evident. Rafferty travelled to Scotland to see his parents, but on arrival took a telephone call from Waiters asking if he was interested in speaking to Carlisle. Rafferty was not enamoured by the prospect but was persuaded by his father that a move back north was a good idea.

Much to the chagrin of Argyle fans, Rafferty signed. To add salt to the wounds, Argyle received a measly £20,000. The fee defied logic, as confirmed when Carlisle eventually sold him to Wolves for a more realistic £125,000. His time at Carlisle produced 27 goals in 72 games, but the move to Wolves in March 1978 saw him form another potentially explosive combination with John Richards. Shortly after Rafferty's arrival at Molineux there was talk of Ipswich buying him to reunite him with Mariner, but nothing materialised. Although Rafferty's pairing with Richards did not spark a torrent of goals, Rafferty's own stock was still rising, and in October 1979 a fee of £175,000 took him to Newcastle. There he teamed up with Peter Withe, another similar player to himself, but they failed to click and after a year on Tyneside Rafferty joined Portsmouth for £80,000.

Fratton Park saw shades of the old Rafferty, who netted 40 times for Pompey in 98 League starts and helped them win the Third Division title in 1983. In February 1984 he joined his final League club, Bournemouth, before he embarked on a three-year spell with Portuguese sides Sporting Club Farense and Loultanos.

Returning to these shores, he set up home in Carlisle, where he has established a successful health club which he still runs. He has also been involved in the centre of excellence at Carlisle United, where he helped develop youngsters such as Matt Jansen and Rory Delap, who have gone on to become Premiership stars.

Rafferty admits that, of all his clubs, he still holds an affection for Plymouth. Whilst it was his partner, Paul Mariner, who reached the heights with England, Rafferty's goal-per-game ratio while at Argyle outshines that of Mariner. Many older supporters still rue the day when their partnership was prematurely ended.

Magic Moment: *Rafferty's power brought him a superb goal against Charlton in February 1975. He soared high to despatch Phil Burrows' inch-perfect cross into the net with a textbook header.*

Worst Nightmare: *In the same match, with the score 1-1, Rafferty stepped up to take a last-gasp penalty but drove the ball against the post to deny Argyle a valuable point in their quest for promotion.*

ARGYLE RECORD	Appearances	Goals
Football League	89 (+1)	35
FA Cup	6	4
League Cup	5	1

No 70. **PHIL BURROWS**

Debut: v Preston, 17 August 1974
Farewell: v Carlisle, 24 April 1976

That unwittingly crucial last match of 1975-76 at Carlisle not only saw the departure of Bill Rafferty, but also of Phil Burrows.

Burrows can be likened in many ways to Pat Jones in the 1940s and 50s. Whilst Burrows' time at Home Park was significantly shorter than that of Jones, both were left-backs, reliable, and popular with the crowd.

Born in Stockport on 8 April 1946, Burrows played for Stockport schools when only fourteen. While studying to become a quantity surveyor, he joined Manchester City as an amateur, progressed through their various sides and signed as a professional in 1964. He became a regular in City's Central League reserve side and acted as understudy to Alan Oakes.

Unfortunately for Burrows, the call to the first team never came. City had an extensive squad and other players were ahead of him. In 1966 a free transfer took him York, where Burrows anticipated a better chance of League action. The gamble of moving down the League ladder, in the hope that he might climb back up, paid off – eventually. Burrows established himself in a York side which had to seek re-election in each of his first four seasons, but also played his part in one of their more success-ful spells. For four consecutive seasons from 1969-70, Burrows was ever present. York twice won promotion in that time, to find themselves in Division Two for the first time. Playing mostly at half-back, Burrows became a highly popular figure and was awarded York's inaugural Clubman of the Year award in 1974.

In eight seasons with York, he played a total of 390 matches, scoring fifteen goals. In the eyes of Argyle manager Tony Waiters, Burrows was an ideal, experienced left-sided player to replace Colin Sullivan. Waiters had been tracking Burrows for some time in the knowledge that Sullivan would inevitably move on to higher things. Little though, did Burrows (or Waiters) know that when he appeared for York in the final game of 1973-74 at Home Park it would be his swansong for York and that his oppo-nents' ground would soon be his home.

Waiters was so desperate to sign Burrows that he tracked him down holidaying in Northumberland. Waiters flew to York to negotiate the deal and Burrows signed for a fee of £16,000 in August.

A direct replacement for Sullivan at left-back, Burrows' debut ended in defeat, but that experience proved to be rare for the remainder of the season. After Waiters' new intake had settled in, the side gelled and stormed to promotion. Every member of the team played his part but none more so than Burrows. Whilst Mariner and Rafferty were grabbing the headlines, the defence was performing no less efficiently. Burrows' consistency marked him out as one of the best players in the lower divi-sions. On the field he seemed totally in control of any situation and rarely did an opposing winger give him a roasting.

Burrows was also a useful attacking force, overlapping at every oppor-tunity. His left-sided link-up with Hugh McAuley was particularly pro-ductive and the pair were responsible for a stream of crosses to Mariner and Rafferty. Nor was Burrows averse to cocking his sweet left foot when within shooting range, so that though his goals were rare they were usu-ally spectacular.

Burrows proved no less competent in Division Two, playing in every game and looking set to become an Argyle fixture for years to come, but with his two-year contract expiring, player and club were unable to agree new terms. He was reluctant to leave the South West but with a family to support he needed to obtain the best deal on offer. Hereford obviously offered more, and a fee of £8,500 took him to Edgar Street.

Groin trouble put him out of action for most of his first season at Hereford. It was the first time Burrows had ever been sidelined for a long spell through injury. He also endured another new experience while with Hereford – relegation, not once but twice, as the side plummeted from the Second to Fourth Divisions. Four seasons at Edgar Street saw him make 110 League appearances, scoring twice.

Burrows then turned his back on League soccer and returned to his original work as a quantity surveyor. He kept active by playing part-time for Witton Albion and Mossley. After his playing days were over he continued to coach and in 1985 became reserve-team manager at Stockport, resigning after one season. His also served on the committee for the Manchester City Players Association and played the occasional game for the club's veterans side. Perhaps surprisingly, bearing in mind his association with City, Burrows confesses to being a Manchester United fan! He now lives in the Stockport area and continues to work in the building industry but often reflects warmly on two highly enjoyable years at Home Park.

Magic Moment: *Having qualified as a quantity surveyor, Burrows never turned his back on the profession. He had continued to study part-time while playing, finally qualifying after eight years' study.*

Worst Nightmare: *Leaving Argyle is a decision Burrows still regrets, as he would have happily settled in the West Country.*

ARGYLE RECORD	Appearances	Goals
Football League	81	2
FA Cup	6	–
League Cup	5	1

No 71. **MIKE GREEN**
Debut: v Preston, 17 August 1974
Farewell: v Bolton, 5 March 1977

Partnering Phil Burrows in the Plymouth Argyle defence during their promotion-winning 1974-75 season was Mike Green, another left-footed player who proved himself to be an influential captain in that successful side.

Green was born in Carlisle on 8 September 1946, and turned professional for his home-town club in September 1964. At the time he was a full-back, but there was little scope for him at Carlisle and, having played only two first-team games in four years, he left in September 1968 on a free transfer to Gillingham.

The Kent club converted Green to a centre-forward, where his 6ft-plus frame proved a useful weapon. He spent three years with the Gills, scoring 24 goals in 131 League starts, and was twice leading scorer. His goals helped Gillingham reach the fifth round of the FA Cup in 1969-70, where they lost to Watford.

Joining Bristol Rovers in July 1971, he again found his chances limited by the likes of ex-Torquay star, Robin Stubbs. More by accident than design, he found himself drafted in at centre-half. Don Megson, father of future Argyle player, Gary, supervised the Rovers reserve side at the time, and it was he who first recommended the switch. Green put his transformation down to the fact that, having been a striker himself, he knew all the tricks of the trade. The elevation of Megson as Rovers manager cemented Green's central defensive position.

In 1973-74 he captained the side through their all-conquering campaign that saw them embark on an unbeaten run of 27 games and thrash Brian Clough's Brighton 8-2. Not surprisingly, Rovers won promotion from the Third Division.

There was a shock in store for Green, however, when he was told that Tony Waiters was interested in taking him to Argyle. Initially, Green, about to taste Second Division soccer, reacted coolly, but agreed to talk with the club. Like other players of the time, Green was impressed with the set up at Home Park and said at the time that he felt he was merely postponing Second Division football for another season. A fee of £19,000 was agreed and Green joined Argyle in time for the 1974-75 season, Waiters appointing him captain in place of the departed Ernie Machin.

Following his debut, there was a quick return to Eastville in the League Cup. Green and his co-defenders had the satisfaction of a clean sheet in the first leg in a 0-0 draw, but Rovers went through after scoring the all-important winning goal at Home Park.

The decision to appoint Green captain proved a wise one. The tall, moustachioed stopper, playing alongside Bobby Saxton, was an excellent leader, his cool and assured performances setting a fine example to his colleagues. Whilst Saxton was the more typical, tough-tackling defender, Green relied on his positional sense and reading of the game. He would mark opponents closely and 'guide' them into less dangerous positions rather than jump in with an impetuous tackle. He was also commanding in the air and used this to good effect from set pieces, where he would occasionally display his striker's instincts.

His first season at Home Park saw him play in every match, testimony to his fair and disciplined approach, and for the second successive season he led a side to promotion. With Second Division soccer arriving at Home Park in 1975-76, Green was again a model of consistency, missing only two matches and nurturing his new young centre-back partner, Dave Sutton.

The 1976-77 season proved something of let-down. The side struggled following the departure of key members of the promotion side, and another central defender, John Peddelty, had arrived as part of the Paul Mariner deal to increase competition for places in the defence. For a while Green was left out, and a 0-3 defeat at Bolton in what proved to be his last game, also marked the beginning of the end for Waiters, who resigned some weeks later.

With local rivals Torquay looking for a new manager, following the temporary appointment of Frank O'Farrell, Green was taken on as player-manager at Plainmoor. He played for a further three seasons, scoring seven goals in 88 League matches before taking a back seat to concentrate on his managerial duties. He remained manager of the Gulls until the end of 1980-81, when his contract was not renewed. He was replaced by Bruce Rioch, ironically a player he had brought to Plainmoor on loan from Seattle Sounders.

Green's managerial philosophy reflected that of his mentors, Waiters and Megson. He fielded attacking sides as well as overseeing a sizeable turnover of players. Unfortunately, he could not lift Torquay out of the Fourth Division.

After his departure from Plainmoor, Green went back to playing at local level for various South Devon sides – Newton Abbot and Hele Spurs. He also purchased a Post Office business in Torquay that he still runs today.

Magic Moment: *Green had the honour of leading the Argyle side out to the applause of the crowd and their opponents, Port Vale, having clinched promotion from Division Three in April 1975.*

Worst Nightmare: *With Argyle leading 5-0 at Bournemouth in January 1975, Green's own-goal sparked a mini-collapse for his side. The Cherries pulled back two more goals to make it 5-3, and threatened to score futher goals before a late rally by the Pilgrims gave them a 7-3 win.*

ARGYLE RECORD	Appearances	Goals
Football League	108	8
FA Cup	7	2
League Cup	7	–

No 72. **HUGH McAULEY**
Debut: v Peterborough, 19 October 1974
Farewell: v Carlisle, 27 November 1976

When Mike Green skippered Argyle to promotion in 1974-75, a player who made a marked contribution to that success was left-winger Hugh McAuley. His individual contribution is largely overlooked, but on his day he was one of the most exciting wingers around. He was the final piece in Tony Waiters' promotion jigsaw.

Born in Bootle on 8 January 1953, McAuley began his soccer career at Liverpool but failed to break into the first team. He was substitute on a number of occasions but, frustratingly, never broke his duck. Competition for places at Anfield was fierce, and McAuley's favoured left-wing position was taken by Steve Heighway, a player with whom he would have a close association many years later.

It was on loan to nearby Tranmere that McAuley tasted League action for the first time, scoring on his debut against Argyle. He also played a part in one of the shock results of the season, supplying the cross from which Eddie Loyden netted the only goal at Arsenal in the League Cup.

During McAuley's time at Anfield, Tony Waiters had been in charge of the youth team. Having now taken over as manager at Argyle, the one missing link in the side was at left wing. Harry Burrows had been wearing No 11 and, although endowed with experience, was in the twilight of his career. Waiters approached McAuley who, faced with the prospect of working again with him, not to mention regular first-team action, was easily persuaded to sign. Liverpool accepted a fee of £12,000.

McAuley's Argyle debut, against Peterborough, was something special. For the first half an hour he was rarely seen, but gradually Argyle imposed themselves on their opponents. The slightly built winger received more possession and then showed why Waiters thought so highly of him. Two pinpoint crosses laid on both the Argyle goals that secured victory.

McAuley retained his place throughout that season and seemed to act as a talisman. It was not until his sixteenth League game that he was on the losing side and his old-fashioned out and out wing play, with Brian Johnson playing a similar role on the right, provided a plentiful supply of chances for Mariner and Rafferty.

Waiters had instructed his side to play in a way that suited McAuley. Rather than chase long balls hit wide for him, he would invariably hang back to receive the ball at his feet, then tantalise his full-back with nifty footwork. When the defender least expected it, McAuley would unleash a burst of acceleration and gain the space from which to deliver a dangerous cross. He also had the ability to centre the ball without breaking his stride and this, matched with his turn of speed, made him a difficult player to nullify. Inevitably, unorthodox tactics were sometimes employed to halt him. But even in the face of severe provocation he would remain impassive, regarding the use of illegal tactics as a moral victory over his opponent.

Following promotion to Division Two, McAuley's inclusion was once again almost automatic – he missed just two matches, through injury, all season. Despite the higher class of football, McAuley still demonstrated that he was a match for anyone. An example of this came at Chelsea. The man responsible for marking him was the highly rated Gary Locke, but McAuley gave him such a wretched 90 minutes that the shattered Locke was thereafter missing from the Chelsea side for some time.

The 1976-77 season proved to be McAuley's last at Home Park. Several of the promotion side had dispersed and the successful 4-2-4 formation was abandoned for a more cautious approach. As a result, only four games into the season McAuley lost his place. His last appearance was made as a substitute and shortly afterwards he signed up for Charlton.

He became a regular at The Valley, making 55 League appearances and scoring nine goals before, in August 1978, he returned to his native Merseyside for a second spell at Tranmere. Rovers were relegated at the end of his first season, whereupon he moved north to Carlisle. After just a handful of games in two seasons at Brunton Park he announced his retirement.

He returned to live in Liverpool, worked for the Merseyside Youth Association, and organised soccer courses for young players. He obtained his FA coaching qualifications and returned to Anfield to work part-time at its School of Excellence. In 1990 he took on a full-time coaching role at Liverpool and is today one of the prime movers of the club's youth academy, run by Steve Heighway. McAuley is manager of Liverpool's under-19s and has witnessed extraordinary talent pass through that side. Michael Owen and Steven Gerrard are just two of today's stars to have graduated through Liverpool's highly successful youth scheme.

One of McAuley's early pupils was his eldest son, Hugh junior, who spectators at Home Park have seen in action over recent times, playing for Argyle's Division Three rivals Cheltenham.

Magic Moment: *Goalscoring was not McAuley's strong suit, but the goal he scored at home to Halifax in March 1975 was special. Collecting the ball in his own half,*

*he skipped past several desperate lunges to score a superb goal and secure two vital
points.*

Worst Nightmare: *McAuley was only substitute for one of Argyle's biggest
matches. 25,000 turned out to see Fulham, with George Best, Bobby Moore and
Rodney Marsh. McAuley played no part.*

ARGYLE RECORD	Appearances	Goals
Football League	76 (+1)	7
FA Cup	6	–
League Cup	5	–

No 73. **CHRIS HARRISON**
Debut: v Carlisle, 24 April 1976
Farewell: v Millwall, 11 May 1985

Chris Harrison was born in Launceston on 17 October 1956 and became
one of the last locally born players to make a sizeable impact at Plymouth
Argyle. He first came to the Pilgrims' attention as a schoolboy player with
Gunnislake, mixing it with the grown-ups in the rough and tumble of the
Plymouth and District League. Harrison was one of Ellis Stuttard's many
discoveries. The youngster trained at Home Park for two nights a week
and was offered an apprenticeship at the club. A year later, under Tony
Waiters, he fulfilled his boyhood ambition of becoming a professional
footballer.

These were exciting times at Argyle, with the club sweeping all before
them in their promotion challenge, but for Harrison the opposite was
true. An unchanged winning team meant little scope for outsiders, let
alone a raw novice.

Harrison continued learning his trade in the reserves until the final
game of 1975-76. Then, with relegation averted, Waiters gave Harrison
his debut at right-back in place of the regular incumbent, Peter Darke.
Darke's disciplinary record was cause for concern and a further booking
in that last fixture would have earned automatic suspension for the start
of the new season.

Harrison held down a regular place in the Argyle midfield until
December 1976. He was versatile, good with both feet, and able to slot
into a variety of midfield or defensive positions.

For the next three seasons he was principally a utility player, covering
for absent colleagues, without an opportunity to establish himself for any
length of time. It was the arrival of Bobby Saxton as manager in January

1979 that acted as catalyst to his career. Saxton used Harrison almost exclusively at right- or left-half, and in two and a half seasons under the ex-Argyle defender's reign, he missed only six games.

Saxton's replacement, Bobby Moncur, who took office in June 1981, was a good judge of a defender if ever there was one. Moncur switched Harrison to a central defensive role. It was here that his best qualities now shone. There was always a touch of class and style about Harrison's play, and at only 5ft 9in he was not the typical Third Division centre-half. What Harrison lacked in brawn, he made up for in brains. His positional sense and anticipation were superb and, because of this, he was rarely called upon to make desperate last-ditch tackles. His passing was simple but shrewd and he always had time on the ball. His play seemed out of place in the hurly burly of the Third Division and was perhaps more suit-ed to a Continental style. Not surprisingly, off the field he was quiet and courteous, always immaculately turned out.

Harrison continued to be a regular choice under Moncur and, subse-quently, John Hore, but it was not until the latter part of his Home Park career that he tasted any measurable success. In 1983-84 Argyle marched to the semi-finals of the FA Cup. Harrison was, by then, the club's longest serving player, taking the field in all but one of the FA Cup rounds.

The following season, his testimonial year, saw Harrison again com-mand a regular place until a losing patch precipitated Hore's departure. When Dave Smith took over, Gerry McElhinney joined the club, and together with Clive Goodyear and Adrian Burrows this meant that Argyle were now awash with central defenders. Harrison, the elder statesman among the quartet, was the one to lose his place.

He played sporadically until the end of the season but his time was up. Argyle granted him a free transfer to assist him to find another club, but not before he was honoured with a testimonial match against Chelsea in August 1985.

Swansea City signed him up a month later and in three seasons at Vetch Field he played 114 League matches, plus three as substitute. His modest goalscoring record was also improved, helped by becoming the Swans' regular penalty taker. Most of his fourteen goals came from the spot.

Harrison was released in 1988 and returned to his native Cornwall. Moving to Looe, he set up his own driving school, a business he still operates today, and continued his soccer career with Saltash, where he was eventually appointed manager. Still living in the Cornish fishing port, he also now works as a part-time fireman.

Magic Moment: *Argyle fans were stunned not only by the FA Cup quarter-final win at Derby, but also by the sight of the shy Harrison climbing the fence at the Argyle fans 'end' to celebrate with them.*

Worst Nightmare: *Harrison's bad back-pass gave Swansea's John Toshack an easy equaliser at Home Park in May 1979. To make matters worse, his error occurred in front of the Match of the Day cameras.*

Argyle record	Appearances		Goals
Football League	315	(+9)	7
FA Cup	25	(+1)	–
League Cup	21		1

No 74. **BRIAN HALL**
Debut: v Exeter, 14 August 1976
Farewell v Portsmouth, 29 October 1977

Another stylish player to join the Argyle ranks in the mid-1970s was Brian Hall, a player with bags of experience at the highest level, but who had entered the professional game at a relatively advanced age.

Born on 22 January 1946, Glaswegian Hall was only two when his father's work took the family to Preston. As a student at Preston Grammar School young Brian focused on an academic career. He had played at an amateur level, but his mathematics degree at Liverpool University took precedence over dreams of professional football. Even then, his break into the professional ranks came almost by accident.

Hall was invited for a trial at Liverpool only after a friend had written to the club on his behalf. He must have done well, as the club signed him on the basis of that one trial match. Having progressed through Liverpool's 'A' and reserve sides, Hall, now a Bachelor of Science, made his full debut in a League Cup Anfield replay against Mansfield. A footballer with a degree was a rarity in itself, but also making his debut in the same match was Steve Heighway, Bachelor of Arts. The two soon earned the nicknames 'Little Bamber' and 'Big Bamber' after the presenter of TV's University Challenge, Bamber Gascoigne.

Hall's early Liverpool appearances were mostly made as substitute. It was not until the autumn of 1970 that he gained a regular place, following the prolonged absence of Ian Callaghan with a cartilage injury. Playing on the right-hand side of midfield, Hall slotted into the star studded Liverpool side with ease. Manager Bill Shankly was impressed enough to retain Hall in his wide role even when Callaghan was fit again.

Hall's first great moment was the 1970-71 FA Cup final, although he finished on the losing side as Arsenal completed one half of their famous 'double'. Inevitably, playing alongside such luminaries as Ray Clemence, John Toshack and Kevin Keegan, further honours were never far away. In May 1973 Liverpool clinched the League title, although Hall had a restricted part in that success – scoring twice in seventeen appearances – in a season when Peter Cormack was often preferred in midfield. Another medal came Hall's way when the Reds beat Borussia Moenchengladbach in a two-legged UEFA Cup final – Hall taking the field as a substitute in the first game. He did, however, play in the 1973-74 FA Cup final, in which Liverpool hardly broke sweat in accounting for Newcastle 3-0.

The following season Hall missed only seven League matches, but the emergence of Jimmy Case and David Fairclough signalled the end of his career at Anfield. He had made over 200 appearances in all competitions. Although Hall was approaching 30, many felt he had much to offer in top-flight football and it was a surprise to many when Tony Waiters tried to persuade him to uproot to Devon for what was then a record fee for Argyle of £50,000.

Fans drooled at the prospect of the club signing a player with such pedigree. The asking price, however, was a stiff hurdle. In an unprecedented move, a 'Hall for Argyle' campaign was launched as supporters throughout Devon, Cornwall and beyond dug deep into their pockets to support various functions and fund-raising events. As a result, a large proportion of the necessary outlay was pledged. Only one question remained. Would Hall actually sign? Other clubs were reputed to be interested, but it was a shopping trip that finally convinced Hall and his wife to take the plunge. Having been down in Plymouth for talks, they were due to return to Liverpool. Mrs Hall decided on some last-minute shopping. Instead of the city-centre hustle and bustle of Liverpool, the Halls were astonished by the leisurely pace of life in Plymouth, and this was what tipped the balance. Hall signed.

Having been promoted two years earlier, Argyle had consolidated in Division Two and, on his arrival at Home Park for the start of 1976-77, Hall declared that it was his intention to lead Argyle into the Promised Land. Many supporters shared this optimism, believing that players of Hall's calibre, masterminded by the managerial skills of Waiters, could finally see a turning point in the club's history. Within a few months that dream was shattered. After a poor start, the sale of Paul Mariner and the departure of Waiters, the club found itself in the nether reaches of the table. The one bright spot was the form of Hall. He lived up to the hype surrounding his arrival, and in reality was probably too good for the level of soccer he found himself in. However, he was no longer playing with the Keegans and Toshacks of this world and his Argyle team-mates were often slow to react to Hall's intelligent play and incisive passing.

His all-action style soon set him apart as a crowd favourite. His small, slightly hunched figure could usually be found in the thick of the action throughout the 90 minutes. He finished his first season as Argyle's top scorer, but to achieve that distinction with just ten goals tells its own story, and Waiters' replacement, Mike Kelly, failed to arrest the slide towards relegation.

When Hall first came to Argyle, the forward thinking Waiters was keen to utilise his new player's intelligence to promote the club. In addition to training and playing, Hall worked in the club's Commercial Department, as well as hosting his own weekly, one hour phone-in show on a local radio station. It was a role that Hall cherished and one that would hold him in good stead later in his life.

He maintained his own high standards at the start of the following season, but the team, despite being back in Division Three, was still losing. One can only surmise how much that was a factor, but Hall confessed to not settling in Devon as well as he had anticipated and, only a few weeks into the new season, he asked to be transferred. In November 1977 he signed for Burnley, which took him and his wife back to the North West. Shortly after arriving at Turf Moor he suffered a serious injury which eventually forced his retirement.

After leaving the game, he went into teaching before moving into local government in Preston. He also set up a consultancy business with Ian St John. The Liverpool connection was subsequently restored when Hall returned to Anfield as public relations manager, a position he still holds today and no doubt due, in part, to those early days at Argyle when he carried out a similar role.

Magic Moment: *Hall scored for Liverpool against Everton in the 1971 FA Cup semi-final at Old Trafford to put the Reds in the final.*

Worst Nightmare: *Hall suffered two broken bones in his back shortly after joining Burnley, which eventually forced him to quit.*

ARGYLE RECORD	Appearances		Goals
Football League	49	(+2)	16
FA Cup	1		–
League Cup	2	(+1)	–

No 75. **JOHN UZZELL**
Debut: v Exeter, 13 August 1977
Farewell: v Oldham, 29 April 1989

Whereas Brian Hall had the talent to grace the First Division and European stages, John Uzzell spent his career in the lower reaches of the League. Nevertheless, it is players like him, loyal and dependable, who are the lifeblood of the game.

Uzzell, born in Plymouth on 31 March 1959, attended Oreston Primary and Plymstock Schools. He was a regular spectator at Argyle's Barn Park End in the early 1970s and achieved one of his ambitions by playing at Home Park when he was selected to play for Plymouth Schools under-15s.

He signed on as an apprentice on leaving school, at a time when Tony Waiters' youth set-up was the envy of other clubs. Uzzell is quick to pay tribute to the likes of Keith Blunt and Bobby Howe who were instrumental in his progress through the youth team and into the Argyle reserve side. .

The quality of the young players coming through at that time was reflected by the reserves finishing second in the 1976-77 Football Combination. Originally a centre-half, second-team manager Mike Kelly converted him to a full-back and on his eighteenth birthday Uzzell was presented with a professional contract. He got a taste of the big time in Jim Furnell's testimonial against an All Star XI in May 1977. With his former reserve-team boss Kelly now in charge, Uzzell and the equally raw Kevin Smart were regularly included in pre-season build-ups and Kelly blooded both young full-backs in a League Cup-tie at Exeter.

A week later, Uzzell and Smart made their League debuts in a 0-0 home draw against Preston. So quickly did Uzzell adapt that he looked to be heading for an ever-present record in his first season, until injury denied him his place for the final two games.

With Malcolm Allison now in charge, Alan Rogers was preferred to Uzzell for the first half of 1978-79, but when Bobby Saxton in turn replaced Allison, one of his first acts was to restore Uzzell. Saxton had second thoughts, however, and for two seasons Uzzell was largely confined to the reserves. Typically, there were no tantrums or transfer-demands. He was prepared to knuckle down and fight for his place. He did have a brief trial with Wimbledon, but never wanted to leave his home-town club.

The arrival of yet another new manager, Bobby Moncur, saw Uzzell installed as first choice left-back and opened up a chapter in which he played some of his best football. By the time John Hore replaced Moncur in October 1983, Uzzell was firmly established. Soon after Hore's arrival, the fairy tale FA Cup-run started to accelerate, ensuring Uzzell a permanent place in the hearts of Argyle fans, who appreciated that his wholehearted style overcame any technical limitations.

There was more to his game than enthusiasm, however. He was a strong, well-built defender, with a left foot that could give the ball a mighty thump. He was dominant in the air, a legacy of his earlier days as a centre-half, and always willing to push forward in attack. His passing occasionally let him down, but he was reliable and rarely had those nightmare games that affect most players.

Dave Smith was the eighth manager Uzzell had served under in ten years. It was not any loss of form but a broken toe and a hamstring strain that forced him onto the sidelines for much of the 1985-86 promotion season.

Uzzell's absence prompted Smith to experiment with midfielder Leigh Cooper at left-back. Seizing his opportunity, Cooper played out of his skin. Once he was fit again, Uzzell found himself only sporadically called into the first team, usually in a central defensive role. There was some consolation to Uzzell when he was granted a testimonial year to honour his service. The highlight of these fund-raising efforts was a match against Brian Clough's Nottingham Forest in November 1986. Despite inclement weather, a 7,000 crowd turned out to acknowledge the popular Uzzell.

Not until November 1988 did Uzzell reclaim his customary No 3 shirt, thanks to the misfortune of Cooper, who broke a leg at Portsmouth. The following summer Uzzell rejected new terms and, along with John Matthews, joined Torquay. At Plainmoor he had no challengers to his place in the first team. With the prospect of a coaching role at the club looming, his cheekbone was shattered in a collision with Brentford forward Gary Blissett. The incident made the national papers and eventually needed legal redress. Uzzell's disfigured face was widely shown, earning him much sympathy.

Two operations followed, whereupon Uzzell continued to train with Torquay in the hope of resuming his career. He even attempted a comeback, but it was soon clear that the injury would not withstand the rigours of football. Uzzell had no choice but to quit.

He took a job as a part-time postman, while coaching youngsters in his home town of Ivybridge and helping his former manager, Dave Smith, with his soccer schools. Uzzell is now a full-time postman and still a regular and popular visitor to Home Park.

Magic Moment: *Uzzell's goals were rare, but none was more vital than his header against Darlington in the FA Cup in January 1984. Argyle were trailing until Uzzell headed in Gordon Nisbet's cross.*

Worst Nightmare: *After playing a second reserve match for Torquay after his horrendous injury, Uzzell felt so much pain in his head that he realised his career was finally over.*

ARGYLE RECORD	Appearances		Goals
Football league	292	(+9)	6
FA Cup	20	(+1)	1
League Cup	16	(+1)	–

No 76. **FRED BINNEY**
Debut: v Shrewsbury, 4 October 1977
Farewell: v Brentford, 27 October 1979

A solid, dependable defender like John Uzzell has little in common with guitar playing, ace goal-poacher Fred Binney except that both were born and bred in Plymouth. Yet Binney was snatched as a youngster from under the noses of Argyle and it was not until the twilight of his career that fans saw what they had missed.

Binney can certainly call himself a true Plymothian, being born on 12 August 1946 in the Mutley area of the city and raised on the Barbican. His early football was played with CM Department juniors and Argyle duly took note. He was watched on a couple of occasions, but Argyle made no move and he joined Launceston in the South Western League and John Conway in the Devon Wednesday League. He scored frequently, but with little thought of a professional footballing career he embarked on an apprenticeship in the Devonport Dockyard as a shipwright.

It was whilst playing for John Conway that he was spotted by Torquay United scout Don Mills. Binney took wing in the Gulls' reserves, scoring over 60 goals in three seasons, and in October 1966 signed professional terms for manager Frank O'Farrell.

Binney's League debut came during 1967-68, but with Torquay legend Robin Stubbs entrenched in Binney's favourite centre-forward position, opportunities were limited. When he did play, he proved he could score, as his record of ten strikes in 24 starts for Torquay illustrates.

In February 1969, Johnny Newman took him on loan to Exeter. Binney's eleven goals in seventeen appearances played a major part in steering City clear of re-election. In March 1970 he signed permanently for a fee of £5,000. At first, injuries curtailed his effectiveness, but 1971-72 saw Binney embark on a run of three seasons as the Grecians' top scorer, establishing a reputation that spread throughout the lower divisions. Stop Binney and you stop Exeter.

In 1972-73 his 28 League goals were equalled by West Ham's Bryan 'Pop' Robson but exceeded by no one. The following season saw him notch another 25 to earn him the PFA Divisional Player of the Year award. With figures of 90 goals in 177 appearances, Binney was too big for Exeter to cling on to, and he transferred in a £25,000-plus-player exchange to Brighton, managed at the time by Brian Clough and Peter Taylor.

The goals continued to flow, with 35 strikes in 68 matches. Binney even picked up Brighton's Player of the Year award, but new manager Alan Mullery freed him to join St Louis All Stars in the North American Soccer League. The stay in the States proved to be an invaluable experience. Crowds of 60,000 flocked to see some of the greats of the game, not just Fred Binney!

In October 1977, 31-year-old Binney returned home and signed for Argyle on a free transfer. At first it was assumed that the passing of the years had dulled his scoring instincts. Manager Mike Kelly preferred Terry Austin up front, but with relegation looming Kelly was pushed aside in favour of Malcolm Allison, who handed Binney the No 9 shirt at Portsmouth. Against the odds, Argyle won 5-1, with Binney scoring twice. The victory gave him an excuse to demonstrate his fluency on the guitar on the journey home.

Binney could hardly be dropped for the remaining ten games, and his seven goals made the difference between relegation and survival. Under Allison's charge the following season, Binney showed what Argyle had been missing for all those years. If a half-chance came his way, it was odds-on that Binney would convert it. There was nothing fancy about his game other than a relentless pursuit of goalscoring opportunities. He was prepared to dive in where it hurts. His game did not rely on speed or agility but pure instinct, a trait that had not diminished with age. Binney, a chirpy character with long shaggy hair and droopy moustache, became a huge favourite, and with 28 League and Cup goals to his name was voted Argyle's Player of the Year. An extrovert character, he collected his trophy, then ran to Argyle's most famous supporter, Umbrella Vi, and planted a kiss on her 'tongues and all'. The highlight of his scoring exploits that season was a twelve-minute hat-trick at Sheffield Wednesday which saw the Pilgrims snatch a 3-2 win after being two goals in arrears.

At the beginning of 1979-80, new manager Bobby Saxton controversially omitted Binney in favour of David Kemp, a similar type of player. At 33, Binney's days seemed numbered and he was left to languish in the reserves. When ex-Argyle forward Frank Lord sought to take him to Hereford, Binney jumped at the chance to extend his career and a fee of £7,000 secured his transfer. Binney played infrequently while at Edgar Street. He concentrated on earning his coaching qualifications and was subsequently appointed as Lord's assistant.

In 1982 Lord and Binney were offered the chance of coaching in Malaysia. After meeting the Sultan of Penang, Binney was offered the post of coach to the Malaysian State team. He remained abroad until 1985 when he returned to Exeter as coach under Colin Appleton. When Appleton was sacked eighteen months later, Binney departed too and returned to live in Plymouth.

For many years Binney has held the post of Recreation Officer for Plymouth University.

Magic Moment: *In 1978 Binney practised bicycle-kicks to imitate Austrian forward Hans Krankl, who had performed them in the World Cup finals. In the first game of the season against Chesterfield, Binney executed a perfect scissors-kick from twenty yards – a stunning goal.*

Worst Nightmare: *Binney failed to score against non-league Worcester City in an FA Cup-tie in November 1978. The underdogs won 2-0 in what was one of Argyle's worst ever performances.*

ARGYLE RECORD	Appearances		Goals
Football League	67	(+4)	39
FA Cup	2		–
League Cup	7		3

No 77. **GARY MEGSON**
Debut: v Portsmouth, 29 October 1977
Farewell: v Brentford, 27 October 1979

Unlike Fred Binney, who made his mark at Argyle late in his career, Gary Megson is arguably the most successful product of the club's youth policy, display his skills at the highest level for a number of years.

The son of ex-Sheffield Wednesday player and Bristol Rovers manager, Don, Gary Megson was born at Wythenshawe, Manchester, on 2 May 1959. The son inherited much of his father's ability and Don had high hopes of Gary making a successful career. To this end, Megson senior approved his son participating in Argyle's superb youth policy established under Tony Waiters.

As an apprentice, Megson was housed in Elm Cottage with other young aspirants, and it is a tribute to the backroom staff of the club at that time that so many of those apprentices progressed, not only into first-team soccer with Argyle, but for some of them – such as Martin Hodge and Megson himself – into the heady heights of Division One. Megson was among the most outstanding youngsters at Argyle and was invited for England youth trials.

On the eve of his eighteenth birthday Megson signed his first professional contract. He did not have to wait long for his debut. Mike Kelly had, by this time, replaced Waiters and the side was losing frequently. The flame-haired Megson was thrown into the fray and, despite looking for all the world like a schoolboy given time off school, he soon showed that he had an old head on young shoulders. He was not overawed by League soccer and exhibited maturity beyond his years, taking control of free-kicks and giving the impression that he had been at this game for years. Operating at the heart of the midfield, he had great vision, distributed the ball well, and his long pumping stride ate up the ground. He retained his place for 28 consecutive games before, under yet another manager, Malcolm Allison, older heads were restored to the side in the bid to stave off relegation.

It was all-change the following season. Megson was back in favour and found the net in each of the first three League games. Despite his tender years, the midfield was soon built around him and other clubs were hovering like vultures. Megson missed only four games, but it was only a matter of time before money talked. It was Bobby Saxton, Megson's fourth boss in as many years, who decided to cash in on his talent, and in December 1979 he was sold to Everton for £250,000, a new record intake for an Argyle player.

The man who signed him, Gordon Lee, hoped to rejuvenate Everton with fresh young faces. Megson did not look out of place in the top division but, after Lee gave way to Howard Kendall, Megson found himself omitted.

Despite being in the reserves, Megson had no thought to leave Goodison Park, knowing that it could only be downhill from there. It was though, perhaps inevitable that sooner or later he would link up with Sheffield Wednesday, whom his father had served for many years. In August 1981, after only 23 games and three goals for Everton, Jack Charlton's Owls bought him for £130,000.

Leaving aside inevitable comparisons with his father, Megson played probably the finest football of his career at Hillsborough. Perhaps inspired by memories of being a spectator at Hillsborough as a lad, Megson became the bulwark of the midfield, playing 148 League and Cup games and scoring twenty goals. He was part of the side that won promotion in 1983-84 under Howard Wilkinson, but then rejected the offer of a new contract, believing he deserved a better deal.

In August 1984 he joined Brian Clough's Nottingham Forest in a £175,000 transfer, but the move was a personal disaster and just three months later Clough wrote off £35,000 of that sum when Megson teamed up again with Jack Charlton at Newcastle. But Megson fared little better in the North East, and 25 games and one goal was a disappointing return.

In December 1985, he was given a second chance at Sheffield Wednesday, his fee now a more modest £60,000. Megson was now back at his spiritual home, playing well, and increasing his worth on the transfer market. His price had risen to £250,000 when Mel Machin signed him for Manchester City in January 1989. Megson scored the winning goal against Oldham on his City debut and became an integral part of the midfield or, occasionally, the back four.

In August 1992 he made his final major move, joining Norwich. Now approaching the veteran stage, he played for three seasons and also took the first steps on the managerial ladder when, in January 1994, he was appointed as assistant to John Deehan.

Leaving Carrow Road in the summer of 1995, Megson's playing career drifted to a close at Lincoln City and Shrewsbury Town. It was not long before Norwich were in need of a new manager and it was to Megson that they turned. He lasted only eight months in the Norwich job before managing Blackpool for one year and Stockport County for two. Despite winning the 'manager of the month' award during his time at Edgeley Park, financial constraints meant he was often forced to sell his better players. He moved from Stockport to Stoke City, and has since been manager of West Brom, whom he guided to the verge of promotion to the Premiership.

Magic Moment: *Only ten minutes into his Argyle debut, Megson's superb crossfield pass to Brian Hall set up Argyle's first goal in a 3-1 win.*

Worst Nightmare: *The highly rated midfielder was not so highly rated at Brian Clough's Nottingham Forest, failing to make any first-team appearance during his three months at the City Ground.*

Argyle record	Appearances	Goals
Football League	78	10
FA Cup	5	–
League Cup	9	–

No 78. **KEVIN HODGES**

Debut: v Bury, 12 September 1978
Farewell: v Stockport, 20 November 1992

Kevin Hodges was a young contemporary of Gary Megson at Home Park. Hodges never experienced life in the top flight as Megson did, but nevertheless is inexorably linked with Argyle. He set an Argyle appearance record that – with the advent of freedom of contract and escalating wages – is unlikely ever to be broken.

Born at Broadwindsor in Dorset on 12 June 1960, Hodges was only eight when he represented the West Dorset under-11s. He later made the Dorset under-13s. Bournemouth signed him on schoolboy forms, and at Dean Court he joined other promising youngsters, including future internationals Kevin Reeves and Graham Roberts. Hodges did not look out of his depth and in December 1975 was selected for the FA Youth squad.

Just when it seemed Hodges was destined for stardom, Bournemouth scrapped its youth policy in a cost-cutting exercise. He had the opportunity to go to Norwich City, but one of his former Bournemouth coaches, Bobby Howe, was now in situ at Plymouth, and he persuaded him that Argyle's youth system would serve him well.

Hodges became one of a number of apprentices who graduated to the full-time professional ranks. His early managers at Home Park were Tony Waiters and Mike Kelly, but it was under caretaker boss Lennie Lawrence that he signed his professional papers in March 1978.

During his schooldays Hodges had been a winger or inside-forward, but had since been converted to full-back, where he played the majority of his games for Argyle reserves. It was as No 2 that he made his Argyle debut, shortly after his eighteenth birthday, when regular incumbent Brian Bason was injured. Occasional appearances followed until, late in the season, he played left-back under Allison's replacement, Bobby Saxton.

1979-80 saw him more or less a regular, either at right-back or as a wide midfield player, and so began a span of twelve seasons when the name of Kevin Hodges was the most familiar on the Argyle team-sheet.

It is a matter of debate as to which was Hodges' most effective position. As a youthful right-back he showed great promise. In midfield, his busyness and short-passing game was an important weapon in Argyle's strategy, but the general consensus is that he was at his best as a right-winger cum midfielder, where his speed and crossing not only created numerous chances, but also allowed him to get forward and try his luck whenever an opportunity presented itself.

It was as part of a four-man midfield that Hodges (and Argyle) reached the 1984 FA Cup semi-final, but unquestionably his best campaign came in 1985-86 under Dave Smith when Argyle won promotion from the Third Division. Hodges was a revelation. He proved to be a real 90-minute player and few full-backs ever fathomed how to stop him. He was not a winger in the conventional sense, and his style seemed uncomplicated. Blessed with close ball-control, Hodges would set off down the touchline in his familiar style, head bobbing and seemingly not looking where he was going or aware of who was around him. Just as his marker would dive in, Hodges would nick the ball away, giving him time and space to whip over a cross. There was, of course, more to his play than that, as sixteen goals in that promotion season confirmed, but he did have the knack of making football look uncomplicated. His partnership with Gordon Nisbet down the right was the focal point of Argyle's attacking strategy and at the end of that memorable season Hodges won numerous awards, including Argyle's Player of the Year and *Match Weekly* magazine's Third Division Matchman of the Year – based on performance ratings throughout the campaign. When Smith produced his 'Promotion Diary', no player earned more praise for 'effort and contribution' than Hodges.

The following season proved to be something of an anticlimax. A knee injury disrupted his pre-season preparations and eventually forced him to seek treatment at Lilleshall. Although he played in 33 League matches, the injury deprived him of pace and confidence, and his own high standards were seldom met.

Early in 1987-88, Hodges' ten-year service was rewarded with a testimonial against the team he supported as a boy, West Ham. Still only 27, Hodges had a good few years left in him. Smith left, and under Bobby Moncur's regime Hodges lost his Argyle place for the first time since his youth. He even appeared on the transfer list, with Brighton taking an interest. Displaying the grit that had served him well over the years, Hodges fought his way back into the side, this time in a more conventional midfield role.

Towards the end of 1990-91 Hodges suffered a persistent hernia problem that forced him to miss much of the following season. In January 1992 he played three matches on loan at Torquay as part of his rehabilitation, but returned to Home Park to add more appearances to his already daunting record.

In August 1992, he became one of the few players ever to be awarded a second testimonial, with Luton providing the opposition to mark Hodges' fifteen years of service. The arrival of Peter Shilton as manager sparked a clear-out, and Hodges was swept away like many others. His last Argyle appearance was as a substitute, but he had long since overtaken Sammy Black's appearance record that had stood since the 1930s. A more surprising statistic is that only seven other Argyle players have outscored Kevin Hodges!

Hodges' playing ties with the club ended in December 1992, when a free transfer took him back to Torquay. His experience was invaluable at Plainmoor, where he was appointed player-coach and youth-team manager, before replacing Eddie May as team boss. Ex-Pilgrims Garry Nelson and Steve McCall joined him to form the Gulls' managerial team.

Hodges carried Torquay to the Wembley play-offs on the back of eight consecutive wins, but lost out on promotion to Colchester. He was a popular manager with the Plainmoor faithful, but the lure of returning to Home Park as manager in succession to Mick Jones in June 1998 proved too hard to resist.

Sadly, Hodges could not reproduce his magic at Home Park. His sides played attractive football but results did not go his way and after a poor start to 2000-2001, which saw the club sliding ominously towards the foot of the Third Division, he lost his job. His reaction to his dismissal said much about his character. There was no animosity or back-stabbing. At the board meeting where he learned he had lost his job, he shook each director by the hand and wished them the best for the future. That summed up Kevin Hodges as a person, honest, loyal and a genuinely good bloke. Some would say too nice to hack it in the brutal world of football management.

Since his dismissal, Hodges has been a regular visitor to Home Park working for local radio and has also secured the role of Football in the Community Officer for Somerset FA.

Magic Moment: *Despite some resentment at his leaving Torquay as manager, a supporters' poll in a football magazine recently voted Kevin Hodges as the Gulls' best ever manager.*

Worst Nightmare: *Hodges seemed to have rescued Plymouth from defeat in the 1984 FA Cup semi-final. His left-foot shot was headed for the corner of the net, but a slight deflection off the turf saw the ball veer tantalisingly wide.*

Argyle record	Appearances	Goals
Football League	502 (+28)	81
FA Cup	38	3
League Cup	31 (+2)	–

No 78. Kevin Hodges played more games for Argyle than any other player
Here he high-steps with Swansea's Ian Callaghan

No 80. Long-serving, coach-driving
goalkeeper Geoff Crudgington

No 81. Leigh Cooper falls in a challenge with Manchester City's Paul Stewart

No 82. Gordon Nisbet gets a rub on the head after Argyle are promoted in 1985-86

No 83. Andy Rogers, Argyle's flying winger of the 1980s

No 85. Tommy Tynan, voted the most popular Pilgrim

Chapter Eight

~ *Cup Fighters* ~

No 79. **DAVID KEMP**
Debut: v Wimbledon, 15 September 1979
Farewell: v Gillingham, 10 October 1981

As with Kevin Hodges, David Kemp's career may have turned out differently had he not left his original club, Chelsea, when a schoolboy.

Born in Harrow on 29 February 1953, Kemp was signed by Chelsea on associated schoolboy terms but was released on the grounds of being too small. He joined Slough Town, and appeared on the scoresheet so frequently that in April 1975 he was back in the League, this time for Crystal Palace. Ten strikes in 32 League appearances earned him a transfer to Portsmouth in November 1976. At Fratton Park he became a hero with 32 goals in only 63 League starts but he was soon on the move again, joining Carlisle in March 1978. Goals continued to flow, prompting Bobby Saxton to pay £75,000, then an Argyle record, to bring Kemp to Home Park in September 1979. Fred Binney was on borrowed time, and with the other forward options comprising the raw Mike Trusson and Mark Graves, a proven goalscorer was a priority.

In Kemp, Saxton bought a player whose style was not dissimilar to that of Binney. A compact player, Kemp had good balance and an eye for a half-chance. He was also brave and would dive in among the flying boots, given a sniff of a goal.

His debut was the stuff of dreams. An uninspiring contest with Wimbledon was brought to life in first-half injury-time, when without thought of personal injury Kemp dived to head in Gary Megson's corner. Two minutes after the resumption Kemp converted Kevin Hodges' through ball, and the Greens went on to record a 3-0 victory.

Kemp scored in his next two matches, too, and briefly teamed up with Binney in what was a potentially lethal strike-force. Their styles, however, duplicated rather than complemented, and Binney soon stood down, then left. Kemp took time to recover from an injury sustained against Colchester, but still finished the season as Argyle's top scorer with fifteen goals, despite starting only 27 games.

1980-81 brought out the best in Kemp. Argyle stayed unbeaten for the first twelve matches, thanks largely to Kemp's ten goals in as many games. These included a hat-trick against his previous club, Carlisle. Although

Kemp grabbed the headlines, much of his success can be attributed to fellow forward John Sims, whose intelligent play created space and time for Kemp to flourish. An injury-free season saw Kemp ever present in the No 8 shirt. His final tally of 28 League and Cup goals meant that supporters did not have to waste time debating who else might be a contender for Player of the Year.

Bobby Moncur replaced Saxton for 1981-82, and for both Kemp and Argyle the consequences could not have been more different. It was not until the twelfth League match that the Pilgrims registered a win. Kemp had played in the first nine without scoring, and stepped down in favour of newly acquired Jeff Cook. Kemp was loaned out to Gillingham and Brentford, and his rapid fall from grace saw him released by Argyle at the end of the season.

The glamour of the North American Soccer League lured Kemp and he joined the Edmonton Drillers. He later played for San Jose Earthquakes and Seattle Sounders before the NASL folded. Sweden then beckoned. He became player-coach with Norrkoping and then coach to Third Division Hagahjodens.

Returning to England, Kemp passed through Slough, Crystal Palace, Wycombe, and Wimbledon before in March 1990 he successfully applied for the Argyle manager's job in succession to Ken Brown. Argyle fans welcomed the return of one of their former heroes. In the weeks available to him he did enough to ensure Division Two safety with an eight-match unbeaten run. He was, however, unable to build on these foundations. A sequence of loan signings and low-cost, second-rate buys – mainly players with little or no League experience – combined with an unappetising long-ball game and the career-ending injury to the influential Andy Thomas, did little to appease a fan base starved of success. The terrace murmurings grew louder, and, as is often the case, a star player returning as manager probably wished he had stayed away.

Kemp was dismissed in February 1992 and returned to Wimbledon in a coaching capacity. After manager Joe Kinnear suffered a heart attack at Hillsborough, Kemp and Mick Harford took joint-control of the Dons. Kemp then took a coaching post at another of his former clubs, Portsmouth, before being given the near-impossible task of keeping Oxford in the Second Division. The task proved beyond him and Kemp was duly replaced.

Magic Moment: *After completing his hat-trick his against former club, Carlisle, in September 1980, Kemp picked up the ball, stuffed it up his shirt and danced back to the halfway line.*

Worst Nightmare: *Kemp was indirectly involved in the abandonment of a League Cup-tie at Chester in September 1981. Kemp's shot was saved by Chester goalkeeper Grenville Millington, who then collided with a goalpost, snapping it near the base beyond immediate repair.*

ARGYLE RECORD	Appearances		Goals
Football League	82	(+2)	39
FA Cup	3		3
League Cup	5		2

No 80. **GEOFF CRUDGINGTON**
Debut: v Chester, 6 October 1979
Farewell: Bradford City, 20 December 1987

Geoff Crudgington was another in a line of outstanding goalkeepers who have served Plymouth Argyle over the years.

'Crudge' was born in Wolverhampton on Valentine's Day 1952. He won three England Schoolboy caps, against each of the home nations, and was signed by his home-town club. Ex-Wolves and England keeper Bert Williams was a friend of Crudgington's father, and knowing there was little chance of breaking through at Molineux he contacted Aston Villa manager Tommy Docherty. Crudgington signed full-time for Villa in September 1969.

Villa suffered the indignity of relegation to the Third Division that season. Crudge played no part, but in January 1971 debuted at Bristol Rovers, replacing first choice John Dunn, hurt in a road accident. He kept his place for a second game but, despite Villa winning both, Crudge was dropped in favour of the fit again Dunn. After that he hardly got a look in, and was farmed out to Barnsley, Bradford City, and Toronto Metros.

A move to Crewe in March 1972 brought better fortunes. In six seasons at Gresty Road, Crudgington was virtually ever present, only the after-effects of flu early in 1974 keeping him sidelined.

After 250 appearances for the Railwaymen, he signed for Swansea in 1978 for £20,000, playing in every game as the Swans gained promotion from the Third Division. Highlight of that season was a 3-1 League Cup win at Tottenham, who included newly recruited Argentinian World Cup stars Ossie Ardiles and Ricardo Villa.

Out of the blue, six matches into 1979-80, Crudgington was dropped by manager John Toshack in favour of new signing Glanville Latheran, and within weeks the Swansea discard was a Plymouth player. Bobby Saxton snapped him up for £40,000. The departure of Martin Hodge had left Argyle short of an experienced No 1. Crudgington went straight into the first team.

He was consistency personified, appearing in 165 consecutive League and Cup matches. In his first five seasons at Home Park he played in all but two games. There were several highs along the way, including an appearance in the FA Cup semi-final and being an ever present in the promotion season of 1985-86.

Not given to theatricals, Crudgington nevertheless possessed a solid, all-round game. He had no real weaknesses: he displayed good handling skills, was an excellent shot-stopper, and positioned himself well. Temperamentally, he was a calm and assuring figure at the back, lending confidence to his defenders.

But goalkeeping is a hazardous occupation, as Crudgington experienced on more than one occasion. On New Year's Day 1986, he dived at a Cardiff forward's feet. The head-wound required a dozen stitches and was described by manager Dave Smith as 'the worst injury of that type that I have seen'.

Crudgington exhibited bravery of a different sort in February 1983. Argyle were due to host Bradford City. Discovering a pan of burning fat at his house, he threw the pan out of the back door, but the flames blew back, melting his sweater and inflicting second degree burns to his waist and back. He reported to the ground as usual and received treatment to his burns. With Crudgington's participation in doubt, full-back Gordon Nisbet prepared to don the keeper's jersey, with manager Bobby Moncur set to name himself as substitute. Defying his pain, Crudgington insisted he was up to playing and did. Argyle won 3-1.

Another 'scare' took place following an away fixture. The team had stopped at a service station. Back on board the coach, Crudgington's team-mates were amazed to see him take the wheel and drive it back to Plymouth. After the initial panic, they learned that Crudgington had for many years held the appropriate licence, and whilst at Crewe had driven heavy trucks. During the summer months it was not unusual to see him driving coaches for Wallace Arnold.

Back on the pitch, Crudgington was appointed captain under Moncur, the first goalkeeper to be so honoured on a regular basis at Argyle since the days of Fred Craig in the 1920s. The beginning of the end of Crudgington's Argyle career came in January 1987. Despite being in his mid-30s he had remained first choice for most of that season, but was controversially dropped for an FA Cup-tie at Arsenal, with Steve Cherry taking over. On reflection it was a good game to miss, as the Gunners blasted Plymouth 6-1, but Cherry was not scapegoated and retained his place for the remainder of the season. In 1987-88 Crudgington remain second choice, playing only seven times before calling time on a career that had seen him make more than 650 appearances in total.

After playing and managing Millbrook in the South Western League and working for an electrical company, Crudgington returned to Argyle as youth-team and reserve-team coach. He is still a familiar figure at Home Park, where he now undertakes the dual role of Football in the Community Officer and goalkeeping coach.

A useful cricketer, he played for Staffordshire County juniors in his younger days and for many years has also swung the willow for Tavistock.

Magic Moment: *Crudgington led out Argyle for his testimonial against a star-studded Spurs side including Gary Lineker and Paul Gascoigne. The evening was made even more memorable when Crudgington was left flat-footed by a superb Gascoigne free-kick.*

Worst Nightmare: *At struggling Bolton in September 1984, Crudge inexplicably attempted to kick clear from Warren Joyce. He kicked air instead to give Bolton an early lead. Argyle collapsed and lost 2-7. Having conceded five goals, Crudgington broke his hand, forcing his withdrawal.*

ARGYLE RECORD	Appearances	Goals
Football League	326	–
FA Cup	28	–
League Cup	20	–

No 81. **LEIGH COOPER**
Debut: v Colchester, 24 November 1979
Farewell: v Stoke, 17 March 1990

One of the defenders to benefit from Crudgington's experience was Leigh Cooper, whose Argyle career was cut short by injury at a relatively early age. Had fortune favoured him, he might have threatened Kevin Hodges' appearance record.

Cooper was born on 7 May 1961 a stone's throw from Reading's former ground at Elm Park and was discovered by Argyle scout Micky Hill. Cooper became an apprentice, joining John Uzzell and Kevin Hodges. Having been part of the Argyle side that won the South West and Wales Youth League, Cooper was one of a number of youngsters from that team offered a professional contract, which he signed on his eighteenth birthday.

He did not have long to wait for first-team action. He was a non-playing substitute at home to Rotherham in October 1979, but a month later was among the starting eleven for an FA Cup-tie at Colchester. He held his place in the Argyle midfield for sixteen games before he was left out to accommodate the return from injury of David Kemp.

Those early games showed that Cooper had what it takes, and the following season he established himself on the left of midfield, until injury against Portsmouth ended his season early.

For the next three seasons Cooper was rarely out of the side and his busy style made him an important cog in the Argyle engine room. When John Hore arrived as manager, Cooper volunteered to captain the side and, at the age of 22, became one of the youngest skippers in League football.

Not even Cooper could have envisaged that, a few months later, he would be leading out Argyle for an FA Cup semi-final. Much press attention focused on the young captain. He handled the pressure well and was far from overawed in the game itself. The occasion was soured – not only by the result, which left him so distraught that he dashed for the dressing room without shaking hands with officials or opponents – but also by the fact that it was his stray pass that led to the only goal.

Whether or not Cooper suffered an adverse reaction, the following season – under first Hore, and then Dave Smith – saw him so under par that he became a target for the Home Park boo-boys.

It was Dave Smith who transformed Cooper's fortunes when, early the following year, he played him at left-back. A stranger to Home Park would have thought he had played there all his career, for he slotted into the position like a glove, putting his speed, distribution, and tackling to good use. He would overlap at every opportunity and his left-flank partnership with Garry Nelson was one of the most prominent features of that promotion season. Cooper continued to perform admirably at No 3 for three seasons, winning rave reviews and adapting quickly to the demands of Division Two soccer. His ex-apprentice colleague, John Uzzell, could not force his way back, and Cooper was grateful that pre-season transfer talks linking him with Orient had come to nothing.

At the age of 27 Cooper's ten years with Argyle were marked by a testimonial against First Division Coventry in August 1988. A few months later, in a match at Portsmouth, he broke his leg. His season was finished, and so began the long haul back to fitness.

Cooper suffered setbacks along the way. He tried to come back too prematurely, which only put him out for longer. Eventually, after fifteen months out, he made a welcome return at Port Vale. Sadly, only one other first-team appearance followed. The club sensed he would never be as good as he once was, and released him on a free transfer at the end of that season.

Having experienced the glamour of the FA Cup and the thrill of promotion, Cooper now experienced football on the other side of the tracks. He joined Aldershot, whose financial plight meant players and staff never knew if they would get paid or not. Cooper spent eighteen months with the Shots, playing 33 League matches and scoring twice, before the inevitable happened. The club folded mid-season, Cooper playing in Aldershot's valedictory League match, at Cardiff.

Having retained his house in Plymouth, Cooper returned to live in the city. He played for Truro City before a second broken leg caused him to say enough was enough. He subsequently managed the Cornish club and led them to two league championships and two Senior Cups. He took over the reins at Saltash United before moving to his present club, Holsworthy, whose fortunes he has transformed.

Cooper has for several years worked for a training and development company in Plymouth.

Magic Moment: *A rare Cooper goal gave him particular pleasure, as it was at Reading, his home-town club, in January 1982.*

Worst Nightmare: *Cooper's goal tally could have been better. He hit the woodwork in his first League match, and in his second, and in his third.*

ARGYLE RECORD	Appearances		Goals
Football League	316	(+7)	15
FA Cup	31		2
League Cup	20		–

82. GORDON NISBET
Debut: v Barnsley, 10 January 1981
Farewell: v Derby, 9 May 1987

Leigh Cooper's fellow full-back during the promotion season was Gordon Nisbet, who is undoubtedly a candidate for a place in a greatest ever Argyle XI.

Nisbet was born on 18 September 1951 at Wallsend-on-Tyne, an area that has produced many great players over the years. Despite selection for Northumberland Schools, Nisbet was overlooked by North Eastern clubs and at the age of sixteen joined West Brom.

At the time, Nisbet was a goalkeeper and it was in this position that he debuted against Coventry in August 1969. The experience was not a happy one, with Willie Carr scoring a hat-trick in the Sky Blues' 3-1 win. Nisbet was generally third-choice keeper behind John Osborne and Jim Cumbes, and, as such, played a number of second and third team matches as an outfield player.

His second League appearance had to wait until December 1971, but this time he was wearing No 2. When Don Howe took charge at the Hawthorns, Nisbet caught his eye, and he was used as a utility player. Eventually, however, he settled into the right-back berth and was rewarded in 1972 with an England Under-23 cap.

After Nisbet had spent four seasons as a first-team regular, clocking up 170 games, new manager Johnny Giles bought Irish international Paddy Mulligan and dumped Nisbet into the reserves. In September 1976 he signed for Hull for £30,000. The Tigers got value for money, with Nisbet playing over 200 games for them. The departure from Hull of manager Billy Bremner ushered in a merry-go-round of managerial appointments, but nothing could prevent relegation to the Fourth Division looming large. Nisbet wanted out, and with Hull needing money to buy someone who could score goals, he accepted a move to Devon. Bobby Saxton signed him for Argyle in December 1980 for a fee of £32,000.

Nisbet was a welcome addition to the Argyle squad in which the full-back positions had been a problem ever since an early season injury to John Uzzell. Nisbet was immediately handed the No 2 shirt, and laid claim to it for the next six and a half seasons, during which he missed only twelve League and Cup matches.

Although principally a defender, the enduring image of Gordon Nisbet is of him flying up the right wing on an overlap. His forceful running would see his moustachioed figure attack at every opportunity. Naturally, his attacking instincts at times left his defensive position exposed, but his speed, determination and strong tackling usually made amends. He was regarded by many as the best full-back in the Third Division, a fact reflected in his regular selection for the PFA divisional sides voted by fellow professionals. Other clubs were said to be interested in buying him, but Nisbet had no intention of leaving the club or the area.

Every now and again Nisbet would treat the Argyle faithful to a goal, usually from long range. Having scored only one League goal in his pre-Argyle career, his tally of seventeen for the Pilgrims showed a startling improvement.

At Home Park, Nisbet finally enjoyed the success that had eluded him beforehand. He played in every round of the 1983-84 FA Cup campaign, including the victory at West Brom, which gave him great personal satisfaction, and the semi-final at Villa Park, where he was asked to mark Watford's John Barnes. He was also ever present in the promotion season of 1985-86, when under Dave Smith he produced probably the best football of his career.

Given his early exploits between the posts, Nisbet was asked to deputise on those rare times when injury forced the early withdrawal of Geoff Crudgington. Nisbet would be the first to admit that these occasions only served to remind him how wise he was in converting to an outfield player. Two such occasions spring readily to mind. On New Year's Day 1986 Crudgington was forced to leave the field with a head wound. Within a minute of Nisbet donning his jersey he was picking the ball out of the net. That game ended 4-4. Again, in September 1984 Crudgington was injured at Bolton. Argyle were already trailing 2-5, and Nisbet was unable to prevent two further goals in the last fifteen minutes. One of these was a tame 20-yarder that squeezed under his body.

At the end of 1986-87 Smith made the difficult decision to release Nisbet. Despite approaching his 36th birthday, he was thought by many fans to have a bit more juice in the tank, a view shared by Exeter boss Terry Cooper, who snapped him up on a free transfer. After just fourteen games for the Grecians, injury forced Nisbet's retirement from League football after a career spanning almost 700 games.

Nisbet thereafter played for Ottery St Mary and for a local pub side in the Plymouth Sunday League. Your author's chief claim to fame in his modest playing career is attempting to man-mark the former England Under-23 international and failing wretchedly, leaving the field at the end of a humbling 90 minutes in awe of how easy a 40-year-old 'has been' could make the game look.

A return to Home Park awaited Nisbet under David Kemp. He ran the youth and reserve sides for three years, and even had an autumn day in the sun when coming on as a substitute for Argyle's reserves against Welton Rovers. Nisbet claimed a goal in a 5-0 victory.

Since then, Nisbet has been a police officer with the Devon and Cornwall constabulary. He continued to play and manage the police side and still turns out for the ex-Argyle side in charity matches.

Magic Moment: *Nisbet gained revenge on his former club West Brom. At Home Park in November 1986, he scored the only goal of the match, a 25-yard piledriver following Leigh Cooper's free-kick.*

Worst Nightmare: *In what turned out to be his last League match, at Scarborough, Exeter's Nisbet tore knee ligaments. A quick look at his leg told him his playing days were over.*

ARGYLE RECORD	Appearances	Goals
Football League	281	14
FA Cup	23	–
League Cup	18	3

No 83. **ANDY ROGERS**
Debut: v Reading, 29 September 1981
Farewell: v Newport County, 6 May 1985

Another hero of the 1984 FA Cup semi-final side was winger Andy Rogers, who – in large part due to one special goal during that cup run – has cemented his place in Argyle history.

Born in Chatteris, Cambridgeshire, on 1 December 1956, Rogers began with Chatteris Town before joining Peterborough United in July 1976. In three seasons at London Road he made just 25 appearances and seemed lost to League soccer when he decided to train as a teacher and play part-time with Hampton. But the offer of a second chance, this time with Southampton, was too good to turn down and, with studies abandoned, he signed for the Saints in February 1980.

These were exciting times at The Dell, with Kevin Keegan, Peter Osgood and Mick Channon strutting their stuff. Whilst the presence of such (fading) stars was great from the fans' point of view, it meant the likes of Rogers were generally restricted to reserve-team football and during his time at The Dell he played only five first-team games, all of them as substitute.

Back at Argyle, the enforced retirement of Brian Johnson meant that the club was short of a specialist winger. The gap was filled in September 1981 when Bobby Moncur brought Rogers to Home Park, initially on a two-month loan. Rogers' arrival, coupled with that of Jeff Cook shortly afterwards, brought about a transformation in fortunes, following a dreadful start, and no doubt encouraged Moncur to make the move permanent. Rogers' fee, £50,000, was not an inconsiderable one, given his relative inexperience.

He played in every remaining match of that season, his slender frame weaving magic on either flank and creating chances for his fellow forwards. At only 5ft 7in and weighing less than 10st, speed was his principal asset. Although he could drift out of games if the mood wasn't with him, defenders had to be on their guard as one flash of inspiration could conjure a goal.

Rogers was now more or less in permanent possession of the No 11 shirt. He was not a heavy scorer himself, but did contribute the occasional important goal. None more so than during the 1983-84 Cup run. Having reached the third round, Argyle hoped for glamour opposition and huge gate receipts. Instead, they were paired at home with Third Division rivals Newport. Two goals from John Aldridge, the first after Rogers fluffed a clearance in his own penalty area, earned Newport a replay, where Rogers' solitary goal saw Argyle through. Following wins over Darlington and West Brom, the Pilgrims finally got their dream quarter-final tie when Derby County were drawn to visit Home Park.

Over 34,000 packed into Home Park to see Argyle win on points but not on goals. The game ended scoreless and most die-hard supporters believed the run was over. Four days later hundreds of Argyle fans squeezed into one end of the Baseball Ground to witness their heroes do battle against an array of international stars. After seventeen minutes Argyle won a corner in front of their fans. Rogers, as he did week in, week out, trotted over to take the kick. If there is such a thing as a perfect corner-kick, this was it. His right-footed, inswinging cross floated into the area. Derby keeper Steve Cherry, who years later would be an Argyle hero at Wembley, came to collect the ball. Instead, all he grabbed was a fistful of cold night air as it sailed over him into the net. Argyle somehow hung on for 73 minutes and, unbelievably, the struggling Third Division side were now just one match away from an FA Cup final.

The semi-final saw Rogers at his best. He teased and tormented the Watford defence all afternoon but was unable to provide the breakthrough Argyle needed to cancel out George Reilly's early header.

After Hore's departure, weeks into the new season, Rogers kept his place under new manager Dave Smith, but that summer felt it was time to move on. He signed for Reading for £15,000, scoring five goals in 44 matches before moving again, in October 1986, to his final League club, Southend. After two seasons at Roots Hall he called time on his League career and went into the probation service.

Rogers' love of the West Country never waned and he has recently relocated to Devon. Now living in Totnes, he works for the probation service in Torquay.

Magic Moment: *Rogers was thrust into the media spotlight to talk through his 'wonder' Cup goal at Derby. The hacks expected tales of endless practice. Instead Rogers admitted 'it was a fluke'. In fact he had been practising corners the previous* *day on a local school pitch, but had been so bad that manager Johnny Hore called a halt!*

Worst Nightmare: *Playing for Reading at Swansea, Rogers made headlines for other reasons. He clashed heads, knocked himself out and swallowed his tongue. Physio Glen Hunter came to the rescue.*

ARGYLE RECORD	Appearances		Goals
Football League	159	(+4)	15
FA Cup	17		3
League Cup	6		—

No 84. **GORDON STANIFORTH**
Debut: v Oxford, 26 March 1983
Farewell: v Millwall, 11 May 1985

Gordon Staniforth was another thorn in Watford's side during that epic FA Cup semi-final. Staniforth was an immensely popular player during his brief stay at Home Park.

Born in Hull on 23 March 1957, Staniforth was a boyhood regular on the Hull City terraces and was hugely thrilled to be taken on as a schoolboy. With professional coaching, he gained England Schoolboy honours and signed professionally with Hull in April 1974. An early League debut turned to frustration. In two and a half years he was restricted to twelve appearances, five as a substitute, scoring twice.

Late in 1976 he was offloaded to York for £7,500. This was a bargain as far as York were concerned, with Staniforth finishing as leading scorer during his two full seasons with the club. Bigger fish were watching, chequebooks ready. Carlisle won the race, having money to burn following the sale of players, including David Kemp to Argyle. Bobby Moncur, then Carlisle manager, splashed out a record £120,000 for his new acquisition, who teamed up with future star (and later best man at his wedding) Peter Beardsley.

Used primarily on the wing, Staniforth did well with Carlisle in 1981-82. The club finished runners-up in Division Three, assisted by winning 3-1 at home to Argyle – Staniforth notching all three.

By this time, Bob Stokoe had taken charge at Brunton Park, and, hoping to repeat the success of the 1970s when Carlisle briefly headed the First Division, brought in new players. Staniforth was allowed to leave, and teamed up with Bobby Moncur at Argyle in a swap with defender Mike McCartney.

Despite being unable to rediscover his scoring boots, 'Stani' – who once described his biggest thrill as 'waking up in the morning' – soon became a favourite with the Argyle fans, who loved his non-stop running, clever use of the ball and infectious enthusiasm. With his droopy moustache and mass of curly hair – reminiscent of the most famous perm in football, that of Staniforth's favourite player, Kevin Keegan – Stani would not have looked out of place sporting a sombrero and strumming a guitar.

The arrival of Tommy Tynan for the start of 1983-84 brought out the best in Staniforth. Whilst they did not prove, that season, especially prolific in front of goal, they linked up well, especially so during the famous Cup run. It was Staniforth's late fourth round winner against Darlington that maintained the momentum. For Stani, that goal came as a welcome relief, not only for taking Argyle through to round five, but for ending his seven-game goal drought. He had become so frustrated at his wayward shooting that, against Darlington, he donned a new pair of boots in the hope that his luck would change.

After the euphoria of the cup run, it was back to the bread and butter of the League. 1984-85 saw Tynan take all the plaudits for his scoring exploits, thanks, in no small part, to his blossoming partnership with Staniforth.

That season saw the expiry of Staniforth's contract. Unhappy with the new terms on offer, he moved to Newport County in a player-swap deal that saw Steve Cooper arrive at Home Park. Thirteen goals, 87 appearances, and two seasons at Newport ended with a free transfer. County were sinking under their financial burden and had to offload.

At the relatively young age of 30, Staniforth built a future for himself as a publican in York, and reacquainted himself with York City, playing nineteen matches in 1987-88 on a non-contract basis. In time he became Football in the Community Officer at Bootham Crescent, and helped to run its social club. His present capacity is as coach to York's youth team.

As a sad footnote, Staniforth's son Tom became a promising professional at Sheffield Wednesday. In August 2001, Tom died at the age of twenty.

Magic Moment: *Despite other players grabbing the headlines during Argyle's FA Cup exploits in 1983-84, Staniforth was rewarded with the Argyle Player of the Year trophy.*

Worst Nightmare: *Few fans present at the FA Cup quarter-final with Derby will forget Staniforth's 20-yard shot that hit both posts. Opposing keeper Steve Cherry* *palmed the shot onto one post. The ball bounced along the goal-line and rebounded out from the other.*

ARGYLE RECORD	Appearances		Goals
Football League	87	(+4)	19
FA Cup	10	(+1)	2
League Cup	8		3

No 85. **TOMMY TYNAN**
Debut: v Wigan, 27 August 1983
Final Farewell: v Watford, 28 April 1990

Partnering Gordon Staniforth up front in that memorable FA Cup semi-final in 1984 was ace goalscorer Tommy Tynan, a man who will go down as a true legend in Argyle history and certainly the club's most popular player of the last 25 years.

Tynan was born in Liverpool on 17 November 1955. His father's soccer career was restricted to Sunday league level, but Tynan and brother Bobby – who played for Tranmere and Blackpool – both became professional footballers.

Tynan began his soccer career in an unusual way. The *Liverpool Echo* launched a Search for a Star competition. Children were invited to collect tokens in order to enter a competition for trials with Liverpool. Tynan, along with 10,000 other teenagers, collected his tokens and played a few matches. Eventually, the wannabes were whittled down to 22 and were invited to a trial at Liverpool's training ground, Melwood, overseen by Bill Shankly. Tynan's team won 5-3. It was little wonder that with Tynan scoring all five goals, he was invited for further trials. Having attained the age of sixteen, he signed as an apprentice.

In his first season at Anfield, Tynan played in the FA Youth Cup final, where Liverpool were beaten by Aston Villa. At the age of seventeen, he signed as a professional and was playing, and scoring, regularly in the Liverpool 'A' team. Notwithstanding a run of thirteen goals in five games, he was unable to break into the reserve side, such was the strength in depth of the Liverpool squad.

His manager of the time, Bob Paisley, loaned him to Swansea to get League experience, and it was at Doncaster Rovers' Belle Vue ground in October 1975 that Tynan's long career began. Of course, he scored on his debut, although Swansea were defeated 1-2.

After six games, Tynan returned to Liverpool. That summer he went to the USA to play for Dallas, and on his return was offered by Liverpool a new two-year contract. But having sampled League football, Tynan felt disillusioned by the prospect of returning to the reserves, and sought to move. Len Ashurst's Sheffield Wednesday bought him for £10,000. Tynan took the transition to League football in his stride, scoring fifteen goals in his first season at Hillsborough. With Jack Charlton taking over, Tynan scored 21 in his next season, clinching the Owls' Player of the Year award. But Tynan and Charlton did not see eye to eye and Tynan left Hillsborough for Lincoln City in October 1978 for a fee of £33,000.

The move to Sincil Bank was disastrous. The man who bought him, Willie Bell, left the club a few days later and his successor, Colin Murphy, wasn't Tynan's greatest fan. A four-month spell at the club saw him play just nine first-team matches, despite scoring goals for a pastime in the reserves, including a run of eighteen in six games.

It was Len Ashurst who rescued Tynan from oblivion and possible retirement. Ashurst was, by then, manager of Newport County and a fee of £25,000 took Tynan to South Wales. It was here that he first made a name for himself. Top scorer for two seasons, Tynan's goals helped Newport to promotion and victory in the 1980 Welsh Cup, which granted a place in the European Cup-Winners' Cup the following season. Tynan teamed up with John Aldridge to form one of the most lethal goalscoring combinations in the lower divisions and helped Newport reach the quarter-finals before bowing out on aggregate to the East Germans of Carl Zeiss Jena. Tynan played in an unfamiliar role in the early rounds but the success of that cup run thrust him and Aldridge into the spotlight.

Financially, Newport always lived on the edge. Players were sold to keep afloat, and Tynan's association with Plymouth began in August 1983 when Bobby Moncur bought him for £55,000.

Looking back, Tynan's early days at Home Park produced one of the most barren spells in his career. In his first fifteen games, he only managed to find the net twice. The team was losing and in September Moncur was replaced by Johnny Hore. League form did not pick up, but this was overshadowed by the FA Cup run. Tynan finished as top scorer with sixteen League and Cup goals, which, far more importantly, saved Argyle from relegation.

Feeble League form the following season cost Hore his job. Dave Smith, the new man at the helm, seemed to inspire Tynan to even greater things. Barely a week passed without T Tynan appearing in the goalscoring column. Not for many a year had Argyle fans witnessed an out and out goalpoacher in prime form. Tynan missed only one game that season and finished with 32 League and Cup goals and a host of awards, including Argyle's Player of the Year and the Golden Boot as the division's top marksman.

Instead of breaking the bank to keep him, as the fans wanted, the club offered Tynan what he considered to be less than fair deal. Added to which, his wife hankered after a move back to Yorkshire. To the mortification of Argyle fans, there was no Tommy Tynan occupying the No 9 shirt when 1985-86 kicked off. A summer move to Rotherham for a paltry £25,000 had assuaged both his financial expectations and his wife's home-sickness.

Seventeen goals in 36 League and Cup games was a reasonable return at Rotherham, but reports of a training ground bust-up with team-mate Phil Crosby saw manager Norman Hunter banish Tynan to the reserves. This happened on the eve of the transfer deadline. The soccer grapevine went into full swing with no less than nine clubs trying to get him on loan, whether to try to secure promotion or avert relegation. But it was Dave Smith who pulled off a masterstroke by bringing Tynan back to Home Park.

Argyle's promotion bid had blossomed in the weeks prior to Tynan's second coming, but no one could have predicted the events of the next few weeks, except perhaps Gordon Nisbet, who famously remarked: 'No one will be more pleased than me if Tommy can score ten goals and we win promotion.'

Tynan's first scheduled appearance was on Easter Monday against Bristol City. But the game was washed out. This proved a blessing in disguise as Tynan's transfer had not been registered in time for him to play.

Few Argyle fans will forget those last nine games of the season. With Nisbet considering a second career as a clairvoyant, Tynan *did* score ten goals and Argyle *did* win promotion. This was not achieved without controversy, as two of Tynan's goals came against the team that he still actually belonged to, Rotherham, who were despatched back to Yorkshire with a 4-0 defeat. Hunter complained that 'his' player should not have played under a gentleman's agreement, of which Dave Smith denied all knowledge.

Promotion was confirmed in the last home match of the season, the re-arranged visit of Bristol City. Tynan's 32nd-minute strike set up a 4-0 victory, and for good measure he added the last goal, a header, to round off an unforgettable evening at Home Park.

Tynan was back with Rotherham for the new season and rewarded them with two goals in the first four games. Smith monitored the situation and eventually brokered a deal that even the Argyle directors were unaware of. In the middle of a board meeting, Smith walked in, introduced Tynan as his new signing, and walked out. Argyle repaid Rotherham the fee of £25,000 and, much to the delight of everyone at Home Park, Tynan was once again an Argyle player.

He was soon back in the scoring groove, finishing as top scorer with nineteen goals. Tallies of seventeen, 26 (including all four against Blackburn in November 1988), and eighteen over the next three seasons saw him establish himself as one of the all-time Argyle greats. An instinctive predator, there was more to Tynan's game than finding the back of the net. Though not tall or big-boned, he could lead the line superbly, always making himself available to receive passes and laying the ball off to colleagues. In the box he was deadly. Close control and a quick turn often created chances out of nothing. Passionate about the game, he was for a while Argyle's captain, but wearing his heart on his sleeve his mouth occasionally got him into trouble with referees.

For Tynan, life revolved around scoring goals. A conscientious trainer, he kept himself remarkably fit and his appearance record, considering the treatment handed out to him by desperate defenders, almost defies belief.

Tynan's almost metronomic supply of goals saw him rise to third in the all-time list of Argyle goalscorers, as well as complete a hat-trick of Player of the Year awards. His one regret was that the opportunity to play at the highest level had passed him by. Given the accomplishments of his former Newport team-mate, John Aldridge, who became a star at Liverpool, Real Sociedad, and for the Republic of Ireland, there is little doubt that Tynan could have done the business in the First Division. Ipswich were known to be watching him closely, and another, unnamed, top division club were said to be on the brink of signing him. The deal collapsed due to their manager returning late from holiday.

The end of 1989-90 saw Tynan out of contract. The opportunity to team up with Dave Smith at Torquay as player-coach was too good to miss, particularly as Tynan had ambitions to go into management. His departure from Argyle coincided with publication of his autobiography, *A Life at the Soccer Factory*, which gave a fascinating insight into Tynan's career and his forthright views on issues and personalities within the game.

Things went well at Plainmoor and Tynan showed that he had still not lost the goal-touch. In late October, against Carlisle, he scored the 300th goal of his career. Tynan's goals helped the Gulls into the play-offs and Torquay became the first side to win a Wembley play-off in a penalty shoot-out against Blackpool. Tynan, however, missed out on an appearance at the Twin Towers. An off-field incident with a team-mate, the details of which have never been revealed, led to his contract being paid up after one year.

In July 1991 Tynan signed for Doncaster but eventually faded from the League scene. A brief spell in America followed, before he returned to these shores to become landlord of a Sheffield pub.

The prodigal son returned to the city of Plymouth to become the landlord of the Golden Hind public house. He was back in the limelight when, in October 1997, he fronted the 'Pilgrims for the People' campaign which hoped to form a consortium to buy out chairman Dan McAuley. The bid failed, but Tynan did return to Home Park a few months later when he was appointed commercial manager. Never far from controversy, Tynan resigned from that post in June 1999, having taken over the nearby Stoke Social Club. 'Conflicts of interest' were cited as his reason for leaving.

Tynan remains the proprietor of that establishment but still occasionally turns out in the green of Argyle in charity games for the ex-players team. He still loves scoring and shows no mercy on hapless opponents.

Tommy Tynan's memory will live on in Argyle for many years to come. Even today, as a chance goes begging, someone in the crowd will invariably say 'Tommy wouldn't have missed that one'.

Magic Moment: *In 1999, Tynan received one vote in Argyle's Player of the Year competition, nine years after his last appearance.*

Worst Nightmare: *After scoring all four of Argyle's goals against Blackburn, the match ball was kicked out of the ground and seemed lost forever. A few days later, however, it was returned to the offices of a local newspaper and Tynan was reunited with the souvenir.*

ARGYLE RECORD	Appearances	Goals
Football League	261	126
FA Cup	23	6
League Cup	17	6

No 86. **ADRIAN BURROWS**

Debut: v Burnley, 25 August 1984
Farewell: v Burnley, 15 May 1994

Adrian Burrows missed out on the FA Cup glory, having joined Argyle in July 1984. Born at Sutton-in-Ashfield, near Nottingham, on 16 January 1959, Burrows' father, Horace, had been an outstanding pre-war footballer for Mansfield and Sheffield Wednesday, with whom he won an FA Cup winners medal in 1935. He was also selected on three occasions for England. Adrian was only ten years old when his father died.

At the age of ten, Burrows was made captain of his school side, despite the fact that he was the midget of the team. While at Quarrydale Comprehensive he captained Nottingham Schools. Physically, he was a late developer but, by the time he joined Hillock Pathfinders in the Mansfield youth league, one of his team-mates was the future Coventry goalkeeper, Steve Ogrizovic.

Mansfield Town initially turned Burrows down on account of his size. But he was invited back for evening training and was eventually signed by manager Billy Bingham on a full-time basis in May 1979. Less than a year later he debuted at Sheffield United and gave a 'man of the match' performance in central defence. He soon became a regular for the Stags, and in three seasons with the club made 77 (plus one sub) appearances, scoring six goals.

When Burrows' contract came up for renewal, Mansfield were in financial difficulty and offered him reduced terms. He signed for Northampton and rarely missed a game, adding another 88 appearances and four goals to his record, but felt that the Cobblers lacked ambition.

Burrows took a chance by writing to Argyle manager, John Hore, enquiring over a possible move to Plymouth, and was invited down for a two-week trial. Burrows was given the nickname 'Shades' by Chris Harrison, as he arrived at Home Park wearing a distinctive pair of sunglasses.

Still only in his mid-20s, and with considerable experience behind him, Burrows' two-week trial was extended to a two-month loan, and then a permanent deal worth £10,000 to Northampton.

The new League campaign started disappointingly and soon cost Hore his job. Dave Smith stepped into the breach, but Burrows kept his place in the side, making 38 League appearances in his first season in Argyle green.

The following two seasons saw Burrows in and out of the side in the face of stiff competition from other central defenders – Gerry McElhinney and Clive Goodyear. When Mark Smith and Nicky Law later joined, it seemed Burrows' days were numbered. In September 1987 he went on loan to Southend. He helped the Shrimpers to a two-legged Littlewoods Cup triumph over First Division Derby, Peter Shilton and all. Southend offered £40,000 for Burrows' services and Dave Smith advised Burrows to sign, but the player decided to fight for his place at Home Park.

Injuries to others saw Burrows drafted into the Argyle side at Oldham. The Pilgrims won 1-0 and the side was unchanged for the next game. Determined not to lose his place, Burrows gave such commanding displays at the heart of the defence that it was impossible to leave him out. He never shirked a tackle, read situations well, and was good in the air. He was also quick, able to use the ball intelligently, and used his aerial power to occasionally score useful goals from set pieces.

For two seasons from 1989 he missed only one match. It was not until 1991-92, when Argyle were relegated from Division Two and managers were coming and going by the month, that he found himself no longer an automatic selection. Nevertheless, he was still an invaluable member of the squad and another new contract saw him complete ten years service, which was rewarded by a testimonial in July 1993.

Under Peter Shilton, Argyle reached the Division Two play-offs in May 1994. Although Burrows did not know it at the time, the first leg at Burnley – ironically, where he had begun his Argyle career – was to be his last appearance in a green shirt. Having been booked earlier in the game, a handball was awarded against Burrows and a red card shown for the first time in his long career. Even die-hard Burnley fans thought the decision harsh.

With Burrows suspended for the home leg, Argyle lost out to Burnley and to promotion. When the retained list was announced, the name of Adrian Burrows was not on it. He stepped down to non-league Saltash United and also captained the Cornwall County side. He then had one final season at Taunton Town.

These days, he lives in Exeter, where he previously worked for Tesco, and is now employed as a postman. He admits to still closely following the fortunes of the Pilgrims.

Magic Moment: *Burrows walked out at Home Park to receive the applause at his testimonial match against his father's former side, Sheffield Wednesday.*

Worst Nightmare: *In January 1989 Home Park was packed for the visit of Everton. After taking a shock lead, Argyle were pulled back by handball against Burrows. TV replays later showed he had been shoved illegally before his arm accidentally touched the ball.*

ARGYLE RECORD	Appearances		Goals
Football League	272	(+5)	14
FA Cup	19	(+1)	–
League Cup	18	(+1)	–

No 87. **KEVIN SUMMERFIELD**
Debut: v Millwall, 22 December 1984
Farewell: v Wolves 22 September 1991

Late in 1984, Adrian Burrows was joined at Argyle by another Midlander, Kevin Summerfield, a player who gave sterling service to several clubs, but remarkably, never cost a penny in transfer fees during the whole of his career.

Born at Walsall on 7 January 1959, Summerfield began as an apprentice at West Brom in 1976 and was a member of their FA Youth Cup winning team in his first season. Progressing to professional status two years later, he soon earned a place on the England Youth tour to Belgium and Monaco. He won a total of six international caps at that level.

1978-79 saw Summerfield's League debut against Derby. Despite scoring four goals in seven (plus four sub) appearances, those games were spread over a four-year period and, with a large squad to choose from, the Baggies free-transferred him to Birmingham in May 1982. His debut for the Blues brought a 1-5 drubbing at Norwich. Three days later Summerfield came on as substitute at West Ham. This time the score was even worse, 0-5.

Again, Summerfield found himself on the fringes of the first team. One of his better performances came in an FA Cup replay with Walsall. Coming off the bench, he scored the only goal of the game in extra-time, and a few weeks later was playing for the club of his birthplace, once again on a free transfer.

Up to that point he had made no more than a handful of League appearances in six years as a professional. All of a sudden he was a first-team regular. The highlight of Summerfield's time at Walsall was a two-legged League Cup semi-final against Liverpool, which saw the Reds come out on top, 4-2 on aggregate.

In July 1984 he was on the move again, this time to Cardiff City, but after only six months at Ninian Park he became Dave Smith's first signing for Argyle, putting pen to paper on the day before his debut.

Summerfield took time to settle at Home Park and was not helped by an injury that sidelined him for the early part of 1985-86. Smith deployed him in a more withdrawn midfield role, as opposed to his earlier days in the forward line. After taking a while to adapt to his new position, he showed Argyle fans what the astute Smith had seen in him.

Tall and upright, the moustachioed Summerfield's ultra slim body would glide gracefully through the midfield. His spindly legs seemed inadequate to withstand the kicking they took, and whilst he suffered his share of injuries, these could be attributed to the kind of tackling that would incapacitate any player. Tackling was not Summerfield's strong point and at times he would frustrate manager and fans alike by drifting along in a world of his own, but he was always capable of turning a match with one pass or a mazy run which would see him ghost past opponents.

Summerfield started 21 games during that promotion season, scoring seven vital goals. The step up to Division Two held no fears for him and during this period he played as well as he had ever done. And none better than in the FA Cup fourth round replay at Everton in January 1989. Summerfield had dominated the midfield exchanges before a 'challenge' by Graeme Sharp left him crumpled on the ground, one of his wafer thin legs broken by the force of the tackle. Although Sharp went unpunished, the nature of the tackle incensed Argyle players and fans alike.

Although he fought his way back to fitness, Summerfield was never the same as he was, and he appeared in a green shirt on only eleven more occasions. With the arrival of David Kemp, numerous new faces soon appeared at Home Park, and Summerfield was one of those to make way. In March 1990 he was loaned to Exeter, playing four games in a side that went on to the Fourth Division title. But it was not until October 1990 that another club – Shrewsbury – signed him permanently.

The move to Gay Meadow gave Summerfield a second lease of life. In six seasons there he was made captain and played over 150 matches, before joining the coaching staff. He scored twice against the Pilgrims in the space of a week in August 1991, as the Shrews put Argyle out of the Rumbelows Cup at the first hurdle.

After Shrewsbury suffered relegation in 1997, manager Fred Davies and Summerfield were replaced, and he returned to Home Park as a youth-team coach. His dedication paid dividends with successive South West Counties championships, and a number of his young charges forced themselves into the first-team reckoning.

With the dismissal of Kevin Hodges and Steve McCall in October 2000, Summerfield was given temporary control of first-team affairs. The players spoke highly of Summerfield's style of management and it looked, at one point, as if he would land the job on a permanent basis. In the end, the directors plumped for the experience of Paul Sturrock, with Summerfield as his right-hand man.

Magic Moment: *Summerfield scored for Walsall in their 2-2 draw at Anfield in the 1983-84 Milk Cup. Alas, there was to be no Wembley appearance, with Liverpool winning the return leg 2-0.*

Worst nightmare: *After giving a superb performance and scoring against Exeter in the 1985-86 Milk Cup, Summerfield suffered a depressed fracture of the cheek-bone in a training accident.*

ARGYLE RECORD	Appearances	Goals
Football League	118 (+20)	26
FA Cup	13	4
League Cup	6 (+1)	3

No 88. **GERRY McELHINNEY**
Debut: v Bournemouth, 26 January 1985
Farewell: v Aston Villa, 27 February 1988

A mix of skills and styles is essential for any team, and this can be no better illustrated than the contrast between the fragile creative Kevin Summerfield and the 'stop them at all costs' gung-ho attitude of Gerry McElhinney.

Born in Londonderry, Northern Ireland on 19 September 1956, McElhinney's sporting career could easily have gone in a different direction. He was a useful Gaelic footballer and also became the Mid-Ulster boxing champion. His 6ft 1in, 14st frame made him a formidable opponent in both disciplines. It will therefore come as little surprise that he made his name on the soccer field as a centre-half.

McElhinney's soccer career began like those of many other Irishmen, with Celtic. He was rejected by the Glasgow giants and returned to Northern Ireland to play for Distillery, where he attracted scouts from various English clubs. In September 1980 Bolton paid £25,000 for his services.

It was after completing a twenty-match loan spell at Rochdale in 1982 that he established himself in the Bolton defence and showed there was more to him than being an out and out 'stopper'. His dominating play brought him full Northern Ireland honours in November 1983, in a European Championship qualifier against West Germany in Hamburg. Norman Whiteside's solitary goal earned one of the greatest upsets in recent international football. A month later McElhinney helped Northern Ireland defeat Scotland 2-0 in Belfast. He kept his place for the next three internationals, including a 0-1 Wembley defeat by England. The last of his six caps was won in September 1984 against Romania in a World Cup qualifier in Belfast.

One of Dave Smith's first tasks when appointed manager in November 1984 was to attend to defensive frailties. Despite a number of experienced defenders on the books, Argyle were leaking goals so badly that they were staring relegation in the face, and McElhinney became one of Smith's first signings when arriving for £32,500 on New Year's Day 1985. Owing to freezing weather, McElhinney had to wait for more than three weeks to make his Argyle debut, but his worth can be assessed by a study of the goals-against column that season. He joined exactly midway through the campaign. Before he arrived, Argyle had conceded 44 League goals; afterwards, just 21.

Smith appointed McElhinney as captain, a natural selection for someone with international experience and who led by example. He gained respect from his colleagues, partly, one suspects, through a sneaking gratitude that they were playing with him and not against. With shaggy hair and a nose and eyes that bore the inevitable marks of his earlier boxing career, his appearance alone gave him a psychological edge over opponents. He became hugely popular with supporters and, for those old enough to remember, there were shades of Jack Chisholm. Tough and uncompromising, McElhinney played the game hard but fair. His bone-shuddering tackles became legendary and were invariably followed by chants of 'Rambo, Rambo' from the Home Park crowd. His clearances sailed huge distances and, adding another string to his bow, for a time he became the club's penalty taker. Despite his hard man image, off the field he had a heart of gold. He attended functions on behalf of the club and on the occasions when appearance money was forthcoming for such events, he would donate it to the local Leukaemia Research Fund.

McElhinney led the Pilgrims to promotion from Division Three in 1985-86. Argyle were awarded penalties in each of the first four games and McElhinney, converting three of them, emerged as an early contender for Argyle's leading scorer.

Not surprisingly, McElhinney's fearless play kept the Argyle physio busy. Rarely did he go through a game without requiring attention to some part of his anatomy, more often than not his head. Manfully he would continue. Being substituted was simply not an option. In October 1986, Argyle entertained Leeds, while defending an unbeaten home record. With the substitute already on, McElhinney was carried off with an ankle injury before half-time. Rather than see his team play a man short, he hobbled back on for the second half and played up front, where, if nothing else, he made a nuisance of himself to the Leeds defence.

For a while, McElhinney was joined at the club by his younger brother Eddie. But Eddie was dogged by injury and was released without making the first team.

1986-87 saw competition at Home Park for centre-half places hot up. With the return to form of Adrian Burrows and the arrival of Nicky Law, McElhinney could no longer be guaranteed a place in the starting line up and over the next two seasons he found himself sliding down the pecking order.

The end of 1987-88 saw him join Peterborough for £10,000. He quickly won over the fans at London Road, who replaced his 'Rambo' tag with 'Gerry from Derry'. He made 87 League appearances for the 'Posh' in three seasons before taking over as youth-team coach.

Following an upheaval in the Posh backroom staff, McElhinney joined Corby Town as a player in February 1992. Towards the end of that season, he was appointed with Bryn Gunn as joint player-manager, a position he held until September 1993. Since then, McElhinney has been out of the game and is now believed to be living back in Ireland.

Magic Moment: *Heading for a benefit game at Stamford, in Lincolnshire, McElhinney got snared in the town's ring-road system. Not wishing to be late, he drove through flower beds and a pedestrians-only street.*

Worst Nightmare: *In the first home game of 1985-86, trailing 0-1 to Reading, Argyle were awarded a last-minute penalty. McElhinney's kick was saved by Reading keeper Gary Westwood and the Pilgrims left the field to a chorus of boos.*

ARGYLE RECORD	Appearances		Goals
Football league	90	(+1)	2
FA Cup	7		–
League Cup	4		1

No 89. **JOHN MATTHEWS**
Debut: v York, 17 August 1985
Farewell: v Oldham, 29 April 1989

Throughout the mid-1980s, Argyle were fortunate to have the creative skills of both Kevin Summerfield and another experienced player, John Matthews, in their midfield.

Matthews was born in Kings Cross on 1 November 1955. He attended Highbury Grove Secondary School in north London and was a fan of nearby Arsenal. Selection for the Islington District side led to an invitation to train with the Gunners. He was offered an apprenticeship in 1971 and realised his boyhood dream when signing professional two years later.

He debuted at Leicester on the opening day of 1974-75, playing in the back four due to a spate of injuries. It turned out to be Matthews' best season in terms of appearances. With the Gunners suffering numerous injury problems, his versatility proved invaluable. His 26 appearances that season boded well for a bright future, but competition at Highbury was fierce. The following season, he was visited by injury, and played only one game. From then on he was never more that on the fringes of the first team, making a total of 48 appearances for the Gunners as well as nine as substitute, scoring five goals.

When Sheffield United bid for him in August 1978, Matthews was reluctant to leave London, but the prospect of regular first-team action settled his doubts. His fee was £90,000. Despite his initial reservations, Matthews enjoyed his time at Bramall Lane, helped, no doubt by scoring the winning goal on his Blades debut, again at Leicester.

A Fourth Division championship medal followed in 1981-82, where-upon Matthews was released by manager Ian Porterfield on a free trans-fer and he joined Mansfield. Two seasons were spent at Field Mill before he moved to Chesterfield on a one-year contract. Honours again came his way when Chesterfield clinched the Division Four title, but once again promotion was followed by the announcement that he was no longer wanted.

Dave Smith had been reserve-team manager at Arsenal during Matthews' early days, and he invited Matthews to Devon. Matthews was a Smith type of player, liking to play football and good on the ball. The Argyle midfield of Matthews, Summerfield and Russell Coughlin was one of the most creative ever seen at the club, and, combined with the marauding wing play of Kevin Hodges and Garry Nelson, the Pilgrims provided a quality of football lacking at Home Park for a number of years.

Matthews soon showed the class befitting a player who had graced the First Division. The tall, dark midfielder regularly dictated the pace of play. Combining neat ball control with vision, he sprayed the ball around to good effect. He strolled through games. The lack of pace which many felt impeded him in Division One was not such a factor in Division Three. His other great asset was his dead-ball skills. A clean striker of the ball, he would take control of free-kicks around the area, and with great precision he would find a team-mate or occasionally have a crack himself. Injury interrupted his first season at Home Park, but he still played 29 League matches and yet again experienced the thrill of promotion.

Life in Division Two gave him yet more time and space to display his repertoire of skills, and he missed only three matches as Smith guided his side to the heady heights of seventh in a division containing the likes of Leeds, Sunderland and Derby.

The following season saw Manchester City and Aston Villa join the Second Division fray, but Matthews, by now approaching the veteran stage, was still a force to be reckoned with. At the end of that season Smith was replaced by Ken Brown. Matthews kept his place, but after Christmas he struggled to last 90 minutes and he was regularly substituted. That summer he was released and – together with John Uzzell – was reunited with Smith at Torquay on a free transfer. By his own admission, Matthews' heart was no longer in the game and after one season at Plainmoor he retired from League football.

He had a brief spell with Dorchester Town before returning to Plymouth where, having gained his FA coaching qualifications, he ran his own soccer schools, before starting up an office furniture business. In 1993 Matthews was short-listed for the position of youth-team manager at Home Park under Peter Shilton, but the position went to Ian Bowyer.

These days Matthews lives in Torpoint and works as a postman. He is still an enthusiastic member of the ex-Arsenal side and plays for them as often as he can.

Magic Moment: *Mathews ran out at his spiritual home, Highbury, when Argyle were drawn against Arsenal in the FA Cup in January 1987. But the Gunners won 6-1 and Matthews was substituted.*

Worst Nightmare: *Just when he was looking to establish himself in the Arsenal side, a broken leg sidelined Matthews for months.*

ARGYLE RECORD	Appearances		Goals
Football League	135	(+4)	4
FA Cup	8	(+1)	1
League Cup	10		–

No 90. **GARRY NELSON**
Debut: v York, 17 August 1985
Farewell: v Derby, 9 May 1987

Winger Garry Nelson relished John Matthews' pinpoint passes. Although he only played at Home Park for two seasons, these confirmed his status as one of the best attacking players in the lower divisions.

Born at Braintree in Essex on 16 January 1961, Nelson began his career at Southend United, spending four seasons at Roots Hall as a professional after graduating through the club's youth system. He debuted as a substitute against local rivals Colchester in October 1979 and went on to make over 100 appearances. The Southend manager at the time was a certain Dave Smith, who was to play a further part in the Nelson story a few years later.

In August 1983 Nelson moved to Swindon, where he formed a potent forward line with Jimmy Quinn and Andy Rowland. In two seasons with the Wiltshire side he made 79 League appearances, scoring seven goals. One of his more spectacular goals for Swindon came against Argyle in a League Cup-tie in September 1983. Despite Argyle winning 4-1, to go through on aggregate, Nelson scored the visitors' goal with a twenty-yard effort that flew past Geoff Crudgington.

With Smith chosen to replace John Hore in November 1984, his pressing task was to stave off relegation. Having achieved that, he looked to build on the FA Cup success from the previous season, but needed to replace players who for various reasons had departed Home Park. One of his priorities was to fill the void created by Andy Rogers' departure to Reading. Aware at first hand of Nelson's ability, Smith prised him away from Swindon for £15,000 in the summer of 1985.

Nelson made his debut on the opening day of 1985-86. Defeats in the first two games were not what Smith had envisaged, but once the new signings had settled the team began to find its feet. The season gathered momentum. Nelson, playing wide on the left, and Kevin Hodges on the right, notched 29 League goals between them. The long serving Hodges was voted Player of the Year, but the honour could justifiably have gone to Nelson. Nimble and quick, he enthralled the crowd with his direct, thrusting wing play. He was not the type of winger who would dribble past his full-back, preferring to run at them, creating space with a twist and a swerve to launch a cross. As his goal record suggests, Nelson was not afraid to cut inside, and his pace caused numerous problems for defences.

The arrival on loan of Tommy Tynan at the rear end of that season completed the jigsaw. His ten goals in nine games confirmed promotion, which was secured following a 4-0 home win over Bristol City. Argyle were unstoppable on that Tuesday evening in April, and it was Nelson who played a large part in the victory, scoring one goal himself and having a hand in two others.

Undaunted by the prospect of Division Two football, the side carried on where they had left off and it was mid-October before they suffered defeat in the League. Nelson, troubled by a mystery virus, missed a number of matches but returned to the side as good as ever. His own goal tally was down on the promotion season, but with Tynan finding the back of the net it mattered little. Argyle finished a creditable seventh, and but for losing the final three games they would have been even higher.

Despite Argyle's potential for yet better things, Nelson had become unsettled and looked to move back to the South East. Brighton wanted him and Smith let him go, rather than try to hang on to a player whose heart was elsewhere. The fee of £72,500, on the face of it, seemed good business. It earned Argyle a healthy profit on the player. But with hindsight, the Seagulls had got away with a steal. Nelson was played in a central role up front, where his pace was even more damaging to the opposition. Brighton, having graced an FA Cup final only five years earlier, were looking to regain past glories, and Nelson's 27 League and Cup goals helped win promotion from Division Three. Another twenty the following season meant he now had a host of admirers among clubs both big and small. His third and final season at Brighton was not so fruitful. Some clubs had lost interest, but not Second Division Charlton, and in August 1991 he signed in a £50,000 transfer.

In 1991-92, while Argyle and Brighton were being relegated, Nelson was establishing himself and becoming a favourite with the Addicks' fans. He remained at the club for five years, making 147 League starts, augmented by 38 substitute appearances, and scoring 37 goals.

His last season for Charlton saw Nelson reveal an unexpected talent. He wrote an award-winning autobiography, *Left Foot Forward*, which chronicled a year in his life, revealing not so much the glamour and excitement of the game, but the daily grind of training and travelling. It also revealed his fears for the future, knowing that a new contract was unlikely to be offered to him at Charlton.

That uncertainty ended when his pal Kevin Hodges was put in charge of Torquay United. One of Hodges' first calls was to Nelson, inviting him to become player-coach at Plainmoor. Nelson accepted the offer and signed a two-year contract. Capitalising on the success of his first book, a sequel, *Left Foot in the Grave*, was published, detailing his first season at Torquay, much of which was spent trying to avoid finishing bottom of the League.

Nelson played regularly in the Torquay side, scoring eight times in 34 games. In 1997, with a year of his contract still to run, Nelson joined the PFA as commercial executive. His playing days were finally over.

As well as his work with the PFA, Nelson also provided expert analysis on radio and this in turn, produced another career change. In the summer of 2001 he accepted an offer to become a football pundit for the new ITV Sports Channel.

Magic Moment: *In October 1985 Walsall were defending a 100% home record. Argyle were 1-2 down in injury-time, but Nelson levelled from a near impossible angle, his second goal of the game.*

Worst Nightmare: *Nelson's famed speed and body swerve failed him during the pitch invasion that followed victory over Bristol City. He disappeared into the throng, to emerge minutes later being carried shoulder high from the pitch.*

ARGYLE RECORD	Appearances		Goals
Football league	71	(+3)	20
FA Cup	7		2
League Cup	4		–

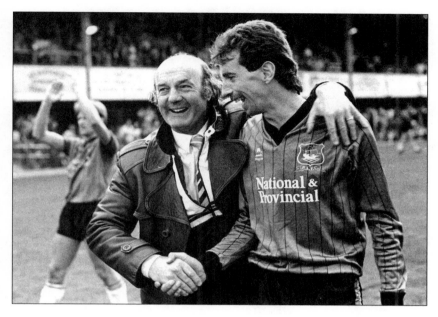

No 87. Kevin Summerfield earns the congratulations of manager Dave Smith

No 66. Paul Mariner (left) and
No 53. Bobby Saxton (right) get shirty

No 88. Gerry McElhinney, Northern
Ireland international centre-half

No 90. Winger and future
author Garry Nelson scores

Manager Dave Smith (back row, left) with the Argyle squad

Chapter Nine

~ *Experience & Potential* ~

No 91. **MARK SMITH**

Debut: v Manchester City, 15 August 1987
Farewell: v Arsenal, 19 September 1989

Mark Smith had already played at the top level before coming to Argyle, and it showed. Undoubtedly one of the classiest defenders to have worn a green shirt, Smith's time at Argyle was all too short.

Born on 21 March 1960, Smith could see Sheffield Wednesday's famous ground, Hillsborough, from the back garden of his parents' house. He dreamed of one day playing in the blue and white of the Owls and, having shown promise in schools football at Shirecliffe Primary and Herries Comprehensive, he was selected for Sheffield Schoolboys from under-11 to under-15 level.

When Wednesday were languishing in the Third Division, they did not seem such a great temptation to a lad with promise. Their great rivals, United, were two divisions higher and offered the prospect of greater things. He trained with United for a while and was a ball boy at Bramall Lane, but blood is thicker than water and, aged sixteen, he was taken on as an apprentice at Hillsborough. One of his duties was to clean the boots of Tommy Tynan.

Initially considered a midfield player, Smith was persuaded by youth-team coach Ken Knighton that he was too tall for that position. Rather, he had the makings of a central defender. Smith did not initially take to this advice, but in the long term it proved well founded. Progressing through the youth and reserve teams, Smith signed as an Owls professional in March 1978, and in the penultimate game of that season debuted at Colchester.

The following season saw him establish himself at the heart of the Owls' defence. He was part of Wednesday's marathon FA Cup third round epic with Arsenal, which, before the advent of penalty shoot-outs, required *four* replays before being settled in the Gunners favour.

His manager, Jack Charlton, pushed Smith's claims for England Under-21 honours and he went on to gain five caps at that level. For a time he was also made captain of Wednesday. Smith's earliest success at Hillsborough came in 1979-80 with promotion from the old Third Division. It was not just his defensive qualities, but also his goals that aided that objective. He became the club's penalty taker and finished the season with eleven goals, all from the spot, including ten in succession without missing.

After playing in the losing side in the 1983 FA Cup semi-final, Smith enjoyed a further promotion in 1983-84 under Howard Wilkinson, when Wednesday reclaimed their place in the top division. In 1986 the Owls again reached the last four of the FA Cup, but Smith missed the semi-final, having injured a foot ten seconds from time in the quarter-final against West Ham. The injury proved serious and it was some months before he regained his place. By then, with his contract about to expire, Smith was considering a change of scene. He was substituted during the final match of 1986-87 and left the pitch sensing that after 352 League and Cup appearances, his eighteen-year association with Hillsborough was over.

Smith was still only 27, and a sideways move to another First Division club seemed most likely. Instead, in July 1987 he signed for Argyle for a record fee of £170,000. For the club to spend that kind of money was unheard of, but Smith's namesake, manager Dave, was not one for rash decisions or panic buys. He had done his homework and felt that the tall defender would prove pivotal to his aim to improve on seventh place in Division Two. The fact that Mark signed suggests that the player thought so, too.

There were no accusations of money wasted. Within a few games, Smith had the Argyle fans purring with delight. He was a 'Rolls Royce' defender. At 6ft 1in he was strong and dominant in the air. On the ground, he possessed a cultured left foot and liked to pass the ball from defence rather than hoof it upfield. Having gained possession, he would calmly sidestep an opponent, before delivering a slide-rule pass to a colleague. Both on and off the field he displayed class. Well groomed and approachable, he became popular with the fans for his pleasant demeanour.

Sadly, Smith's performances were not matched by those of certain colleagues. Visions of promotion to Division One soon faded, and in each of his two full seasons at Home Park the Pilgrims finished in the bottom half.

1989-90 kicked off with rumours of Mark Smith being unsettled in the South West and seeking a return to his northern roots. The rumours were true. Nine games into the season, he was off to Barnsley. It was fitting that his farewell appearance in Plymouth colours was made in a League Cup-tie at Highbury, on a stage better suited to his ability. Smith made over 100 appearances for Barnsley, before transferring to Notts

County, from where he spent loan spells at Port Vale, Huddersfield and Chesterfield.

His final season as a player came in 1983-84 at Lincoln, after which he became the Imps' youth-team coach under former Argyle striker Frank Lord. Smith subsequently became reserve-team and then assistant manager at Notts County, before moving to his present role, working with the under-19 squad at Barnsley.

Magic Moment: *The man who initially signed Smith for Sheffield Wednesday, George McCabe, was so worried that other clubs might poach him that he got Smith to sign apprentice forms and then locked them in the club's safe until he had left school.*

Worst Nightmare: *In 1986, bending down to have his photo taken with the mascots, Smith injured his knee before his testimonial for Sheffield Wednesday against city rivals United.*

ARGYLE RECORD	Appearances	Goals
Football League	82	6
FA Cup	5	–
League Cup	9	1

No 92. **NICKY MARKER**

Debut: v Swindon, 14 November 1987
Final Farewell: v Hull, 20 March 1999

Nicky Marker was a classy defender in the Mark Smith mould. He was tipped for the top from his early days and fulfilled that potential.

Born in the Devon seaside resort of Budleigh Salterton on 3 May 1965, he attended Exmouth Comprehensive and played for his home-town club in the Exeter and District League. When only thirteen he impressed in trials for Exeter and signed schoolboy forms. Marker made the Grecians' reserve side when only fifteen, and in October 1981, still only a 16-year-old apprentice, he made his League debut at centre-half at Burnley. He held his place for the next two games and was then asked to mark Liverpool debutant Ian Rush in a home League Cup-tie. With Exeter already 0-5 down from the first leg, hopes of an upset were non-existent, but 11,000 still packed into St James Park for a glimpse of the Liverpool All Stars. Sadly for Marker, Liverpool turned on the style to record a 6-0 victory.

Despite his tender age, Marker impressed everyone with his cool unflappable style and versatility. Equally at home in central defence or in midfield, Marker wore seven different shirt numbers at Exeter, in the days when numbers still largely dictated positions. He even played centre-forward on a couple of occasions, but wherever he played he always looked to support the attack.

Although Exeter supporters were resigned to the fact that Marker would go to a bigger club, they did not expect him to sign for fierce rivals Argyle. Dave Smith bought him in October 1987 for a fee of £95,000, plus striker Darren Rowbotham in exchange.

Marker's signature was something of a coup for Argyle, who had signed a player who was only 22 but had 200 games under his belt. Marker soon showed the Argyle supporters that he was a class act. Commanding in the air, he was also – for a big man – deceptively skilful on the ball, passing intelligently and often taking the ball from deep to set up attacks.

Whatever position he was asked to fill, Marker was rarely out of the side, becoming one of the outstanding players in Division Two. In the course of 1989-90 he succeeded Tommy Tynan as club captain and at the end of that campaign took the Argyle Player of the Year honours.

But what goes around, comes around. This time it was Argyle fans who were resigned to losing Marker, and relegation to Division Three in 1991-92 merely accelerated the process. Marker could not be expected to languish in Division Three for long, and in September 1992 cash rich Blackburn bought him for £200,000. Under the deal, Argyle also acquired defender Keith Hill and winger Craig Skinner.

Marker arrived at Rovers when Jack Walker was bankrolling the club onwards and upwards, even bringing in Kenny Dalglish as manager. With fierce competition for places at Ewood Park, Marker was restricted to a total of 48 League and Cup appearances, with a further fifteen as substitute, in five years. But at least he could boast he was a Premiership player and played in the Champions League.

In August 1997 his Blackburn contract was not renewed and Marker joined Sheffield United. At the end of his first season he was voted Blades Player of the Year, but the appointment of Steve Bruce as manager saw Marker fall out of favour. There was speculation about a return to Home Park, and in February 1999 he did return on a month's loan. Marker played four games but lacked match practice. There were occasional flashes of the old Marker, but his general midfield contribution was minimal. His four matches for Argyle were winless and goalless.

In November 1999 Marker joined Cheltenham, newcomers to the League, but although named as substitute he never made an appearance. Injuries over the years had taken their toll. Back problems required painkillers and he had arthritis in his knees. He called it a day and returned to live in the Plymouth area. In January 2000 he joined Tiverton Town.

Magic Moment: *Marker's versatility was evident at Newcastle in September 1991. With goalkeeper Rhys Wilmot injured, Marker took over in goal and pulled off some fine saves as Argyle drew 2-2.*

Worst Nightmare: *In March 1988 Marker received a bad press following a clash with Blackburn's World Cup star Ossie Ardiles at Home Park. A hefty challenge by Marker resulted in Ardiles being forced to retire. Argyle went on to record an emphatic 3-0 win.*

ARGYLE RECORD	Appearances		Goals
Football League	205	(+1)	13
FA Cup	9		1
League Cup	15		3

No 93. ANDY MORRISON
Debut: v Aston Villa, 27 February 1988
Farewell: v West Brom, 12 April 1993

Nicky Marker was not the only Argyle central defender to progress to top-flight football during the 1990s. Whilst his progress was not so rapid, Andy Morrison also found himself in Premiership football. Although not the most naturally gifted player ever to have worn Argyle green, few have been more committed to giving their all for the club.

Having been born in Inverness on 30 July 1970 – hence his nickname 'Jock' – Morrison's family moved to Plymouth when he was only seven. He was eventually offered a place at Argyle through the Youth Training Scheme, having been noticed playing for Plymouth junior side, Elm United.

Able to play in defence or midfield, Morrison made rapid strides and made his first-team debut as a substitute at Villa Park when only seventeen. He came on for his boyhood hero when standing on the Home Park terraces, Gerry McElhinney. That proved to be Morrison's only appearance that season, and he did not get a look in until the final two games of the following one, lining up from the start against Oxford and Bournemouth.

Twenty League and Cup games in 1989-90 established Morrison's reputation as a truly gifted youngster. He was fiercely competitive, and despite his tender years was vociferous on the pitch, berating or cajoling senior team-mates. Powerfully built, he was strong in the tackle and dominant in the air, where he could head the ball huge distances. Supporters were soon comparing him to McElhinney.

Morrison's appearance said everything about his never say die spirit. His scowling face would turn crimson, and Vaseline around his eyebrows lent a pugilistic appearance. With his Scottish blood he would not have looked out of place brandishing a spear alongside Mel Gibson in 'Braveheart'. His confirmation as Argyle Young Player of the Year in 1989-90 was never in doubt.

The arrival of David Kemp saw Morrison employed mainly in midfield, where his ball winning proved fundamental to Kemp's style of play. The ferocious nature of Morrison's game inevitably led to injury and suspension, but his performances continued to receive rave reviews.

The first half of 1991-92 was interrupted by an ankle ligament injury, but Morrison returned, and such were his leadership qualities that he was named skipper whenever Nicky Marker was absent. Morrison's long-term future was clearly not going to be at Home Park, and in the summer of 1993 he was transferred for £500,000 to mega-bucks Blackburn, where he again teamed up with Marker.

This dream move to a Premiership club was more of a nightmare, so far as Morrison was concerned. Rovers finished runners up to Manchester United, but Morrison played only one full game, and appeared four times as a substitute towards the end of the campaign. The following season saw Blackburn win the Premiership, but they did so without Morrison, who in December 1994 departed for Blackpool in a transfer valued at £245,000.

Morrison rediscovered the form that had made him such a hot prospect at Argyle, and in July 1996 Blackpool cashed in their main asset by selling him for £500,000 to Huddersfield.

In October 1998 Morrison went on loan to Manchester City, who a month later bought him for a knock-down £80,000. He assisted City in their promotion to the Premiership. His physical presence shored up City's defence while earning him one red and thirteen yellow cards in his first season at Maine Road.

Once in the Premiership, Morrison's lack of pace was exposed. With City struggling to stay up, numerous defensive permutations were tried out. Morrison, out of favour following a 0-4 FA Cup thrashing at Liverpool in February 2001, was loaned in turn to Blackpool, Crystal Palace, and finally Sheffield United. With City relegated and manager Joe Royle sacked, Morrison did not feature in new boss Kevin Keegan's plans and, out of contract, he was released that summer. As 2001-02 kicked off, Andy Morrison was still clubless.

Magic Moment: *Most of Morrison's goals came from bullet headers from set pieces, but he volleyed a classic goal against Shrewsbury in August 1991.*

Worst Nightmare: *Morrison was sent off in an FA Cup-tie at Wimbledon in January 1999, which did little to help City's cause as they went down to a single-goal defeat.*

ARGYLE RECORD	Appearances		Goals
Football League	105	(+8)	6
FA Cup	6		–
League Cup	10	(+1)	1

No 94. SEAN McCARTHY
Debut: v Walsall, 27 August 1988
Final Farewell: v Rochdale, 5 May 2001

Like Andy Morrison, Sean McCarthy also graduated from Home Park to higher things. McCarthy was not without his critics, but he belongs to that elite band of players who have scored more than 200 League goals in their career.

Born in Bridgend in South Wales on 12 September 1967, McCarthy began his League career with Swansea in October 1985. As a swashbuckling forward, he became The Swans' leading scorer in both of his two full seasons at the Vetch, prompting Argyle manager Ken Brown to fork out £50,000 for his services in the summer of 1988.

The burly McCarthy became the perfect foil for Tommy Tynan. Whilst Tynan grabbed the headlines with his prolific goalscoring, he would be the first to acknowledge McCarthy's contribution in bearing the brunt of defenders' battering. McCarthy himself scored thirteen League and Cup goals in that first season as a Pilgrim, none more important than his strike which gave Argyle a shock lead against Everton in the FA Cup.

The following season was blighted by injury, but McCarthy came good towards the end, when – with relegation still a threat – he hit a hat-trick in a 3-0 win at West Brom, followed by two goals at home to Oldham two days later. The final game at Bradford City saw McCarthy on the scoresheet again, notching the only goal of the game. Within weeks he returned to Valley Parade, this time as a player, with Argyle receiving a record fee of £250,000.

McCarthy added much-needed firepower to City's forward line, and in three and a half seasons averaged almost a goal every two games. Had it not been for Wales being blessed with the talents of Ian Rush and Mark Hughes, McCarthy might have won full international honours. Instead he had to be content with selection for the Wales 'B' side.

McCarthy's scoring exploits saw his market value shoot up, and in December 1993 he joined Premiership Oldham for £500,000. His goals were unable to keep Oldham from tumbling out of the Premiership at the end of that season. He remained at Boundary Park for four and a half years, in which time he scored 43 goals in 117 (plus 23 sub) appearances. On transfer deadline day in March 1998 he joined Bristol City on loan.

It was his ex-Argyle colleague, Kevin Hodges, who brought him back to Home Park that summer. Hodges felt that the Welshman would add experience to his squad, although the offer of a three-year contract to a 30-year-old player surprised many.

The first two seasons of McCarthy's second spell at Home Park were punctuated by injury, and as a result his best form eluded him. Obviously past his peak, he was less mobile than Argyle fans had remembered him, ten years earlier, and did not score goals with the same regularity, but he maintained the ability to hold the ball up and was a handful for any defender in the air.

McCarthy's third and final season was his best. Largely free from injury, he was employed by Hodges as a central defender for pre-season friendlies, although he was restored to his familiar forward role when the gloves came off in August 2000. The absence of other experienced players also saw him handed the captain's armband.

Whilst always a physical player, McCarthy's latter years saw him use his bulky 6ft frame to stretch the laws to their limits. There was no doubt that opponents 'knew they had been in a game', but two red cards and a spate of yellows incurred suspensions which did nothing to help Hodges – and later Paul Sturrock – field the best forward combination.

Although McCarthy's lack of finesse was not to everyone's taste, his contribution was perhaps more appreciated when he was not in the side. The local derbies at Torquay and Exeter showed what he was still capable of. At Plainmoor, McCarthy led the line well, posing all sorts of problems, before an accidental collision saw him depart early with a broken arm. A month later, with arm strapped, he delighted the travelling Pilgrim Army with both goals in a 2-0 win at Exeter, to give the Greens their first away win of the season.

The return to Home Park of Michael Evans, a player similar in style, signalled the end of McCarthy's Argyle career. Out of contract, he was offered a two-year deal by his ex-Bradford City colleague, Noel Blake, to sign for Exeter.

Magic Moment: *McCarthy's goal against York on 19 February 2000 was the 200th of his career. McCarthy, Paul McGregor and Chris Hargreaves stripped off their shirts to reveal the figure 2-0-0. They had been waiting since McCarthy's previous goal on Boxing Day to reveal their work of art.*

Worst Nightmare: *McCarthy lost his scoring touch at Oldham in the 1995-96 season when he failed to score for seventeen games.*

ARGYLE RECORD	Appearances	Goals
Football League	133 (+19)	38
FA Cup	11	1
League Cup	10 (+2)	8

No 95. **ALAN MILLER**
Debut v Oldham, 26 November 1988
Farewell v Chelsea, 18 February 1989

Alan Miller was recommended to Argyle by London-based scout Ken Trace. Despite arriving only on loan, Miller became an instant hit with the Argyle fans and was a contender for the club's Player of the Year award on the basis of just fifteen games for the club.

Born in Epping on 29 March 1970, Miller won England Schoolboy caps and was snapped up by Arsenal. He was selected to attend the FA School of Excellence and became its first graduate to be selected for the England Under-21s – an honour that came his way before he had played a full game for the Gunners. He won four Under-21 caps in total, as well as an FA Youth Cup winners medal with Arsenal.

Arsenal were happy to allow their talented young keeper to gain experience with Argyle, who were in need of a No 1 when Steve Cherry returned to the Midlands to join Notts County.

For Argyle manager Ken Brown, it was a gamble to throw a rookie keeper into League action, particularly in a tough division that contained sides such as Leeds, Chelsea and Manchester City. Miller, to his credit, put such misgivings to shame. On his debut he made a blinding save from Oldham's Andy Ritchie that impressed even manager Joe Royle. There appeared to be no weakness in his game. At 6ft 3in, and weighing over 14st, he made an imposing figure. But despite his size, he was agile, a superb shot stopper, and a clean handler of the ball. This was curious, because at Arsenal some critics felt Miller could have been more commanding of his penalty area.

Off the field, Miller also enjoyed the spotlight, proving to be an amiable young man willing to take on promotional duties for the club. When his three-month loan spell was over, Argyle fans hoped that, at worst, it would be extended, and, at best, he would sign on a permanent basis. The latter option was never on. Miller's likely transfer fee would be beyond Argyle's reach. And besides, Arsenal foresaw a great future for the lad at Highbury.

And so Miller came and went in the blink of an eye. He was recalled to Highbury to cover for first choice David Seaman. To acknowledge his brief but telling contribution to the Pilgrims, he was presented with a gold watch by the Argyle directors.

Back at Highbury, Miller had to settle for playing second fiddle to Seaman and it was not until November 1992 that he made his Premiership debut, coming on as substitute when Seaman was hurt at Leeds. Miller appeared to put something of a hex on Arsenal, finishing on the winning side only once in eight appearances, although that 1-0 win over Sheffield Wednesday was largely down to the keeper. Not only did he pull off spectacular saves, but his massive throw set up Ian Wright for the only goal.

In 1991-92 Miller was loaned to West Brom and then Birmingham, but with Seaman immovable in goal Arsenal sold him to Middlesbrough in August 1994 for £500,000. In his first season at Boro, Miller won a First Division championship medal, and on his Premiership debut he single-handedly denied Arsenal a win, ruining the much-hyped debuts of David Platt and Dennis Bergkamp. For much of his time at Boro, however, Miller was second choice behind Gary Walsh. In 1997 he was loaned to Grimsby and West Brom, who then bought him for £400,000. Miller had made 62 League and Cup appearances for Middlesbrough.

For three years at the Hawthorns, Miller enjoyed a virtually unbroken run, making over 100 League and Cup appearances. Albion fans voted him as Player of the Year in 1997-98. That season also saw him voted by his fellow professionals into the PFA First Division select XI.

Back problems midway through 1998-99 contributed to him losing his place at the Hawthorns, and when he failed to regain it he was sold in February 2000 for just £50,000 to Blackburn. To date, he remains at Ewood Park but has played little and been loaned out to Bristol City and Coventry. Now in his 30s, his best years are perhaps behind him, but the memory of his saves for Argyle will linger in the memory of those privileged to see them.

Magic Moment: *Miller received a standing ovation from Home Park as he stepped out for his last appearance.*

Worst Nightmare: *After a superb start, Miller was injured in only his third Premiership match for Middlesbrough and lost his place for virtually the rest of the season.*

ARGYLE RECORD	Appearances	Goals
Football League	13	–
FA Cup	2	–

No 96. **RHYS WILMOT**
Debut: v Manchester City, 25 February 1989
Farewell: v Grimsby, 31 March 1992

The man to replace Alan Miller was another goalkeeper with Arsenal connections, Rhys Wilmot. Born at Newport in South Wales on 21 February 1962, Wilmot attended Chepstow Comprehensive School, but with a lack of competitive soccer in the area, he travelled to play for the Ebbw Vale school district side, where his performances saw him gain Welsh schoolboy caps.

In 1975, at the invitation of Arsenal scout Harold Joy, Wilmot went to Highbury for trials, and after four games in the Gunners youth side he was taken on as an apprentice. Welsh youth caps were added to his collection, and as soon as he turned eighteen years of age he signed professional terms.

Benefiting from being coached by former Arsenal and Scotland keeper Bob Wilson, Wilmot learnt quickly. But with Pat Jennings and John Lukic ahead of him, first-team opportunities were at a premium, although this did not prevent him from earning six Welsh Under-21 caps. His Arsenal debut came in a televised Milk Cup-tie at Aston Villa, when he learnt of his inclusion 30 minutes before kick-off.

In total, Wilmot played only nine first-team matches for Arsenal, but gained League experience on loan to Hereford, Swansea and Leyton Orient, for whom he was ever present in 1984-85. When Alan Miller returned to Highbury, Ken Brown simply asked to replace him with Wilmot until the end of 1988-89. From day one, Wilmot looked a star, leaving Argyle fans marvelling at the array of goalkeeping talent available to Arsenal.

Ironically, it was due partly to Miller's good form while at Argyle that Arsenal were persuaded to release Wilmot. After playing in the final seventeen games of his first season at Home Park, he was signed by Argyle for the not inconsiderable sum of £100,000.

His first season as a signed-up Pilgrim saw him continue his amazing form. At 6ft 1in, and weighing almost 14st, Wilmot was an imposing figure, but he possessed agility as well as bulk. He also dominated his area and his handling skills were second to none. His form even earned him a call up to the full Welsh squad, where he understudied for Neville Southall.

Wilmot played every match of 1989-90, and other than through injury was the regular choice until the arrival of Peter Shilton in March 1992. Notwithstanding Shilton's former glories, there was a strong case for arguing that Wilmot's youth gave him the edge. But with Shilton wanting to combine playing with managing, Wilmot stepped aside as Shilton inched his way to his 1,000th first-team game.

Unhappy with the idea of reserve-team football, Wilmot moved firstly to Grimsby, where he played 33 matches in two years, and then to Crystal Palace, where he saw action in only five League games. Injury was beginning to take its toll, and when he moved to Torquay in August 1996 he was not the keeper he had been at Argyle. Knee problems eventually forced his retirement from the game.

Wilmot became a publican in the Herefordshire village of Shobdon, before returning to live in Plymouth in December 2000. In mid-2001 he joined the Devon and Cornwall Police.

Magic Moment: *At home to Tranmere in March 1992, Wilmot dived to his right to keep out a penalty from ace taker John Aldridge. It was a vital save, for Argyle won 1-0.*

Worst Nightmare: *In a daunting match at Newcastle in September 1991, Wilmot left the field with a badly bruised thigh after 30 minutes. Nicky Marker took over in goal and helped fight a rearguard action which saw Argyle snatch a 2-2 draw.*

ARGYLE RECORD	Appearances	Goals
Football League	116	–
FA Cup	2	–
League Cup	8	–

No 91. Classy defender Mark Smith tries to recover the ball

No 92. Nicky Marker forces West Brom's Arthur Albiston into desperate measures

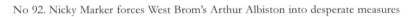

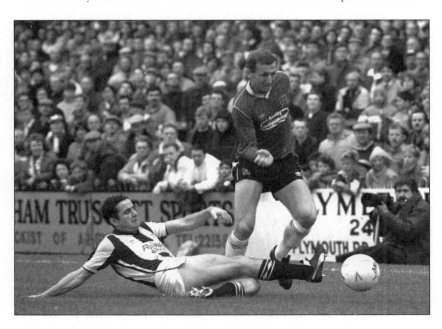

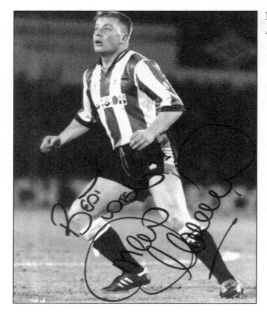

No 93. Tough-tackling defender
Andy 'Jock' Morrison

No 94. Sean McCarthy (left) celebrates the 200th goal of his career

Chapter Ten

~ *Wembley at Last!* ~

No 97. **MARTIN BARLOW**
Debut: v Oxford, 6 May 1989
Farewell: v Carlisle, 17 February 2001

A good friend of Rhys Wilmot, on and off the field, Martin Barlow gave loyal service to Argyle throughout the 1990s. His father served with the RAF in North Devon, and Martin was born in Barnstaple on 25 June 1971. But having moved to Plymouth when he was only two, he is deemed an honorary Plymothian.

Educated at Honicknowle Secondary Modern, he represented Devon schools and also played for local side Prince Rock. He was invited to join Argyle's centre of excellence and subsequently joined the club as an associated schoolboy. There were doubts that he was big enough to make the grade and his father had arranged trials with Exeter. However, Barlow's performance in a trial match at Harper's Park, albeit at full-back, convinced Argyle to take him on as an apprentice. He turned professional, under Ken Brown, in July 1989.

Barlow thought of himself as a right-winger, making his first-team debut as a substitute for Darren Garner – a one-time team-mate of Barlow with Prince Rock. His hopes of a more regular spot in 1989-90 were dashed by the need for a hernia operation.

It was David Kemp who gave Barlow his chance in place of David Byrne on the right wing. Barlow soon settled and scored a cracker at Brighton in front of former England manager Ron Greenwood, that earned him the Barclays Young Eagle of the Month award. Aston Villa then tabled a bid that was rejected by Argyle and kept secret from Barlow.

The impish winger had never lacked confidence. He was nicknamed 'Chopsy', on account of his constant chirping at senior players in training, and this inner belief surfaced in his play. Barlow always wanted the ball and was not one to 'disappear'.

The 1990s were a decade of turmoil at Home Park, with managers and players coming and going as if through a revolving door. Barlow was the one constant, but when Peter Shilton arrived he signed another winger, Craig Skinner, and dropped Barlow into the reserves.

It was Shilton's assistant, John McGovern, who suggested that Barlow switch to midfield. He was used as a wide midfield player, and later in the centre, where his non-stop running and prompting were best suited. Barlow was only 5ft 7in, but buzzed around like a fly, collecting the ball from deep and threading passes to team-mates. Close markers were left leaden-footed by his sudden twists and turns.

The arrival of Neil Warnock in June 1995 seemed to signal the end of Barlow's Argyle career. He was out of contract and unimpressed with the new terms on offer. Cardiff took an interest, but then cooled, leaving Barlow on a week to week contract at Home Park. But with the Pilgrims on a roll, he fought his way back into contention and finally signed a new two and a half year contract.

His form at the end of 1995-96, with Argyle pushing for the play-offs, was electrifying. Two goals in a 5-1 demolition of Scarborough earned him one of *six* awards for 'man of the match' during the run in. But in the play-offs at Colchester, Barlow had a stinker. Warnock intended to play Chris Billy in the home leg, but had second thoughts and stayed true to Barlow, who rewarded his manager's faith by supplying the cross from which Paul Williams took Argyle to Wembley. Barlow's performance that night sealed his place in the final, and although it was no classic, it goes down as the highlight of his long career.

In 1997 Barlow was plagued by a groin strain. Never one to shirk training, he played through the pain for two years. At one stage Barlow needed pain-killers to see him through a game, and had difficulty in getting out of bed the next day. Not that his performances were diminished, as his award for the 1997-98 Argyle Player of the Year (jointly with Carlo Corazzin) confirmed.

Surgery could no longer be postponed, which meant he could not play in his own testimonial against Fulham in July 1999. Unable to even jog, he hobbled onto the pitch to receive the acclaim of the crowd, kicked-off and was then 'substituted' two seconds later.

But for the appointment of Kevin Hodges as manager in June 1998, that testimonial may not have taken place. Barlow was again out of contract, and when he finally relented he cited the arrival of Hodges – whose boots he had cleaned as an apprentice – as a major reason for signing.

The first operation – to repair stomach and groin – was not wholly successful, and a second visit to the operating theatre set back Barlow's recovery by another six weeks. After seven months out, he came on as a substitute against Rotherham and played from the start at home to Chester. After just seventeen minutes, Barlow suffered knee ligament damage which ended his season.

July 2000 saw protracted talks before a new contract was signed, but Hodges' departure in October 2000 and the arrival of Paul Sturrock raised yet more doubts about Barlow's future. More often than not, Sturrock left him out, and the player was advised that he would not be retained and should look for a new club. Easier said than done, when a knee injury then necessitated a cartilage operation.

The summer of 2001 saw Barlow train on his own to regain full fitness. He now wears the colours of bitter rivals Exeter City, but Pilgrim fans will wish this whole-hearted advocate of Argyle's cause the best of luck.

Magic Moment: *Barlow scored one of the greatest goals ever seen at Home Park. Against Shrewsbury in April 1999 he volleyed a headed clearance from a tight angle into the far corner of the net.*

Worst Nightmare: *Barlow's dream appearance at Wembley in the 1995 play-off final did not start as planned. After a few seconds the ball came to him, hit a divot, and bounced comically over his foot.*

ARGYLE RECORD	Appearances	Goals
Football League	297 (+35)	27
FA Cup	19	–
League Cup	11 (+1)	2

No 98. **STEVE McCALL**
Debut: v Port Vale, 28 March 1992
Final Farewell: v Mansfield, 6 May 2000

Steve McCall had a huge influence on Martin Barlow's career, having a wealth of top division and European experience. He came to Argyle late on, but proved to be a highly influential figure in the Argyle midfield.

Born in Carlisle on 15 October 1960, McCall was educated at Morton Comprehensive. He played for the Cumbrian County side and was spotted by Ipswich scout, John Carruthers. Ipswich were riding on a crest of a wave at that time, having won the FA Cup, and a certain Paul Mariner was banging in the goals. McCall soon tasted success, being part of the side that won the Southern Junior Floodlit Cup and the following year was called into the England Youth squad which – under Brian Clough and Peter Taylor – won an international tournament in Las Palmas. McCall won a total of six youth caps and at the end of 1978-79 was voted Ipswich's outstanding young player.

His first-team break came during the summer of 1979 on a tour of the USA. What with injuries and international call-offs, McCall was the only left-footed player in the squad. His debut came at left-back in a match against Minnesota.

The 1979-80 League season started poorly for Ipswich, who were not helped by a glut of injuries. McCall made his competitive debut in a UEFA Cup-tie at Skied Oslo, and a few days later made his League bow in a 1-1 home draw with Everton.

From that point he became a useful squad member, able to slot in at left-back or midfield with equal effectiveness. His first major honour arrived at the end of 1980-81, when Ipswich – having missed out on the League title – lifted the UEFA Cup after a 5-4 aggregate win over AZ 67 Alkmaar of Holland.

Further international honours followed, with McCall joining the England Under-21s' tour of Switzerland and Hungary, keeping his place in the squad that triumphed in the European Championship in October 1982. In all, McCall won six Under-21 caps and added an England 'B' cap to his collection in 1984. As for Ipswich, in April 1985 McCall set a new club record by playing in 175 consecutive matches and went on to make over 300 appearances.

Ipswich's downfall was also McCall's. Relegation in 1986 saw him out of contract and sold to Sheffield Wednesday in June 1987. His fee, £300,000, went some way to reducing Ipswich's mounting debts following major ground improvements.

His time at Hillsborough was dominated more by injuries than anything else. In only his fifth game, he broke his leg and underwent five knee operations, not to mention suffering hernia and Achilles problems. In contrast to his record at Ipswich, McCall managed only 29 appearances for Wednesday in almost five years. A fee of £25,000, as Peter Shilton's second signing for Argyle in March 1992, seemed to represent a major gamble.

Nicknamed 'Zimmer' by his new team-mates, McCall's battle-hardened image was not helped playing without his false teeth. But in reality he was one of the most astute signings in Argyle's history. Any doubts that McCall had been put out to graze at Home Park were soon dispelled. Firstly, he was simply too nice a chap to let anyone down, and secondly, he had the knack of making the game look terribly easy. Years of playing with the likes of Arnold Muhren, Frans Thijssen and John Wark had clearly rubbed off. There was good reason why he adopted the more complimentary nickname 'Professor'. His passing was immaculate. There was nothing elaborate about this; he just did the right thing time and time again. Occasionally he would show an eccentric streak with a deft flick or nonchalant back-heel but usually it was a simple short pass made with his trusty left foot. He also had the ability to drift past opponents as if they were not there. There was no perceived change of pace, just a drop of one of those familiar hunched shoulders and he was in the clear.

McCall missed few games in his first full season, winning the Player of the Year award. His class shone through as Argyle reached the 1993-94 play-offs, and despite losing out he became only the second Argyle player – after Paul Mariner – to win successive Player of the Year awards.

In March 1995, after the acrimonious departure of Peter Shilton, the directors turned to McCall to take charge of team affairs. Initially he was given the title of temporary player-manager. Shilton had not yet officially left his post, being merely 'suspended' by the club.

After a daunting first game in charge at Nottingham Forest in the FA Cup, McCall concentrated on pulling Argyle away from the drop zone. But after just two wins in eleven games, the board sought to lighten his load by bringing in an experienced coach to assist. McCall declined. Five games later, and with time running out, the board repeated their offer. McCall, a proud man, felt that the repeated suggestion undermined his position and resigned. He had been in charge for just two months.

McCall stayed at Home Park as a player to help the new boss, former Ipswich team-mate Russell Osman. But the die was cast, and relegation to the basement division of the League for the first time in Argyle's history became reality.

The arrival of Neil Warnock saw the injection of new players and new ideas. A succession of injuries meant McCall was largely unavailable. He was called upon only four times, twice as substitute, towards the end of the season when Warnock needed his experience in the play-off push. For the play-off final at Wembley, McCall's big-match experience demanded a place, if only on the bench, but Warnock kept faith with the regular players who had taken Argyle that far.

McCall, a qualified FA coach, ended up at Plainmoor as assistant to Kevin Hodges. Despite his advancing years he continued to play, and made another trip to Wembley for the 1997-98 play-off final. When Hodges returned to Home Park, McCall followed, and, injuries permitting, he continued to turn out whenever asked, but at 38 his battle-weary legs struggled to last for 90 minutes. He was interviewed for the vacant managerial position at his home-town club, Carlisle, but lost out to another Ipswich old boy, Ian Atkins, and remained at Argyle.

Although still registered as a player for 2000-01 he had played his last game and, following a poor start, left the club with Hodges in October 2000. Still living in Plymouth, McCall is currently working as a scout for Ipswich.

Magic Moment: *McCall got a huge reception from the Home Park crowd when coming on as substitute against Mansfield in April 1996 after a season-long absence.*

Worst Nightmare: *McCall's record-breaking run of appearances for Ipswich was halted by a controversial sending off against Everton in an FA Cup-tie.*

ARGYLE RECORD	Appearances	Goals
Football League	222 (+11)	9
FA Cup	16 (+2)	–
League Cup	13 (+1)	–

No 99. **MICK HEATHCOTE**
Debut: v Colchester, 12 August 1995
Farewell: v Halifax, 23 December 2000

Mick Heathcote was a wily campaigner, known affectionately to fans and colleagues as 'Hector'. Born in Kelloe, County Durham, on 10 September 1965, Heathcote was more interested in cheering on his beloved Newcastle United than actually playing, but eventually he joined Spennymoor United and became a regular in the side which competed in the tough Northern League.

The big 6ft 2in defender was briefly on Middlesbrough's books, but carried on playing part-time for Spennymoor and working as a delivery driver for a company owned by the club's chairman. Sunderland were the next to take a shine to Heathcote, but their manager, Lawrie McMenemy, balked at Spennymoor's £20,000 asking price.

McMenemy's successor, Denis Smith, invited 22-year-old Heathcote to join the squad for pre-season training, and in August 1987, after two reserve matches, he was given a two-year contract.

Heathcote found the transition in playing standards relatively easy to adjust to. What was not so easy was the training. Used to training only two evenings a week, the demands of daily exertions soon took their toll and at one point he was given a week off to recharge his batteries.

His first League appearance came in November 1987, when he came on as substitute for Richard Ord in a 7-0 win over Southend. It was to be over two years before he pulled on another first-team Sunderland shirt, although a loan spell at Halifax gave him his first taste of regular League football. On the verge of breaking through at Roker Park, he suffered a back injury which required surgery, and which lost him eighteen months in recuperation. The operation was only partially successful, and to this day he still suffers from back problems.

Sunderland were sympathetic, extending his contract to give him time to show his mettle. But first-team appearances were rare and being loaned out to York was not the answer, so in July 1990 he joined Shrewsbury for a fee of £55,000. Fourteen months later, he moved again, this time to Cambridge for a club record fee of £150,000.

He spent four years at Cambridge, captaining the side and winning their Player of the Year award. He was an integral part of John Beck's long-ball revolution which carried Cambridge from the Fourth Division to the brink of the Premiership. Big clubs were keeping tabs, not just on Dion Dublin, but also on Mick Heathcote. But 1994-95 brought a pelvic injury to Heathcote and relegation to Cambridge. Heathcote was out of contract and not enthusiastic about the one on offer. Waiting in the wings, new Argyle boss Neil Warnock was about to swoop.

Warnock had watched Cambridge play Huddersfield and been impressed by the way Heathcote set about subduing Andy Booth. Heathcote, despite blood pouring from his battle scars, refused to leave the pitch. The story goes that after the final whistle Warnock approached the big defender and told him 'Wherever I am next season, I'm going to sign you.' With Warnock joining Argyle that summer, he was true to his word, signing Heathcote for £70,000 after making a few phone calls from the Maldives, where Warnock was honeymooning.

It was clear that Heathcote was pivotal to Warnock's plans and he was immediately appointed captain. That first season culminated in the Wembley play-off triumph that saw him become the first Argyle player to climb the famous steps to collect a trophy. He was also voted into the PFA divisional side by his fellow professionals.

Already guaranteed a place in Argyle history, Heathcote continued to perform like a rock at the heart of the defence. He continued as captain, where his experience and quiet efficiency brought out the best in others. His colleagues, to a man, admired his dedication and manner in which he conducted himself. Off the field, Heathcote was a great ambassador for the club, always willing to spend time with fans and usually leaving them in fits of laughter with one of his classic one-liners delivered in a thick Geordie accent.

On the field, Heathcote would never win any prizes for style, but there were few more effective 'stoppers'. In the air he was as good as anyone, and on the ground various parts of his anatomy were put to use to ensure ball or man did not pass. Many a time it seemed an opponent's through-ball was past him, until a shin, knee or even a foot would suddenly appear to clear the danger. Another trait was the sudden urge to dribble the ball out of defence, accompanied by great cheers from the crowd.

To anyone watching Heathcote for the first time, all this would have seemed highly improbable. Each pre-match warm-up – no matter the weather – would end with him trudging back to the dressing room sweating and red faced. He looked ready to be substituted there and then, but would return to play a blood and guts 90 minutes.

Heathcote rarely had a bad game, but his last official match for Argyle will not linger long in his memory. Shortly afterwards he suffered a serious groin injury that kept him out for the season and, at one time, threatened his career. He fought his way back and manager Paul Sturrock allowed him the 2001-02 pre-season build up to prove his fitness. One of those matches came in his testimonial against his first club, Sunderland. Heathcote was given an emotional reception from the crowd and a few days later was offered a new one-year contract. To the dismay of his manager and supporters, another of his former clubs, Shrewsbury, had offered him a two-year deal. Understandably, at his age, he accepted the longer contract and within days of his testimonial he had gone.

Fate brought a return to Home Park for the opening game of the new season. Apart from a few numbskulls with short memories, Heathcote was given a warm reception. He ably marshalled the Shrews, who, playing with ten men for much of the game, sneaked a 1-0 win.

Having undertaken a UEFA coaching course, Heathcote hopes to stay involved in soccer once his playing days have ended.

Magic Moment: *Heathcote raised the biggest cheer of the day against York. Out on the touchline he executed a perfect 'Cruyff' turn, befuddled the opponent confronting him, and sent over a wicked left-foot cross.*

Worst Nightmare: *Heathcote had to break the news to his son that he was leaving Plymouth. Both of them ended up in tears.*

ARGYLE RECORD	Appearances		Goals
Football League	199	(+4)	13
FA Cup	18		3
League Cup	9		1

No 100. **RONNIE MAUGE**
Debut: v Colchester, 12 August 1995
Farewell: v Cambridge, 1 May 1999

Shortly before the arrival of Mick Heathcote, Ronnie Mauge (pronounced 'Mojay') became another of new manager Neil Warnock's numerous signings. Mauge was born in Islington on 10 March 1969. He passed through Charlton's hands and in September 1988 moved to Fulham on a free transfer.

The move paid off. Mauge made over 50 appearances for the Cottagers in two seasons, prompting a £40,000 move to Bury in time for the 1990-91 season. In five seasons at Gigg Lane, the tough-tackling midfielder made 126 appearances, scoring fourteen goals.

With Warnock rebuilding at Argyle, he cast his mind back to a clash between his previous club, Huddersfield, and Bury, a game in which Mauge had ran the show from midfield. Warnock saw him as the ideal ball-winning replacement for Steve Castle and – despite interest from other clubs – Mauge signed in July 1995 for £40,000.

Argyle were listed in some quarters as favourites for the Third Division title, but Warnock's early games were disastrous. With hindsight, perhaps, it was little wonder. The curtain raiser at Colchester saw the travelling Green Army having to check their matchday programme to confirm the identities of their new heroes. No fewer than seven players debuted that day, ruling out hopes of cohesion.

Argyle were pointless after six games. By the end of August they were out of the Coca-Cola Cup and – for the first time in their long history – propping up the whole Football League. If Warnock was panicking, he hid it well, defusing the situation by promising that sooner or later someone would feel the brunt of Argyle's new line up.

Saturday, 2 September saw Argyle travel to meet Mauge's old side, Bury. The Shakers were defending a 22-match unbeaten home run. Mauge had been highly regarded by Bury supporters, many of whom were sorry to see him leave, and he was handed the Argyle captain's armband for the day. By 5pm, Plymouth's stay at home fans must have assumed a dyslexic Teletext operator was on duty. But no, the result was correct, Bury 0 Argyle 5. It proved to be the turning point of the season. The Pilgrims lost just one more match before Christmas, and Mauge showed his true colours with some battling performances in midfield.

Retaining the captaincy, he also scored vital goals, such as that at Hartlepool in November, when heading in full-back Mark Patterson's free-kick. As the season unfolded, an air of optimism pervaded Home Park. The team began to perform as Warnock had envisaged, and no one wanted to miss out, least of all Mauge, who played on through the pain of a fractured toe. He eventually succumbed to the injury at a vital part of the season. Argyle were now in play-off country and Mauge was only on the bench for the first leg semi-final at Colchester. He was back in the starting eleven for the home leg and kept his place for the Wembley final.

After 65 minutes of a drab encounter, the moment came when Ronnie Mauge wrote himself into the annals of Argyle greats. In a pre-planned move, Chris Leadbitter's corner was played into space. Mark Patterson flighted the ball over and Mauge headed it beyond the reach of Darlington keeper Paul Newell for the only goal of the game. It earned Plymouth promotion.

Assured of permanent hero status, Mauge continued to police the Argyle midfield for a further three seasons, whenever injuries and, more commonly, suspensions permitted. No one could claim that Mauge was the most talented player ever to wear a Pilgrims shirt, but there have been few more committed to the cause. He was the sort of midfield player every side needs. Eating up the ground, he would win the ball and play short simple passes to team-mates. International honours came his way when he was picked for Trinidad and Tobago. The fans loved his combative style, referees, not always so. 1998-99 saw him sent off twice in the space of four weeks and yellow cards were flashed before his eyes with the frequency of strobe lights.

It was Neil Warnock who described Mauge as a 'likeable rogue'. Anyone who met Mauge could not help but warm to him. Arriving on matchday in a natty suit, his flashing smile, revealing two gold teeth, was never far away. Unfortunately, a spate of off-field incidents – involving the police and courts – marred his time in Plymouth. Showing his better side, he fronted a 'Kick Racism out of Football' campaign.

His final season saw his frustration at Argyle's failings come to a head. The euphoria of Wembley was a forgotten yesterday, as subsequent relegation saw the team slide back whence they had come. With his contract on the point of expiry, Mauge made noises about leaving. Supporters feared the worst, and his solo lap of honour – exchanging applause with the crowd after the last home fixture of 1998-99 – said it all. It proved to be his final Argyle appearance: he was omitted for the final two away matches.

A 'Bosman' transfer to his current club, Bristol Rovers, followed. Needless to say, Mauge has established himself as one of Rovers' most popular players.

Magic Moment: *Mauge set up Argyle's first goal in their stunning 5-0 win at Bury in September 1995 that changed Argyle's season.*

Worst Nightmare: *Having established himself with his new club, Bristol Rovers, Mauge broke a leg whilst on international duty with Trinidad in February 2000, keeping him out till the end of the year.*

ARGYLE RECORD	Appearances	Goals
Football League	119 (+16)	13
FA Cup	12	2
League Cup	6	–

101. **CARLO CORAZZIN**
Debut: v Fulham, 30 March 1996
Farewell: v Burnley, 2 May 1998

Like Ronnie Mauge, Giancarlo Corazzin was another Argyle player who had won international honours for his country.

A Christmas Day baby, Corazzin was born in Vancouver, Canada, in 1971 of Italian parents. His father had hopes of his son becoming a cyclist but the young Corazzin started playing soccer at the age of five and was soon a devotee of Vancouver Whitecaps, whose side boasted luminaries such as Bruce Grobbelaar, Peter Beardsley and Frans Thijssen. Corazzin progressed to having trials for the Canadian under-16s.

A family holiday in Italy changed the course of Corazzin's career. He was invited to play for the local under-18s and after his parents returned to Canada he stayed in Italy with his grandmother. For four years he played for Giorgione and Pievigina in the Italian equivalent of the English Fourth Division. He returned home to take his place in the Canadian national squad for an Olympic qualifying tournament. He won a Canadian Soccer League champions medal with Winnipeg Fury before moving back to the city of his birth to join Vancouver 86ers.

While playing in Los Angeles, he took the eye of former Arsenal defender Bob McNab, who arranged a trial at Stoke City. He was set to sign, but, when manager Lou Macari quit to join Celtic, Corazzin signed for Cambridge United instead. They had seen him in action for Stoke reserves and agreed a £20,000 fee with his Canadian club. Corazzin made his English League debut in December 1993.

He soon proved himself a consistent scorer. His second season with Cambridge saw him finish top of their scoring charts and he was voted Player of the Year. He had impressed Argyle chief Neil Warnock for some time and on transfer deadline day in March 1996 he got his man for £150,000. Corazzin's arrival was intended to carry the Pilgrims to promotion from Division Three. He was used mainly as a substitute, but his first goal – in only his second game – could not have proved more vital.

A Tuesday evening visit by Mansfield seemed likely to earn Argyle three vital points. Ian Bowling's goalkeeping, however, kept the home side at bay. Three minutes from time Corazzin was sent on. Within a minute, his goal-bound header was saved by Bowling, but in injury-time he was felled inside the area. Mark Patterson grabbed the ball to take the penalty, but Warnock recalled a spot-kick Corazzin had converted against Argyle some weeks earlier, and screamed from the touchline that he should take this one. Corazzin duly scored to take the Pilgrims a step closer to the play-offs. The Wembley final brought mixed emotions for Corazzin, who was a non-playing substitute, but it was a proud moment when he climbed the famous steps to collect his medal.

The following season saw him established in the side as first-choice striker. Although goals were hard to come by, Corazzin was an excellent target man, always making himself available, shielding the ball well, and showing some delightful touches. Although solidly built, at 5ft 9in he was short for a central striker, but surprised many a defender with his heading ability.

Corazzin was also a hit off the field, particularly with the ladies, who took to his dark Latin looks and flashing smile. He was always ready to spend time with the fans, signing autographs or posing for photos.

1997-98 did not start brightly. Corazzin was sent off in the opener at Bristol Rovers, but bounced back after suspension and regularly appeared on the scoresheet. His seventeen goals, each of which sparked a celebratory cartwheel, saw him finish top scorer and share the Player of the Year award with Martin Barlow. But his goals were not enough to fend off relegation, which was confirmed by a defeat in what proved to be his final game.

Several clubs – including Watford, Gillingham, Bournemouth and Wycombe – were aware that Corazzin's contract was up and were monitoring the situation closely. There were even stories of him returning to Italy with Empoli. Argyle fans wanted him to stay, but with the club stating publicly that they could not meet his wage demands, he was snapped up by Northampton under a 'Bosman', which meant Argyle did not recoup a penny of their outlay two years previously.

At Northampton, Corazzin scored 31 times in 71 games (plus fifteen substitute appearances). In his first year he won another Player of the Year award for being top scorer, but in July 2000, after helping the Cobblers to promotion in his second season, he was transferred on another 'Bosman' to Oldham. He finished his first season at Boundary Park with only nine strikes to his name, four of them in 90 minutes against Wrexham in February 2001.

All through his years in English soccer, Corazzin has jetted across the Atlantic as a member of the Canadian national side. To date he has won 53 caps for his country, scoring ten goals. To his credit, despite a sometimes hectic schedule, he has rarely missed a League game due to his international commitments.

Magic Moment: *Corazzin was part of the Canadian side that won the CON-CACAF Gold Cup in February 2000, beating Colombia in the final. He was also presented with a 'Golden Boot' award as the tournament's top scorer.*

Worst Nightmare: *On his return to Home Park with Northampton in April 2000, Corazzin was booed by a small section of Argyle 'fans'. He silenced those idiots by scoring to give the Cobblers an early lead.*

ARGYLE RECORD	Appearances	Goals
Football League	64 (+13)	23
FA Cup	2 (+2)	1
League Cup	2 (+1)	–

No 96. Rhys Wilmot and No 94. Sean McCarthy

No 97. Martin Barlow, Argyle's midfield dynamo

No 98. Steve McCall nearly gets chopped in half by this Derby challenge

No 99. Skipper Mick Heathcote lifts the 1996 play-off trophy at Wembley

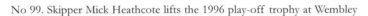

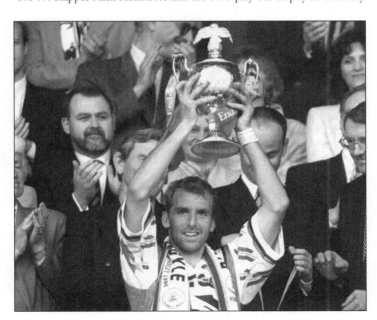

No 100. Ronnie Mauge heads the all-important goal at Wembley against Darlington

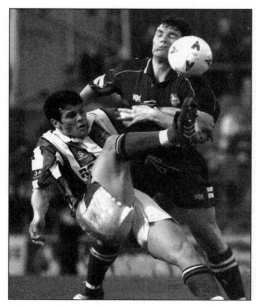

No 101. Canadian international striker Carlo Corazzin

Neil Adams	Ronnie Mauge	Tom Finnie	Mike Bickle
Paul 'Grizzly'		Sam Fleet	Steve Castle
Adams	Garry Nelson	Michael Foster	Tommy Tynan
Geoff Allman	Paddy Ratcliffe	Nick Fowler	Martin Phillips
C M Aston	Gordon Fincham	Terry Fowler	Michael Evans
N D Aston	Adrian Burrows	Ivor W H Francis	Wilf Carter
Arthur Atkins	Jack Chisholm	Warwick Franklin	Tommy Tynan
John Atkinson	Paul Mariner	Lisa Anne Fray	Adrian Littlejohn
Paul Bartlett	Barrie Jones	Paul Fray	Tommy Tynan
John Baskerville	Paul Mariner	Graham Gardner	Kevin Hodges
Peter Batchelor	Tommy Tynan	David Peter Gates	Mark Patterson
George Bate	Ernie Machin	Tim Gear	Dwight Marshall
Dave Beck	Tommy Tynan	Martyn Getson	Steve McCall
Steve Billing	Tommy Tynan	Neill Getson	Tommy Tynan
Barry Bowden	Jimmy Gauld	M V Gibbs	Tommy Tynan
Jon Brain	Michael Evans	Geoffrey E Gilbert	Pat Jones
Paul R Brewer	Wilf Carter	Andrew Gillbard	Tommy Tynan
Syd Brooks	Andy 'Jock' Morrison	Bernard Gillbard	Johnny Williams
David Brown	Tommy Tynan	James Gray	Paul Mariner
Phil Buse	Tommy Tynan	Kenneth P Griffin	Jack Chisholm
P Cannan		John Haley	Paul Mariner
Colin Carr	Jim Furnell	Colin James Hall	Tommy Tynan
Alan J Churchill	Tommy Tynan	Andy Hancock	Dwight Marshall
Simon Coates	Kevin Hodges	Bill Hansford	George Dews
John Coker	Barrie Jones	James Harries	Tommy Tynan
Mike Cole	Wilf Carter	David Harris	Johnny Williams
Chris Coleman	Paul Mariner	Jennie Harris	Johnny Williams
David Coles	Tommy Tynan	Paul Thomas Hart	Tommy Tynan
Ian W Collins	Tommy Tynan	Mike Healy	Bill Shortt
John Condon	Tommy Tynan	Gary Hoare	Gordon Nisbet
Ian Connor	Paul Mariner	Kevin Hoare	Paul Mariner
Ian Cory	Paul Mariner	Paul Hobbs	Wilf Carter
Julian Cosson	Tommy Tynan	Phil Hollow	Jimmy Gauld
Howard Cottrell	Johnny Williams	Dave Horn	Tommy Tynan
Gordon Couch	Johnny Williams	Gary Horrell	Tommy Tynan
Robert Cowan	Paul Mariner	Dennis Horswell	Tommy Tynan
Malcolm Cowl	Johnny Williams	Michael Hoskin	Paul Mariner
Paul Curtis	Billy Rafferty	Kevin Ireland	Paul Mariner
David A S Dane	Tommy Tynan	Ian F S Jackson	Tyrone Jones
Steve Dean	Billy Rafferty	G Jennings	Barrie Jones
David Dicker	Paul Mariner	Brian Jervis	Maurice Tadman
Callum Douglas	Wilf Carter	Mark Joannes	Paul Mariner
Jeff Down		Gary Johnston	Tommy Tynan
Dr John Eales	Gordon Nisbet	Alan H Jones	Johnny Williams
Peter Eastman	Tommy Tynan	Jenny Julian	David Friio
Paul Edmonds	Barrie Jones	Paul Julian	Tommy Tynan
Colin Eynon	Nicky Jennings	Simon Kearney	Tommy Tynan
Daniel Eynon	Gordon Nisbet	Vernon Kerswell	Maurice Tadman
Lee Finn	Paul Mariner	A G Knox	Maurice Tadman

J M Leask	Tommy Tynan	I Saunders	George Dews
Philip Lee	Wilf Carter	Richard Saunders	Michael Evans
Mr J Leonard	Ernie Machin	Trevor Scallan	Tommy Tynan
Gordon Littlejohns	Tommy Tynan	Ken Sellek	Jack Chisholm
Colin MacDonald	Gordon Nisbet	John Simmonds	Paul Mariner
Clive MacTavish	Tommy Tynan	Jim Smart	Mike Bickle
Russell McAulay	Tommy Tynan	Andy Soper-Hall	Ernie Edds
Paul 'Chunker'		John Robert Spry	Tommy Tynan
McClellan	Alan Rogers	Lee Stentiford	Happy 18th Birthday
Stanley McFarlane	Maurice Tadman		Gran & Grandad
In memory of		Richard Stocken	
Alain Marks	Paul Mariner	Alderman Joan	
Jeff Marlow	Leigh Cooper	Stopporton	Kevin Hodges
Robert Martin	Paul Mariner	Laurie Strike	Tommy Tynan
Christopher May	George Robertson	Irving Sweet	John Uzzell
Charles Mills	Paul Mariner	Ronald Symons	Tommy Tynan
'Pigpen'	Paul Mariner	Neil Taylor	Paul Mariner
Frank Netherton	Bill Shortt	Ann Telfer	Kevin Hodges
Gary O'Connell	Paul Mariner	Brian Treharne	George Dews
Paul O'Riley	Tommy Tynan	J Treleven	Paul Mariner
Peter Ogley	Paul Mariner	Neil Tucker	Tommy Tynan
Nigel Ormerod		Tyhee Slim	Paul Mariner
Raymond John		Gary Wake	John Newman
Owens	Geoff Crudgington	Jan Walaszkowski	Paul Dalton
Derek Palmer	Billy Strauss	James Wallace	David Friio
Martin Palmer	Gordon Nisbet	John T Warne	David Burnside
Colin Parsons	Sammy Black	Justin White	Mick Heathcote
Les Partridge	Bill Shortt	Mike 'Chalkie'	
Andrew Pearce	Paul Mariner	White	Tony Book
Andy Pengelly	Paul Mariner	Paul White	Tommy Tynan
Mike Pengelly	Paul Mariner	John Willcocks	Jimmy Gauld
Mike Pengelly	Tommy Tynan	Clive Willis	Gordon Nisbet
Andy Perrow	Paul Mariner	Jeremy Wills	Wilf Carter
David J Perry	Paul Mariner	Graham Wilton	Paul Mariner
Josh Perry	Tommy Tynan	Chris Wise	Tommy Tynan
Richard Phillips	Garry Nelson	Marc Woodward	Kevin Hodges
Malcolm Pine	George Dews	Paul Worman	Ian Stonebridge
Martin Piney	Tommy Tynan	Harry Yelland	Tommy Tynan
John A Pitts	John Hore	Peter Yolland	Jimmy Hinch
Peggy Prior	Paul Mariner		
R J Rapson	Steve McCall	Most popular Plymouth Argyle players	
Dave Revell	Paul Mariner	(48 different players received votes)	
Paul, Karen & Harry			
Richardson	Tommy Tynan	1st	Tommy Tynan
Chris Ridley	Paul Mariner	2nd	Paul Mariner
Martin Rogers	Paul Mariner	3rd=	Wilf Carter
Bernard A Roe	George Dews	3rd=	Johnny Williams
Mike Rundle		5th	Gordon Nisbet
Owen Ryles	Tommy Tynan	6th=	George Dews
		6th=	Kevin Hodges